THIS BOOK IS DEDICATED TO THE BREEDERS, SPINNERS, AND DYERS,
WHO MAKE ALL THE WONDERFUL YARNS AVAILABLE TODAY,
AND TO THE DESIGNERS WHO SHOW US NEW AND CREATIVE WAYS TO USE THEM.

The mission of Storey Publishing is to serve our customers by
publishing practical information that encourages
personal independence in harmony with the environment.

Edited by Judith Durant and Gwen Steege
Technical editing by Dorothy T. Ratigan
Cover design by Mary Winkelman Velgos and Leslie Anne Charles, LAC Design
Art direction and book design by Mary Winkelman Velgos
Text production by Jennifer Jepson Smith

Photographs © Alexandra Grablewski
Photo styling by Leslie Siegel
Credits for props appear on page 255
Technical illustrations by Alison Kolesar

Indexed by Christine R. Lindemer, Boston Road Communications

© 2007 by Storey Publishing

All rights reserved. No part of this book may be reproduced without written permission from the publisher, except by a reviewer who may quote brief passages or reproduce illustrations in a review with appropriate credits; nor may any part of this book be reproduced, stored in a retrieval system, or transmitted in any form or by any means — electronic, mechanical, photocopying, recording, or other — without written permission from the publisher.

The information in this book is true and complete to the best of our knowledge. All recommendations are made without guarantee on the part of the editor or Storey Publishing. The editor and publisher disclaim any liability in connection with the use of this information. For additional information, please contact Storey Publishing, 210 MASS MoCA Way, North Adams, MA 01247.

Storey books are available for special premium and promotional uses and for customized editions. For further information, please call 1-800-793-9396.

Printed in the United States by R.R. Donnelley
10 9 8 7 6 5 4

Library of Congress Cataloging-in-Publication Data

Durant, Judith, 1955–
   101 designer one-skein wonders / Judith Durant.
     p. cm.
   Includes index.
   ISBN 978-1-58017-688-0 (pbk. : alk. paper)
   1. Knitting—Patterns. I. Title. II. Title: One hundred and one designer one-skein wonders.
TT825.R286 2006
746.43'2041—dc22

2007029371

INTRODUCTION

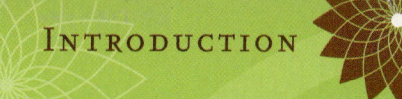

WELCOME TO OUR NEW COLLECTION OF PATTERNS that use only one skein of yarn, 101 Designer One-Skein Wonders. The contributors to this volume come from all areas of the knitting and crocheting world. Some design for yarn companies, some are published in magazines, some write books, some work in yarn shops, and some knit for family and friends. Whatever the background, we all have one thing in common: We love yarn and can't have too many different ways to use it.

The patterns presented here are organized by yarn weight, so whether you're tempted by a skein of bulky-weight merino, a ball of novelty ribbon, or a skein of lace-weight alpaca, you can easily find an idea for using it within these pages. Projects include scarves, hats, socks, purses, even toys, so there's sure to be something just right for you and your yarn. You'll find a list of common abbreviations and an illustrated glossary of techniques at the back of the book. Everything else you need to know is included with each pattern. Browse through the photo gallery on the following pages to discover the patterns you'd like to try, then pick up your needles and yarn and start knitting!

Enjoy these designs, and when you've finished a wonder, visit www.oneskeinwonders.com to post your accomplishment and see what others are up to. We look forward to hearing from you. Knit and crochet on!

4 LACE-WEIGHT YARN PROJECTS

47 Christening Shawl

51 Forest Park Dresser Scarf

38 Three-Season Lace Vest

43 Tucson Lattice Shawl

LACE-WEIGHT YARN PROJECTS 5

44 Alpaca Warmers

36 Dogwood Blossom Wrap

41 Rhea Lace Stole

42 Oriel Lace Scarf

6 FINGERING-WEIGHT YARN PROJECTS

60 Magic Loop Minis

81 Picot Edge Socks

83 Catch-Me-If-You-Can Socks

65 Ostrich Plume Baby Bonnet

FINGERING-WEIGHT YARN PROJECTS   7

71 Megan's Ruffled Neck Warmer

73 Wave Jumper

75 Marialis End-to-End Scarf

8 FINGERING-WEIGHT YARN PROJECTS

Blue-Wave Baby Sweater

FINGERING-WEIGHT YARN PROJECTS

59 Sock-It-To-Me Scarf

64 Missy's Checkbook Cover

70 Knitted Humbug Bag

79 BlueBells Socks

10 FINGERING-WEIGHT YARN PROJECTS

66 *Grampie's Tie*

56 *Lola Flip-Top Mittens*

68 *Scrunchie Hand Warmers*

77 *Horseshoe Cable Socks*

SPORT-WEIGHT YARN PROJECTS 11

94 Lacy Beanie

90 Garter Stitch Loop-Through Scarf

99 Plaited Cable Men's Belt

12 SPORT-WEIGHT YARN PROJECTS

96 Ring Bearer Pillow

88 Guilty Pleasures Socks

92 Feather and Fan Baby Sweater

DK / LIGHT WORSTED-WEIGHT YARN PROJECTS | 13

105 Pink Tweed for Baby

103 Simple Mistake Rib Vest

112 Baby Squash Hat

109 Between-Seasons Cap

14 DK / LIGHT WORSTED-WEIGHT YARN PROJECTS

102 Scallop-Edge Beaded Necklace

107 Sachets and Keepsake Pouches

104 Elegant-and-Easy Garter Stitch Tie

111 Child's Hat with Pompom

MOHAIR YARN PROJECTS

120 *Lace Spiral Scarf*

116 *Lace Kid Merino Cowl*

117 *Chicly Chevroned "Broadway" Hat*

118 *Tiers-of-Waves Beaded Scarf*

16 WORSTED-WEIGHT YARN PROJECTS

167 *Basket Lattice Cap*

135 *Boy-O-Boy*

161 *Crochet Ruffle Scarf*

138 *Broken Rib Socks*

WORSTED-WEIGHT YARN PROJECTS 17

172 *Not-Your-Average Washcloths*

151 *Mini Messenger Bag*

133 *New Directions Hat*

WORSTED-WEIGHT YARN PROJECTS

154 Baby Basket Hat

178 Blossom Belt

129 Ribbed Headband

128 His 'n' Hers Shower Soap Holders

WORSTED-WEIGHT YARN PROJECTS 19

140 Elegant-and-Easy Cable Mittens for the Family

173 La Cancion Amulet Purse and Flower Brooch

131 Garterlac Bath Rug

181 Fishbowl Baby Hat

146 Indian Cross Scarf

20 WORSTED-WEIGHT YARN PROJECTS

137 *Tweed Silk Scarf*

165 *Edge-of-Lace Hat and Cuffs*

175 *Elizabeth's Perfect Hat*

142 *Four Egg-Cozy Hats*

WORSTED-WEIGHT YARN PROJECTS 21

160 Lavender Lace Beanie

WORSTED-WEIGHT YARN PROJECTS

164 | *Spiral Hat*

150 | *Hugs-and-Kisses-with-Love Headband*

130 | *Knitted Notebook Cover*

147 | *Hugs-and-Kisses-with-Love Hand Warmers*

WORSTED-WEIGHT YARN PROJECTS

158 *Essentials Mini-Purse*

169 *Cabled Baglet*

124 *Kat's Hat*

24 WORSTED-WEIGHT YARN PROJECTS

162 Little Green Wristlets

WORSTED-WEIGHT YARN PROJECTS 25

177 Poems Easy Headband

179 Eyelet Shruglet

155 Little Monster Bear

126 Taos Slippers

26 HEAVY WORSTED-WEIGHT YARN PROJECTS

207 | Blanket Buddy

200 | Mitered Square Belt with Beads

209 | Power Flowers

197 | Vermont Felted Bag

HEAVY WORSTED-WEIGHT YARN PROJECTS 27

202 *Waterfall Scarf*

196 *Smock-a-Ruche Scarf*

186 *Cross-Stitch Scarf*

203 *Square Hole Hat and Wristlets*

28 HEAVY WORSTED-WEIGHT YARN PROJECTS

188 Cozy Socks for Kids

187 April-in-Paris Beret

212 Infant's Rolled Neck Pullover

190 Zigzag Scarf

195 Nano Nanny

HEAVY WORSTED-WEIGHT YARN PROJECTS

199 *Zane's Coming Home Sweater*

193 *Saw-Tooth Companion Bowl*

192 *Loop's Centipede*

30 HEAVY WORSTED- / BULKY-WEIGHT YARN PROJECTS

218 *Fuchsia Felted Bowl*

205 *Felt Ruffle Bag*

216 *Two-Hour Handbag*

NOVELTY YARN PROJECTS 31

224 | *Neck Warmer*

228 | *Soft Clutch Purse*

229 | *Tokyo Scarf*

32 NOVELTY YARN PROJECTS

226 *Square-Hole Shrug*

222 *Flirty Ribbon Purse*

223 *Catnip Kick Pillow*

230 *Buttons on Belts*

Contents

Project Photos 4
Introduction 33
Lace Weight 35
Fingering Weight 55
Sport Weight 87
DK/Light Worsted Weight 101
Mohair Yarn 115
Worsted Weight 123
Heavy Worsted Weight 185
Bulky Weight 215
Novelty Yarn 221
About the Designers 232
Glossary 244
Index 252

Dogwood Blossom Wrap

Designed by Catherine Devine, photo on page 5

This elegant wrap is knitted with 100% cultivated silk yarn that is beautifully painted at Schaefer Yarns. The coloring is very subtle, so it does not interfere with the lovely lace patterning.

MEASUREMENTS	Approximately 16" (41 cm) wide and 66" (168 cm) long
YARN	Schaefer Yarn Andrea, 100% cultivated silk, 3.5 oz (100 g)/1093 yds (999 m), one-of-a-kind color
NEEDLES	US 2 (3 mm) straight needles or size you need to obtain correct gauge and US 7 (4.5 mm) straight needles for cast-on/bind-off
GAUGE	22 stitches = 4" (10 cm) in lace on smaller needle, smoothed flat but unblocked
OTHER SUPPLIES	Stitch markers, tapestry needle, blocking pins
ABBREVIATIONS	**pm** place marker

Getting Started

- **NOTE:** Slip the first stitch of every row purlwise with yarn in back.
- With larger needle, cast on 103 stitches. Change to smaller needle and knit 11 rows.
- **SET-UP ROW (WS):** Slip 1, K6, pm, K11, pm, K22, pm, K22, pm, K22, pm, K12, pm, K7.

Knitting the Wrap

- Keep the first and last 7 stitches in garter stitch and work Dogwood Blossom Lace Chart (facing page) between these stitches, purling all even-numbered (wrong-side) rows.
- Work Rows 1–72 of chart a total of 7 times, then repeat Rows 1–41.
- Knit 12 rows in garter stitch for ending border, then bind off loosely using larger needle.

Finishing

- Weave in ends. Thoroughly dampen the wrap and pin out to a 19" × 67" (48 × 170 cm) rectangle. Allow the wrap to dry completely.

Lace Weight

Dogwood Blossom Lace Chart

- ☐ knit
- ◯ yarn over
- ╲ slip 1, slip 1, knit 2 slipped stitches together through the back loop
- ╱ knit 2 together
- ⋀ slip 1 as to knit, knit 2 together, pass the slip stitch over
- ▢ pattern repeat

⊢ Work these 11 sts once ⊣ ⊢ Work Pattern Repeat 3 times ⊣ ⊢ Work these 12 sts once ⊣

NOTE: Only right-side rows are charted. Purl all wrong-side rows.

Three-Season Lace Vest

Designed by Linda Burt, photo on page 4

This is a soft, light, and airy vest that's great for layering in spring, summer, and fall. The pattern is written for three sizes.

MEASUREMENTS	Approximately 35 (42, 48)" (89 [107, 123] cm) chest
YARN	Valley Yarns 2/14 Alpaca/Silk, 80% alpaca/20% silk, 8 oz (227 g) cone/ 1736 yds (1587 m), Nile Green
NEEDLES	US 7 (4.5 mm) and US 4 (3.5 mm) straight needles or size you need to obtain correct gauge
GAUGE	20 stitches = 4" (10 cm) in pattern on larger needles
OTHER SUPPLIES	Stitch markers, tapestry needle
ABBREVIATIONS	**p2sso** pass two slipped stitches over **ssk** slip 1, slip 1, knit 2 slipped stitches over **yo** yarn over

Knitting the Back

- With smaller needles, cast on 87 (103, 119) stitches.

Knitting the Edging

- Beginning with a purl row, work stockinette stitch for 7 rows.
- **NEXT ROW:** *K2tog, yo; repeat from * to last stitch, K1.
- Beginning with a purl row, work stockinette stitch for 7 rows.

Knitting the Lace Pattern

- **NOTE:** Incorporate increased stitches into lace pattern.
- Change to larger needles and work 2 rows stockinette stitch.
- Begin Snowflake Lace pattern and increase 1 stitch on each end of every 22 rows 3 times. You now have 93 (109, 125) stitches.
- Continue even until piece measures 10" (25 cm). Place marker at each end of row to indicate beginning of armhole.
- Continue in Snowflake Lace pattern, increasing 1 stitch on each end of every 7 (8, 9) rows 7 times. You now have 107 (123, 139) stitches. Continue even in Snowflake Lace pattern until piece measures 7.5 (8.5, 9.5)" (19 [22, 24] cm) from armhole marking. Bind off 8 (10, 12) stitches at the beginning of the next 8 rows. Bind off remaining 43 stitches.

stitch pattern

SNOWFLAKE LACE

Worked over a multiple of 8 + 5 stitches.

ROW 1: K4, *ssk, yo, K1, yo, K2tog, K3; repeat from * to last stitch, K1.

ROW 2 AND ALL EVEN-NUMBERED ROWS THROUGH 12: Purl.

ROW 3: K5, *yo, slip 2, K1, p2sso, yo, K5; repeat from *.

ROW 5: Repeat Row 1.

ROW 7: Ssk, yo, K1, yo, K2tog, *K3, ssk, yo, K1, yo, K2tog; repeat from *.

ROW 9: K1, *yo, slip 2, k1, p2sso, yo, K5; repeat from * ending last repeat K1 instead of K5.

ROW 11: Repeat Row 7.

Repeat Rows 1–12 for pattern.

Knitting the Left Front

- Using smaller needles, cast on 47 (55, 63) stitches.
- Work edging as for Back.

Knitting the Lace Pattern

- **NOTE:** Incorporate increased stitches into lace pattern.
- Change to larger needles and work 2 rows stockinette stitch.
- Begin Snowflake Lace pattern and increase 1 stitch at beginning of right-side rows every 22 rows 3 times. You now have 50 (58, 66) stitches.
- Continue even until piece measures 10" (25 cm). Place marker at beginning of a right-side row to indicate beginning of armhole.
- Continue in lace pattern, increasing 1 stitch at armhole edge every 7 (8, 9) rows 7 times and at the same time when piece measures 16" (41 cm) bind off on every other row at neck edge 16 (14, 12) stitches once, 3 stitches once, 2 stitches once, and 1 stitch 4 (6, 8) times. Continue even in lace pattern until piece measures 5 (5.5, 6)" (13 [14, 15] cm) from armhole marking. Bind off 8 (10, 12) stitches at the beginning of the next 4 right-side rows.

Knitting the Right Front

- Using smaller needles, cast on 47 (55, 63) stitches.
- Work edging as for Back.

Knitting the Lace Pattern

- **NOTE:** Incorporate increased stitches into lace pattern.
- Change to larger needles and work 2 rows stockinette stitch.
- Begin Snowflake Lace pattern and work as for Left Front reversing shaping.

Knitting the Edgings

- Sew shoulder seams together.

Knitting the Front Edgings

- With smaller needles, right side facing, and beginning just above bottom edging, pick up and knit 79 stitches along right front to neckline.
- Beginning with a purl row, work stockinette stitch for 7 rows.
- **NEXT ROW:** *K2tog, yo; repeat from * to last stitch, K1.
- Beginning with a purl row, work stockinette stitch for 7 rows, binding off on last row.

Three-Season Lace Vest continued

- Work for Left Front as above, but pick up stitches beginning at the neckline and work down to bottom edging.

Knitting the Neck Edging

- With smaller needles right side facing, and beginning just above Right Front edging, pick up and knit 91 (105, 115) stitches along neckline.
- Beginning with a purl row, work stockinette stitch for 7 rows.
- **NEXT ROW:** *K2tog, yo; repeat from * to last stitch, K1.
- Beginning with a purl row, work stockinette stitch for 7 rows, binding off on last row.

Knitting the Armhole Edgings

- With smaller needles, right side facing, and beginning at Right Back armhole marking, pick up and knit 69 (79, 89) stitches along armhole edge.
- Beginning with a purl row, work stockinette stitch for 7 rows.
- **NEXT ROW:** *K2tog, yo; repeat from * to last stitch, K1.
- Beginning with a purl row, work stockinette stitch for 7 rows, binding off on last row.
- Work left armhole as for right, but begin at the front armhole edge.

Finishing

- Fold edgings to inside along picot edge and loosely stitch in place. Block, stretching as necessary. Sew side seams. Weave in ends.

Rhea Lace Stole

Designed by Kirsten Hipsky, *photo on page 5*

Named for the Ancient Minoan mother of the gods, this stole combines old and new, and surprisingly easy lace patterns that emphasize the beauty of the hand-dyed alpaca-silk yarn.

MEASUREMENTS	Approximately 24" (61 cm) wide and 72" (183 cm) long, blocked
YARN	Valley Yarns 2/14 Alpaca Silk Hand Dyed, 80% alpaca/20% silk, 4 oz (113 g)/865 yds (791 m), Rainforest
NEEDLES	US 5 (3.75 mm) straight needles or size you need to obtain correct gauge
GAUGE	20 stitches = 4" (10 cm) in pattern, blocked
OTHER SUPPLIES	Tapestry needle
ABBREVIATIONS	**SK2P** slip 1, knit two together, pass slipped stitch over **ssk** slip 1, slip 1, knit 2 slipped stitches over **yo** yarn over

Knitting the Edgings (make two)

- Cast on 10 stitches. Knit 2 rows. Work Rows 1–6 of Rhea Lace Edging 24 times. Knit 2 rows. Bind off loosely.

Knitting the Body

- Pick up 111 stitches along the long straight edge of one lace edging. Work Body pattern for about 60" (152 cm) or until you have about 5 yds (4.5 m) of yarn remaining.
- Knit each stitch from the needle together with a loop from the other edging, binding off loosely as you go.

Finishing

- Weave in ends. Soak stole in Eucalan (a wool wash) following manufacturer's directions. Block rigorously. Preferred blocking method is to find or construct an adequately sized wooden frame, place damp stole within it, and whip stitch each edge independently to the frame with a strong but thin yarn.

stitch pattern

Rhea Lace Edging

Row 1: K2, yo, P2tog, (K1, P1, K1, P1, K1) in next stitch, yo, P2tog, K1, yo, K2. You now have 15 stitches.

Row 2: K2, (K1, P1, K1) in next stitch, K1, yo, P2tog, K5, yo, P2tog, K2. You now have 17 stitches.

Row 3: K2, yo, P2tog, K5, yo, P2tog, K6.

Row 4: K6, yo, P2tog, K5, yo, P2tog, K2.

Row 5: K2, yo, P2tog, K2tog, K1, ssk, yo, P2tog, K6. You now have 15 stitches.

Row 6: Bind off 3, K2, yo, P2tog, SK2P, yo, P2tog, K2. You now have 10 stitches.

Repeat Rows 1–6 for pattern.

Body

Row 1: K2, *yo, K1, SK2P, K1, yo, K1; repeat from * to last stitch, K1.

Row 2: Knit.

Repeat Rows 1 and 2 for pattern.

Oriel Lace Scarf

Designed by Anne Carroll Gilmour, photo on page 5

This lovely lace pattern is rumored to have come from Ireland around 1880, specifically from the Oriel District around County Monaghan. Although it has a "right" and a "wrong" side, it is equally attractive on both.

MEASUREMENTS	Approximately 10" (25 cm) wide and 56" (142 cm) long
YARN	The Wooly West Nordic Lites, 100% wool, 3.5 oz (100 g)/475 yds (434 m), Birch
NEEDLES	US 8 (5 mm) straight needles or size you need to obtain correct gauge
GAUGE	24 stitches = 4" (10 cm) in pattern
OTHER SUPPLIES	Stitch markers, tapestry needle
ABBREVIATIONS	**pm** place marker

stitch pattern

Oriel Lace

ROWS 1, 3, AND 5 (RS): P1, *ssk, K3, yo, P1, yo, K3, K2tog, P1; repeat from *.

ROWS 2, 4, 6, AND 8: K1, *P5, K1; repeat from *.

ROW 7: P1, *yo, K3, K2tog, P1, ssk, K3, yo, P1; repeat from *.

ROW 9: P2, *yo, K2, K2tog, P1, ssk, K2, yo, P3; repeat from *, ending last repeat with P2.

ROW 10: K2, *P4, K1, P4, K3; repeat from *, ending last repeat with K2.

ROW 11: P3, *yo, K1, K2tog, P1, ssk, K1, yo, P5; repeat from *, ending last repeat with P3.

ROW 12: K3, *P3, K1, P3, K5; repeat from *, ending last repeat with K3.

ROW 13: P4, *yo, K2tog, P1, ssk, yo, P7; repeat from *, ending last repeat with P4.

ROW 14: K4, *P2, K1, P2, K7; repeat from *, ending last repeat with K4.

ROWS 15, 17, AND 19: Repeat Row 7.

ROWS 16, 18, 20, AND 22: Repeat Row 2.

ROW 21: Repeat Row 1.

ROW 23: P1, *ssk, K2, yo, P3, yo, K2, K2tog, P1; repeat from *.

ROW 24: K1, *P4, K3, P4, K1; repeat from *.

ROW 25: P1, *ssk, K1, yo, P5, yo, K1, K2tog, P1; repeat from *.

ROW 26: K1, *P3, K5, P3, K1; repeat from *.

ROW 27: P1, *ssk, yo, P7, yo, K2tog, P1; repeat from *.

ROW 28: K1, *P2, K7, P2, K1; repeat from *.

Lace Weight

Knitting the Scarf

- Cast on 47 stitches. Work 8 rows of garter stitch (knit every row).
- **NEXT ROW (RS):** K5, pm, work Row 1 of Oriel Lace pattern to last 5 stitches, pm, K5.
- Continue knitting the first and last 5 stitches on every row and working Oriel Lace between the markers, working a total of 17 full repeats of the 28-row pattern.
- Remove the markers and work 8 rows of garter stitch. Bind off loosely.

Finishing

- Weave in end. Wash and block.

Tucson Lattice Shawl

DESIGNED BY NANCY MILLER, photo on page 4

The lovely variegation in this yarn makes a very simple shawl look wonderfully complex. The fiber blend makes this a year-round item of wearable art.

MEASUREMENTS	Approximately 19" (48 cm) wide and 80" (203 cm) long
YARN	Lorna's Yarn Helen's Lace, 50% silk/50% wool, 4 oz (113 g)/1250 yds (1143 m), Tuscany
NEEDLES	US 8 (5 mm) straight needles or size you need to obtain correct gauge
GAUGE	16 stitches = 4" (10 cm) in pattern, blocked
OTHER SUPPLIES	Tapestry needle, blocking pins
ABBREVIATIONS	**psso** pass slipped stitch over **yo** yarn over

stitch pattern

LACE

ROWS 1 AND 3: Purl.

ROW 2: K1, *yo, K2tog; repeat from *.

ROW 4: *Slip 1, K1, psso, yo; repeat from * to last stitch, K1.

Repeat Rows 1–4 for pattern.

Knitting the Shawl

- Loosely cast on 75 stitches. Work Lace pattern to desired length. Bind off loosely.

Finishing

- Weave in ends. Block to desired size.

Alpaca Warmers

Designed by Judith Durant, *photo on page 5*

These warmers are knitted from lace-weight yarn and offer just enough warmth for a drafty old house. Unlike most warmers, these have finger holes, so they stay in place while allowing for complete freedom of finger movement. The lovely lace pattern makes them appropriate for a winter bride.

Measurements	Approximately 8" (20 cm) circumference
Yarn	Misti International Misti Alpaca Lace, 100% baby alpaca, 1.75 oz (50 g)/437 yds (400 m), NT100 Natural
Needles	Set of five US 0 (2 mm) double-point needles or size you need to obtain correct gauge
Gauge	20 stitches = 2" (5 cm) in pattern
Other Supplies	Stitch markers, tapestry needle
Abbreviations	**psso** pass slipped stitch over **ssk** slip 1, slip 1, knit 2 slipped stitches together **yo** yarn over
Note	One skein will make two pairs of warmers

Knitting the Left Warmer

- Holding two needles together, cast on 72 stitches. Place 24 stitches on each of three needles and join into a round. Place marker. Work K2, P2 rib for 1.5" (3 cm), increasing 1 stitch on the last round. You now have 25 stitches on needle 1 and 24 stitches each on needles 2 and 3.

Beginning the Lace Pattern

- **Next round:** Knit, placing a marker after stitch 37 to mark side; at 4 stitches from end of needle 3, place marker for thumb gusset, K1, place marker for thumb gusset, K3.
- Continue working Lace pattern beginning with Round 2 over first 37 stitches for back of warmer and stockinette stitch over remaining 36 stitches for the palm until you have worked Rounds 1–8 of Lace pattern five times total and *at the same time* increase 1 stitch after the first and before the second thumb gusset markers on every 4 rounds beginning with Round 4. You now have 93 stitches.

---

stitch pattern

Lace

Rounds 1, 3, 5, and 7: Knit.

Round 2: K1, *yo, ssk, K1, K2tog, yo, K1; repeat from *.

Round 4: K1, *yo, K1, (slip 1, K2tog, psso), K1, yo, K1; repeat from *.

Round 6: K1, *K2tog, yo, K1, yo, ssk, K1; repeat from *.

Round 8: K2tog, *K1, yo, K1, yo, K1, (slip 1, K2tog, psso); repeat from * to last 5 sts, K1, yo, K1, yo, K1, ssk.

Note: On Round 8, slip first stitch from needle 2 to needle 3 to work the ssk.

Isolating the Thumb Gusset

- Work Round 1 of Lace pattern on back stitches and knit palm stitches to first thumb gusset. Place 21 thumb gusset stitches on string to hold. Cast on 1 stitch, join and knit last 3 stitches from needle 3. You again have 73 stitches.
- Continue working patterns as established beginning with Round 2 until you have worked Rounds 1–8 of Lace pattern two more times. Knit 1 round.
- Work Round 2 of Lace pattern over 25 stitches on needle 1 and first 3 stitches on needle 2; place remaining 9 back stitches and first 9 palm stitches on string to hold for Little Finger. On Needle 2, cast on 6 stitches, rejoin and knit to end of round. You now have 61 stitches: 25 on needle 1, 12 on needle 2, and 24 on needle 3.
- Continue in patterns as established until you have completed Rounds 1–8 of Lace pattern one more time, working the first 3 stitches on needle 2 as follows:
- ROUND 4: Yo, K1, ssk.
- ROUND 6: K2tog, yo, K1.
- ROUND 8: K1, yo, K1.
- NOTE: On Round 8, work last 5 stitches on needle 1 as K1, yo, K1, yo, K1, ssk.
- Discontinue Lace pattern. Knit one round.

Knitting the Index Finger

- Knit 12 back stitches, place remaining 16 back stitches and first 23 palm stitches on string to hold. Cast on 6 stitches on new needle, rejoin and knit remaining 11 stitches. You now have 29 stitches. Knit one round, decreasing 1 stitch. Work 2 rounds of K1, P1 rib, bind off loosely in rib.

Knitting the Middle Finger

- Place 8 palm stitches on needle, join new yarn and knit these stitches. With a new needle, pick up and knit the 6 stitches cast on for Index Finger (see No Holes). Place 8 back stitches on needle and knit, cast on 6 stitches. Join and knit one round. Work 2 rounds of K1, P1 rib, bind off loosely in rib.

Knitting the Ring Finger

- Place remaining 23 stitches on two needles. With a new needle, pick up and knit the 6 stitches cast on for Middle Finger (see No Holes). Join and knit one round, decreasing one stitch. Work 2 rounds of K1, P1 rib, bind off loosely in rib.

Alpaca Warmers continued

Knitting the Little Finger

- Place 18 held stitches on two needles. With a new needle, pick up and knit the 6 stitches cast on for Ring Finger (see No Holes). Join and knit one round. Work 2 rounds of K1, P1 rib, bind off loosely in rib.

Knitting the Thumb

- Place 21 Thumb Gusset stitches on two needles. With new needle, pick up and knit 9 stitches into the space at the inside of the thumb. Knit one round. Work 2 rounds of K1, P1 rib, bind off loosely in rib.

Knitting the Right Warmer

- Work the cuff as for Left Warmer.

Beginning the Lace Pattern

- **NEXT ROUND**: K3, place marker for thumb gusset, K1, place marker for thumb gusset, K32 and mark side.
- Continue as for Left Warmer until you have 93 stitches and are ready to work the thumb gusset.

Isolating the Thumb Gusset

- Knit 3 and place 21 thumb gusset stitches on string to hold. Cast on 1 stitch, join and continue round in patterns as established. You again have 73 stitches.
- Continue working patterns as established beginning with Round 2 until you have worked Rounds 1–8 of Lace pattern two more times. Knit 1 round.
- Work in patterns to 9 stitches before side marker. Place 9 palm stitches and 9 back stitches on string to hold for Little Finger. Cast on 6 stitches, rejoin and work in pattern to end of round.
- Continue as for Left Warmer, knitting the Ring Finger, the Middle Finger, and then the Index Finger, using the same number of stitches specified for Left Warmer for each finger. Knit the Little Finger and Thumb as for Left Warmer.

Finishing

- Weave in all ends, using the tails to close up any holes at the base of the fingers that may have developed despite your best efforts.

NO HOLES

To prevent holes from forming at the base of thumbs and fingers in mittens and gloves, pick up an extra stitch on each side of the stitches you need to pick up for the thumb or finger. When you work the next round, knit the first extra stitch together with the one before it and the second extra stitch together with the stitch after it.

Christening Shawl

Designed by Anne Dill, *photo on page 4*

This shawl is intended to enhance the lives of the people who use it, and it is too lovely to fail. The beautiful lace border is knitted with tussah silk and attached to a rectangle of linen. Use it as a christening blanket or as a decorative cloth.

Measurements	Approximately 44" (118 cm) square
Yarn	Pine Tree Yarns 1-Ply Tussah Silk, 100% tussah silk, 3.5 oz (100 g)/437 yds (400 m), Rapunzel
Needles	Three US 7 (4.5 mm) straight or double-point needles 7" (18 cm) long or size you need to obtain correct gauge
Gauge	28 stitches = 4" (10 cm) in stockinette stitch
Other Supplies	Stitch markers, 1 yd (1 m) linen, silk sewing thread, sewing needle, quilting and blocking pins, crochet hook, fine tapestry needle, needle stoppers to fit ends of double-point needles
Abbreviations	**KB** knit in back of stitch on right-side row **PB** purl in back of stitch on wrong-side row **SK2P** slip 1 knitwise, K2tog, pass slipped stitch over **ssk** slip 1, slip 1, knit 2 slipped stitches together **yo** yarn over

stitch pattern

Lace

Row 1: Slip 1, K3, yo, K2tog, P3, K2, yo, K2tog, yo, K3, yo, K2tog, P1, yo, P1, K2, yo, K2tog, P1, ssk, K5, K2tog, P1, K2, yo, K2tog, K2.

Row 2: Slip 1, K3, yo, K2tog, K1, P7, K3, yo, K2tog, K1, PB, K3, yo, K2tog, K4, yo, K2tog, K1, PB, K3, yo, K2tog, K1, P1.

Row 3: Slip 1, K3, yo, K2tog, P1, yo, KB, yo, P1, K2, yo, K2tog, yo, K4, yo, K2tog, P1, yo, KB, yo, P1, K2, yo, K2tog, P1, K7, P1, K2, yo, K2tog, K2. You now have 46 stitches.

Row 4: Slip 1, K3, yo, K2tog, K1, P7, K3, yo, K2tog, K1, P1, PB, P1, K3, yo, K2tog, K5, yo, K2tog, K1, P1, PB, P1, K3, yo, K2tog, K1, P1.

Row 5: Slip 1, K3, yo, K2tog, P1, K1, yo, KB, yo, K1, P1, K2, yo, K2tog, yo, K5, yo, K2tog, P1, K1, yo, KB, yo, K1, P1, K2, yo, K2tog, P1, ssk, K3, K2tog, P1, K2, yo, K2tog, K2. You now have 49 stitches.

Row 6: Slip 1, K3, yo, K2tog, K1, P5, K3, yo, K2tog, K1, P2, PB, P2, K3, yo, K2tog, K6, yo, K2tog, K1, P2, PB, P2, K3, yo, K2tog, K1, P1.

Christening Shawl continued

ROW 7: Slip 1, K3, yo, K2tog, P1, K2, yo, KB, yo, K2, P1, K2, yo, K2tog, yo, K6, yo, K2tog, P1, K2, yo, KB, yo, K2, P1, K2, yo, K2tog, P1, ssk, K1, K2tog, P1, K2, yo, K2tog, K2. You now have 52 stitches.

ROW 8: Slip 1, K3, yo, K2tog, K1, P3, K3, yo, K2tog, K1, P3, PB, P3, K3, yo, K2tog, K7, yo, K2tog, K1, P3, PB, P3, K3, yo, K2tog, K1, P1.

ROW 9: Slip 1, K3, yo, K2tog, P1, K3, yo, KB, yo, K3, P1, K2, yo, K2tog, yo, K7, yo, K2tog, P1, K3, yo, KB, yo, K3, P1, K2, yo, K2tog, P1, (slip 1, K2tog, psso), P1, K2, yo, K2tog, K2. You now have 55 stitches.

ROW 10: Slip 1, K3, yo, K2tog, K1, P1, K3, yo, K2tog, K1, P4, PB, P4, K3, yo, K2tog, K8, yo, K2tog, K1, P4, PB, P4, K3, yo, K2tog, K1, P1.

ROW 11: Slip 1, K3, yo, K2tog, P1, K9, P1, K2, yo, K2tog, yo, K2, yo, K2tog, P2, K2, yo, K2tog, P1, K9, P1, K2, yo, K2tog, P1, K1, P1, K6. You now have 56 stitches.

ROW 12: Bind off 3, K4, pass 4 stitches over the last stitch worked, K3, yo, K2tog, K1, P9, K3, yo, K2tog, P4, yo, K2tog, P3, yo, K2tog, K1, P9, K3, yo, K2tog, K1, P1. You now have 49 stitches.

ROW 13: Slip 1, K3, yo, K2tog, P1, ssk, K5, K2tog, P1, K2, yo, K2tog, yo, K3, yo, K2tog, P1, yo, P1, K2, yo, K2tog, P1, ssk, K5, K2tog, P1, K2, yo, K2tog, P1, K1. You now have 47 stitches.

ROW 14: Slip 1, K3, yo, K2tog, K1, P7, K3, yo, K2tog, K1, PB, K3, yo, K2tog, K4, yo, K2tog, K1, P7, K3, yo, K2tog, K1, P1.

ROW 15: Slip 1, K3, yo, K2tog, P1, K7, P1, K2, yo, K2tog, yo, K4, yo, K2tog, P1, yo, KB, yo, P1, K2, yo, K2tog, P1, K7, P1, K2, yo, K2tog, K2. You now have 50 stitches.

ROW 16: Slip 1, K3, yo, K2tog, K1, P7, K3, yo, K2tog, K1, P1, PB, P1, K3, yo, K2tog, K5, yo, K2tog, K1, P7, K3, yo, K2tog, K1, P1.

ROW 17: Slip 1, K3, yo, K2tog, P1, ssk, K3, K2tog, P1, K2, yo, K2tog, yo, K5, yo, K2tog, P1, K1, yo, KB, yo, K1, P1, K2, yo, K2tog, P1, ssk, K3, K2tog, P1, K2, yo, K2tog, K2. You now have 49 stitches.

ROW 18: Slip 1, K3, yo, K2tog, K1, P5, K3, yo, K2tog, K1, P2, PB, P2, K3, yo, K2tog, K6, yo, K2tog, K1, P5, K3, yo, K2tog, K1, P1.

ROW 19: Slip 1, K3, yo, K2tog, P1, ssk, K1, K2tog, P1, K2, yo, K2tog, yo, K6, yo, K2tog, P1, K2, yo, KB, yo, K2, P1, K2, yo, K2tog, P1, ssk, K1, K2tog, P1, K2, yo, K2tog, K2. You now have 48 stitches.

ROW 20: Slip 1, K3, yo, K2tog, K1, P3, K3, yo, K2tog, K1, P3, PB, P3, K3, yo, K2tog, K7, yo, K2tog, K1, P3, K3, yo, K2tog, K1, P1.

ROW 21: Slip 1, K3, yo, K2tog, P1, (slip 1, K2tog, psso), P1, K2, yo, K2tog, yo, K7, yo, K2tog, P1, K3, yo, KB, yo, K3, P1, K2, yo, K2tog, P1, (slip 1, K2tog, psso), P1, K2, yo, K2tog, K2. You now have 47 stitches.

ROW 22: Slip 1, K3, yo, K2tog, K1, P1, K3, yo, K2tog, K1, P4, PB, P4, K3, yo, K2tog, K8, yo, K2tog, K1, KB, K3, yo, K2tog, K1, P1.

ROW 23: Slip 1, K3, yo, K2tog, P3, K2, yo, K2tog, yo, K2, yo, K2tog, K4, yo, K2tog, P1, K9, P1, K2, yo, K2tog, P1, K1, P1, K6.

ROW 24: Bind off 3, K4, pass 4 stitches over the last stitch worked, K3, yo, K2tog, K1, P9, K3, yo, K2tog, K4, yo, K2tog, K3, yo, K2tog, K5, yo, K2tog, K1, P1. You now have 41 stitches.

Knitting the Lace Leaf Border

- Using waste yarn and a provisional method (see page 248), cast on 41 stitches. Purl 1 row. Begin following the chart at Row 1, placing markers for each eyelet and leaf pattern. Note that the motifs are separated by a column of purl stitches.
- Work Rows 1–24 of pattern 28 times. Edging measures approximately 112" (284 cm).
- Carefully unpick waste yarn from cast-on edge and place these stitches on a needle. Join ends together with a 3-needle bind-off.

Christening Shawl Chart

| | knit on right side; purl on wrong side
| - | purl on right side; knit on wrong side
| s | slip stitch purlwise
| o | yarn over
| \ | slip, slip, K2 slipped stitches together tbl
| / | k2 tog
| * | knit in back of stitch on right-side; purl in back of stitch on wrong-side
| • | knit 4 marked stitches; pass 4 stitches one at a time over last stitch worked
| ⌒ | bind off
| ▲ | slip 1, K2tog, pass slipped stitch over

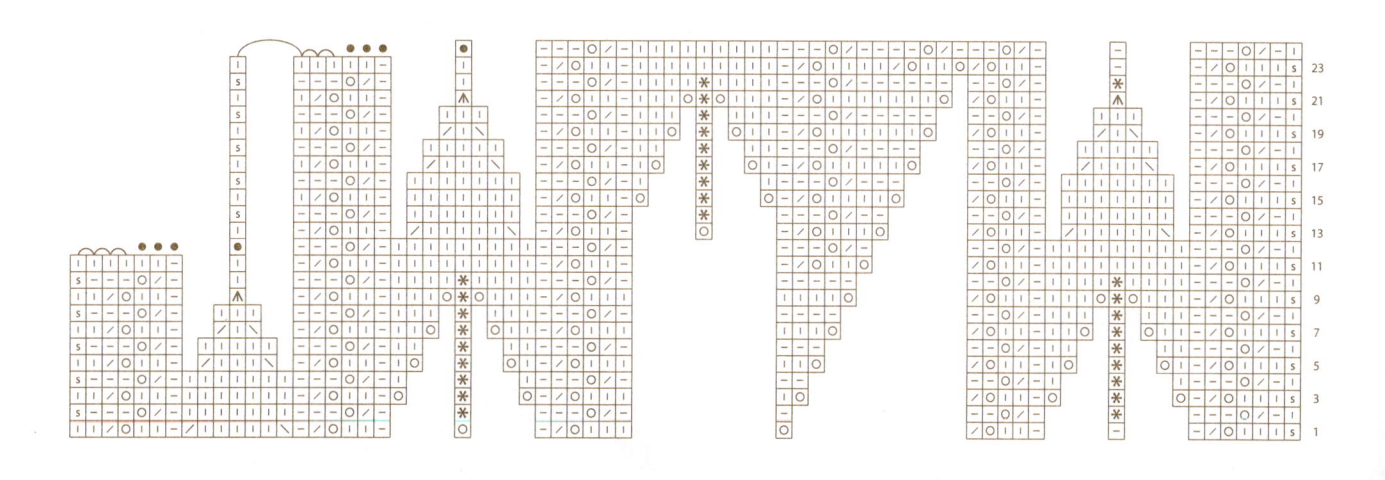

Christening Shawl continued

Preparing the Fabric Center

- Cut a square of linen 30" × 30" (76 × 76 cm). Press a 1" (2.5 cm) hem along all four sides. Fold the hem allowance under .5" (1.25 cm). Cut and miter the corners and pin hem in place. With sewing needle and thread, invisibly stitch hem in place. Press and steam well. Mark the center of each side of the square with a quilting pin.

Attaching the Edging

- Beginning at the 3-needle join, divide the lace into four equal lengths (7 repeats per side), and mark with a quilting pin. With right sides together and beginning at the 3-needle join, pin the edging to the corners of the fabric square. Find the center of each quadrant of lace and pin it to the center of each fabric side. Stretching the lace gently as necessary, pin the lace to the fabric from the centers to the corners, allowing the excess to gather at the corners so that it will block out flat around the corners.

- With sewing needle and thread, stitch each chain selvedge to the fabric twice, catching both sides of the chain selvedge stitch.

Blocking

- On a deeply padded ironing surface, pin the fabric upside down at 2" (5 cm) intervals in straight lines. Stretch the lace out at the corners to 7" (18 cm) and pin in place. Stretch and pin each lace point out to 7" (18 cm) and pin in place. Using heavy steam, block the lace. Do not let the iron touch the yarn.

Forest Park Dresser Scarf

Designed by Jolene Treace, photo on page 4

The simple geometric shapes featured in this dresser scarf were inspired by the architecture of Frank Lloyd Wright. The delicate quality of the lace-weight yarn combined with the luxurious feel of alpaca result in nothing short of pure elegance. You'll knit the body of the scarf vertically and attach the edging to the scarf as you knit it.

Measurements	Approximately 16" (40 cm) wide and 50" (127 cm) long
Yarn	The Alpaca Yarn Company Suri Elegance, 100% suri alpaca, 3.5 oz (100 g)/875 yds (800 m), 3001 Pearl Harbor
Needles	One US 3 (3.25 mm) circular needle and two US 3 (3.25 mm) double-point needles or size you need to obtain correct gauge
Gauge	About 20 stitches = 4" (10 cm) in pattern
Other Supplies	Stitch markers, tapestry needle, blocking pins
Abbreviations	**psso** pass slipped stitch over **ssk** slip 1, slip 1, knit 2 slipped stitches together **tbl** through the back loop **yo** yarn over

Working Short Rows

Short rows are worked in the corners of the edging to ease it around the corners. The top part of the edging chart shows these short rows. The arrow in the chart indicates a turning stitch, which is worked on a wrong-side (purl) row as follows: Slip the turning stitch from the left needle to the right needle. Bring the yarn from front to back between the needles and slip the turning stitch back to the left needle. Bring the yarn to the front between the needles. The turning stitch is now wrapped. Turn the work and begin the next row.

Getting Started

- Cast on 57 stitches using the long tail method (see page 246) and working over two needles held together. Purl one row.

Following the Body Chart

- To create a chained selvedge, slip the first stitch of every row knitwise and purl the last stitch of every row. These edge stitches are shown on the charts (page 53). Only right-side rows are charted and you follow the charts from right to left. All wrong-side rows are purled. The first two rows of the Body Chart are worked as follows:
- **Row 1:** Slip 1, K2tog, *yo, K1, K2tog, yo, K2, K2tog, yo, K1, yo, ssk, K2, yo, ssk, K1, yo, slip 1, K2tog, psso; repeat from * 2 more times, ending last repeat with ssk, P1.
- **Row 2:** Slip 1 as to purl, purl to end of row.
- Continue to work the selvedge chain at the beginning and end of every row and follow the Body chart between these stitches until you have worked the 32-row chart 12 times. After completing the last wrong-side row, break the yarn and slide the stitches to the other end of the circular needle.

Knitting the Edging

- Cast on 10 stitches onto double-point needle using the long-tail method and working over two needles held together. Purl one row.
- When you work these wrapped stitches on Row 12, pick up the wrap with the tip of the right needle and place it on the left needle. Work a P2tog with the wrap and the stitch it wrapped.
- Slipping the first stitch of every row (these stitches are included on the chart), work Rows 1–12 of the Short-Row Edging chart. Remember on the last row to work the wraps together with their stitches (see Working Short Rows). When you get to the last stitch of Row 12, slip it to the right needle without working it. Put down the empty double-point needle.
- With purl sides of both pieces facing you, hold the needle with the scarf stitches in your left hand and the needle with the edging stitches in your right hand. The working yarn of the edging stitches is between the last two stitches on the right needle. With the tip of the left needle, slip the last stitch from the right needle to the left and P2tog (the last edging stitch together with the first body stitch) through the back loop.
- Turn the work and begin working the Lace Edging chart beginning with Row 1. This is the top edge of the scarf, and you need to alternate between P2tog tbl and P3tog tbl when attaching the edging (see Attaching the Edging).
- When you have one scarf body stitch left on the needle, work a short row point following the top part of the chart. Work Rows 1–12 of short-row point twice.
- Once you have completed the short-row corner, you will work edging along the side of the scarf. With the circular needle, pick up 192 chain selvedge stitches. Increase one stitch at the beginning and end by picking up the outside and inside loops of these two stitches separately. Slipping the first stitch of every row knitwise, follow the chart for the edging, attaching it to the scarf body on wrong-side rows with P2tog tbl (see Attaching the Edging). You will work 32 points along the edge. When you have one body stitch left, work another short-row point.
- To work the edging along the cast-on edge, pick up one loop for each cast-on stitch. You have 57 body stitches. Work the second point of the short-row corner, then work edging along the bottom as for the top, alternating between joining to the body with P2tog tbl and P3tog tbl. When you have one body stitch remaining, work a short-row corner as before and work edging along the second long side as for the first.
- When you have one body stitch left, work a short-row point to complete the first corner. Bind off loosely. Sew bind-off to cast-on edge.

ATTACHING THE EDGING

The edging is attached to the body of the scarf on wrong-side rows. On the long edges of the scarf, work to the last stitch of the edging and work a P2tog tbl (purl 2 together through the back loops), working this last stitch together with a chained selvedge stitch. This method puts the scarf body stitch on top of the last edging stitch on the right side of the work and will not make a line along the attaching points.

When attaching edging to the top and bottom of the scarf, you will need to alternate between the P2tog tbl described above and a P3tog tbl — this will keep the knitting from flaring out along these edges. P3tog tbl is worked the same as P2tog but purl three stitches together: the last edge stitch and the next two body stitches.

Finishing

- Weave in all ends and block. Completely wet the lace and stretch it enough that the pattern opens up but not so much that the stitches are strained. Pin in place and allow at least eight hours for it to dry.

Forest Park Dresser Scarf Charts

Symbol	Meaning	Symbol	Meaning
s	slip 1 as to knit	⅄	slip 1, knit 2 together, pass slipped stitch over
□	knit on right side, purl on wrong side	O	yarn over
•	knit on wrong side, purl on right side	OO	yarn over twice
╱	knit 2 together	⌒	bind off
╲	slip 2 stitches one at a time to right hand needle; knit both stitches through back loops	■	remaining stitch on the needle after bind off

Short-row Edging

Lace Edging

Body

Row 2 and all even-numbered rows: Slip 1, purl to end of row.

Fingering Weight

Lola Flip-Top Mittens

Designed by Laura Nelkin, photo on page 10

These flip-top mittens are knitted in wonderfully bright hand painted yarn and the pattern is sized for everyone from a two-year-old to a large adult. A loop at the top of the mitten fits around a button on the back of the cuff to keep the flip-top out of your way while open.

MEASUREMENTS	Approximately 5.5 (6, 6.5, 7, 7.5, 8)" (14 [15, 17, 18, 19, 20] cm) circumference
YARN	Schaefer Yarn Company, Lola 100% superwash merino wool, 4 oz (113 g)/280 yds (256 m)
NEEDLES	Set of five US 2 (2.75 mm) double-point needles or size you need to obtain correct gauge
GAUGE	28 stitches = 4" (10 cm) in stockinette stitch
OTHER SUPPLIES	Stitch markers, tapestry needle, crochet hook, sewing needle and thread, 2 small buttons
ABBREVIATIONS	**Kfb** knit into front and back of stitch (one stitch increased) **M1L** make 1 left slanting increase (see page 247) **M1R** make 1 right slanting increase (see page 247) **pm** place marker **sm** slip marker

Knitting the Cuff

- Cast on 38 (42, 44, 48, 52, 56) stitches and divide evenly onto 4 double-point needles. Pm and join into a round, being careful not to twist stitches. Work in K1, P1 rib until cuff measures 1.75 (2.25, 2.5, 2.5, 2.75, 2.75)" (4 [5, 6, 6, 7, 7] cm).

Knitting the Hand and Shaping the Thumb Gusset

- **SET-UP ROUND 1:** Knit to last stitch, Kfb.
- **SET-UP ROUND 2:** K19 (21, 22, 24, 26, 28) stitches, pm, M1L, K1, M1R, pm, knit to end of round.

For All Sizes

- **ROUNDS 1 AND 2:** Knit.

- **ROUND 3:** Knit to marker, sm, M1L, knit to next marker, M1R, sm, knit to end of round.
- Repeat last 3 rounds 4 (5, 5, 5, 6, 7) more times, ending with Round 1.
- You now have 13 (15, 15, 15, 17, 19) thumb gusset stitches between markers.
- **NEXT ROUND:** Knit to marker, remove marker, and place thumb gusset stitches on holder, remove second marker, cast on 1 stitch, knit to end of round. You now have 39 (43, 45, 49, 53, 57) stitches.
- Knit 2 (2, 2, 3, 4, 5) rounds.

Setting Up for the Flap

Right Mitten

- Knit to last 3 (3, 3, 3, 4, 4) stitches of round. Kfb in next 24 (26, 28, 30, 34, 36) stitches, removing beginning of round marker.

Left Mitten

- K16 (18, 19, 21, 22, 24), Kfb in next 24 (26, 28, 30, 34, 36) stitches, removing beginning of round marker.

Both Mittens

- **NEXT ROUND:** Knit to increased stitches, pm for beginning of round, knit to end of round placing the 24 (26, 28, 30, 34, 36) increased stitches on holder for flap, knit to marker.
- Knit 1 (2, 3, 6, 7, 7) round even.
- Work K1, P1 rib for 3 (4, 4, 4, 5, 5) rounds. Bind off in pattern.

Knitting the Flap

- **ROUND 1:** Cast on 12 (14, 16, 18, 18, 20) stitches and distribute evenly onto 2 double-point needles, K24 (26, 28, 30, 34, 36). You now have 36 (40, 44, 48, 52, 56) stitches. Pm, join into a round.
- Distribute stitches so you have 6 (7, 8, 9, 9, 10) stitches on needles 1 and 2 and 12 (13, 14, 15, 17, 18) stitches on needles 3 and 4.
- Work in garter stitch on needles 1 and 2 and stockinette stitch on needles 3 and 4 for 3 rounds.
- Redistribute stitches so you have 9 (10, 11, 12, 13, 14) stitches on each of 4 needles. Work even in stockinette stitch until piece measures 4.75 (5.75, 6.5, 7, 7.75, 8.25)" (12 [15, 17, 18, 20, 21] cm) from beginning of cuff.

Lola Flip-Top Mittens continued

Shaping the Top

- **ROUND 1:** *Knit to last 2 stitches on needle, K2tog; repeat from *.
- **ROUND 2:** Knit.
- Repeat Rounds 1 and 2 until you have 28 (32, 32, 32, 36) stitches.
- Repeat Round 1 only until you have 4 (4, 4, 4, 8) stitches.
- Cut yarn leaving a 24" (61 cm) tail. Thread tail onto tapestry needle and draw through remaining stitches twice. Pull up snug and use crochet hook to make a chain long enough to go around button. Draw end of yarn through first chain stitch and then to inside of mitten. Fasten off on the inside.

Knitting the Thumb

- Place held thumb gusset stitches onto 3 double-point needles. Pick up and knit 1 stitch over the gap. Join into a round. You now have 14 (16, 16, 16, 18, 20) stitches.
- Work even in stockinette stitch until thumb measures .75 (1, 1.25, 1.25, 1.5, 1.75)" (2 [2.5, 3, 3, 4, 4.5] cm).
- **ROUND 1:** [K2tog, K3 (3, 3, 3, 4, 5)] twice, K2tog, K2 (4, 4, 4, 4, 4).
- **ROUND 2:** Knit.
- Repeat Rounds 1 and 2, working 1 fewer stitch between decreases and working 1 round even between decrease rounds 2 times.
- Repeat Round 1 only, working 1 fewer stitch between decreases 0 (1, 1, 1, 1, 2) times. You now have 5 (4, 4, 4, 6, 5) stitches.
- Cut yarn leaving a 10" (25 cm) tail. Thread tail onto tapestry needle and draw through remaining stitches twice. Pull up snug and fasten off on the inside.

Finishing

- Weave in ends, closing any gaps that appear at base of thumb. With sewing needle and thread, sew button to center back of cuff, where the mitten body begins.

Sock-It-To-Me Scarf

Designed by Carol Scott, photo on page 9

Who says sock yarn is for knitting socks? We think it looks pretty good as a scarf, too. This one is done in a wavy stripe pattern that shows off the self-striping yarn to great advantage. The pompoms make a whimsical finishing.

MEASUREMENTS	Approximately 7" (18 cm) wide and 54" (137 cm) long
YARN	Online Supersocke, 75% superwash wool/25% polyamide, 5 oz (142 g)/ 410 yds (375 m), Winter
NEEDLES	US 7 (4.5 mm) straight needles or size you need to obtain correct gauge
GAUGE	24 stitches = 4" (10 cm) in pattern
OTHER SUPPLIES	Stitch holder, pompom maker, tapestry needle
ABBREVIATIONS	**ssk** slip 1, slip 1, knit 2 slipped stitches together **yo** yarn over

stitch pattern

Wavy

row 1: K1, *K1, yo, K4, K2tog, ssk, K4, yo; repeat from * to last 2 stitches, K2.

row 2: K2, purl to last 2 stitches, K2.

Knitting the Pieces

- Cast on 42 stitches. Knit 1 row.
- Work in Wavy pattern until piece measures 26" (66 cm) and ending with Row 2. Place stitches on holder. Knit a second piece like the first, beginning and ending at the same place in the yarn stripe repeat.

Finishing

- Use Kitchener stitch to graft the two sets of live stitches together. Following the directions on page 248, make 6 pompoms. Sew pompoms to bottom points. Weave in ends.

Magic Loop Minis

Designed by Libby Beiler, photo on page 6

The Magic Loop method of knitting in the round is all the rage. With this method you can knit these minis on a 40" (100 cm) circular needle. Use the minis to decorate a Christmas tree or adorn a gift package.

MEASUREMENTS	Each mini is approximately 4" (10 cm) or smaller
YARN	Claudia Hand Painted Fingering Weight, 100% merino wool, 1.75 oz (50 g)/175 yds (160 m), Roasted Chiles
NEEDLES	One US 1 (2.25 mm) circular needle 40" (100 cm) long and set of two US 1 (2.25 mm) double-point needles or size you need to obtain correct gauge
GAUGE	6–7 stitches = 1" (2.5 cm) in stockinette stitch
OTHER SUPPLIES	Tapestry needle, crochet hook, stitch markers
ABBREVIATIONS	**Kfb** knit into front and back of stitch (one stitch increased) **pm** place marker **sm** slip marker **ssk** slip 1, slip 1, knit 2 slipped stitches together

Knitting the Hat

- Cast on 24 stitches. Following instructions for Working the Magic Loop, work garter stitch (knit 1 round, purl 1 round) for 6 rounds.
- Knit 8 rounds.

Decreasing for the Crown

- **ROUND 1:** *K4, K2tog; repeat from *. You now have 20 stitches.
- **ROUNDS 2, 4, AND 6:** Knit.
- **ROUND 3:** *K3, K2tog; repeat from *. You now have 16 stitches.
- **ROUND 5:** *K2, K2tog; repeat from *. You now have 12 stitches.
- **ROUND 7:** *K2tog; repeat from *. You now have 6 stitches.
- **ROUND 8:** *K1, K2tog; repeat from *. You now have 2 stitches on each needle.

Finishing the Crown

- Slip 4 stitches to one double-point needle making sure working yarn is at beginning of row. K2tog twice. Following instructions on page 245, work 2-stitch I-cord for 1" (2.5 cm). Bind off. Tie knot in I-cord.

Working the Magic Loop

Cast on required number of stitches. Slide the stitches onto the cable and divide in half, drawing out a loop of cable between the two halves. Slide the stitches back onto the needle points. This is the home position — you'll have half the stitches on each needle point.

*Hold the work so that the stitches you are about to knit are in the front and the working yarn is coming off the last stitch on the right of the back needle point. Slide the back stitches onto the cable and use the point to knit the front stitches. Turn the work and slide the stitches back onto the needle points (half on each needle point). Repeat from *, sliding the stitches from points to cable and back again as necessary.

Knitting the Earflaps

- With top of hat facing you and tail from cast-on on the left, use one double-point needle to pick up and knit 6 stitches in middle of cast-on edge.
- **ROW 1:** Knit.
- **ROW 2:** Purl.
- **ROW 3:** K1, K2tog twice, K1.
- **ROW 4:** Knit.
- **ROW 5:** K2tog twice.
- Work 2-stitch I-cord for 2.5" (6 cm).
- Work second earflap opposite the first.

Finishing

- Bind off. Weave in ends.

Knitting the Mittens (make two)

- Cast on 24 stitches leaving a 12" (30 cm) tail. Following instructions for Working the Magic Loop (see facing page), work K1, P1 rib for 8 rounds.
- **ROUND 9 AND ALL ODD-NUMBERED ROUNDS THROUGH 17:** Knit.
- Three stitches are taken from the original 24 to work the thumb. This leaves 21 working stitches plus the 3 thumb stitches.
- **ROUND 10:** Kfb, K1, Kfb; knit to end of round.
- **ROUND 12:** Kfb, K3, Kfb; knit to end of round.
- **ROUND 14:** Kfb, K5, Kfb; knit to end of round.
- **ROUND 16:** Kfb, K7, Kfb; knit to end of round.
- **ROUND 18:** K1 and slide stitch onto cable. Slip 9 stitches to holder for thumb, cast on 1 stitch, join and knit to end of round. You are now working on 24 stitches.
- Knit 8 rounds even.

Shaping the Top of the Mitten

- **ROUND 1:** *K2, K2tog; repeat from *.
- **ROUND 2:** Knit.
- **ROUND 3:** *K1, K2tog; repeat from *.
- **ROUND 4:** Knit.
- **ROUND 5:** *K2tog; repeat from *.
- Cut yarn leaving a 10" (25 cm) tail. Thread tail onto tapestry needle and draw through remaining 6 stitches. Pull up snug and fasten off on the inside.

Magic Loop Minis continued

Knitting the Thumb

- Starting with first stitch at bottom of hand, slide 9 held stitches onto needle points, 5 on front and 4 on back point. Attach yarn K2tog, knit to end of round. Knit 3 rounds.
- **NEXT ROUND:** *K2tog; repeat from *.
- Cut yarn leaving a 10" (25 cm) tail. Thread tail onto tapestry needle and draw through remaining 4 stitches. Pull up snug and fasten off on the inside.

Finishing

- Using tail at cast-on edge, single crochet a chain to desired length and knot the end. Weave in ends. Tie chains of two mittens together.

Knitting the Sweater

- Sweater is worked from neck down.
- Cast on 20 stitches. Following instructions for Working the Magic Loop, work K1, P1 rib for two rounds. Change to stockinette stitch. Begin at center back of sweater.
- **ROUND 1:** K4, pm, K2, pm, K8, pm, K2, pm, K4.
- **ROUND 2:** Increase 1 stitch before and after each marker.
- **ROUND 3:** Knit.
- Repeat Rounds 2 and 3 four more times. You now have 60 stitches.

Working the Sleeves

- Knit to first marker and remove. Slide stitches onto cable. Grasp cable behind next marker and pull it out to make a loop. Return to home position and pull out back needle. Work back and forth on 12 sleeve stitches in stockinette stitch for 10 rows, decreasing 1 stitch at each end of seventh row. Work K1, P1 rib for 2 rows. Bind off in rib.
- With right side facing and needle points facing right (all stitches are on cable), grasp cable behind next marker and pull it out to make a loop. Pull out back needle and slip 20 stitches from front needle onto empty needle. Remove marker. Slide all stitches onto cable. Pull out loop of cable behind remaining marker. Attach new yarn at beginning of front needle. Pull out back needle and work back and forth in stockinette stitch on these 12 stitches for 10 rows, decreasing 1 stitch at each end of seventh row. Work K1, P1 rib for 2 rows. Bind off in rib.
- Using tails from sleeve bind off, sew under side of sleeves together.

Knitting the Body

- Return to home position with 18 stitches on each needle. Attach new yarn and knit in the round until piece measures 2.5" (6 cm) from top of neck. Work K1, P1 rib for 3 rounds. Bind off in rib.

Finishing

- Weave in ends.

Knitting the Socks *(make two)*

- Cast on 24 stitches. Following instructions for Working the Magic Loop, work K2, P2 rib for 5 rows. Change to stockinette stitch and work 14 rounds.

Knitting the Heel Flap

- Heel is worked back and forth on 12 stitches (no magic loop).
- **ROW 1:** *Slip 1, K1; repeat from *. Turn.
- **ROW 2:** *Slip 1, P11. Turn.
- Repeat Rows 1 and 2 four more times, then work Row 1 again.

Turning the Heel

- **ROW 1:** Slip 1, P6, P2tog, P1, turn.
- **ROW 2:** Slip 1, K3, ssk, K1, turn.
- **ROW 3:** Slip 1, P4, P2tog, P1, turn.
- **ROW 4:** Slip 1, K5, ssk, K1, turn. You now have 8 heel stitches.

Knitting the Gusset

- **REPOSITION THE STITCHES AS FOLLOWS:**
- Slip 4 stitches from back to front needle.
- Slide all stitches onto cable.
- From right side, count across 6 instep stitches and pull cable loop out after this stitch.
- Slide stitches onto two needle points.
- Hold needles so the one with the yarn attached to the center is in front. You are now in the home position with the yarn in the center of the front needle. Pull out back needle and begin Working the Magic Loop.
- Slip 4, knit to end of needle. With same needle point, pick up and knit 5 stitches along heel flap, pm, K6 instep stitches. Return to home position and K6 instep stitches, pm. With same needle point, pick up and knit 5 stitches along heel flap. Knit remaining 4 heel stitches.
- **ROUND 1:** Knit.
- **ROUND 2:** Knit to within 2 stitches of marker, K2tog, sm, knit to next marker, sm, K2tog, knit to end of round.
- Repeat Rounds 1 and 2 until you have 24 stitches.

Magic Loop Minis continued

- Continue working even until foot measures about 1.5" (4 cm).

Shaping the Toe

- **ROUND 1:** *K4, K2tog, K1 (mark this stitch) ssk, K3; return to home position and repeat from *.
- **ROUND 2:** Knit.
- **ROUND 3:** *Knit to 2 stitches before marked stitch, K2tog, K1, ssk, knit to end of needle; return to home position and repeat from *.
- Repeat Rounds 2 and 3 until you have 8 stitches. Knit 1 round.
- Cut yarn leaving a 6" (15 cm) tail. Thread tail into a tapestry needle. Place all stitches onto needle and pull tightly.
- **LAST ROUND:** Slide all stitches onto cable. Grasp cable at center of work and pull out a loop. Slide stitches back to needle points (4 stitches each). Graft stitches together with Kitchener stitch (see page 245).

Finishing

- Weave in ends. Crochet ties as for mittens.

Missy's Checkbook Cover

DESIGNED BY DIANA FOSTER, *photo on page 9*

Writing checks to pay the bills will be much more fun with a custom checkbook cover. You could even consider knitting covers for all your desk accessories.

MEASUREMENTS	To fit a standard checkbook, approximately 6.25" (16 cm) wide and 7" (18 cm) tall before folding in half
YARN	O-Wool Balance, 50% wool/50% cotton, 1.75 oz (50 g)/130 yds (120 m), Sustone
NEEDLES	US 1 (2.25 mm) straight needles or size you need to obtain correct gauge
GAUGE	28 stitches = 4" (10 cm) in pattern
OTHER SUPPLIES	Tapestry needle, stitch markers
ABBREVIATIONS	**pm** place marker **sm** slip marker

stitch pattern

ROW 1: K3, pm, *K3, P3; repeat from * to last 6 stitches, K3, pm, K3.

ROW 2: K3, sm, *P3, K3; repeat from * to last 6 stitches, P3, sm, K3.

ROW 3: K3, sm, *K3, P3; repeat from * to last 6 stitches, K3, sm, K3.

ROW 4: Repeat Row 1.

ROW 5: Repeat Row 2.

ROW 6: Repeat Row 3.

Repeat Rows 1–6 for pattern.

Knitting the Cover

- Cast on 45 stitches. Work garter stitch for 1.5" (4 cm). Change to pattern stitch and work for 6.5" (17 cm). Change to garter stitch and work for 2" (5 cm). Bind off.

Finishing

- With wrong sides together fold over 1.5" (4 cm) at each end and sew sides at top and bottom. Weave in ends.

Ostrich Plume Baby Bonnet

Designed by Ranée Meuller, photo on page 6

Fingering-weight yarn of cashmere and extra fine merino combined with a delicate lace stitch produces this heirloom baby bonnet. The body of the bonnet is knitted in one shaped piece with two small seams, and ribbing is picked up and knit along the bottom edge.

stitch pattern

Ostrich Plume Lace

Row 1 and all other wrong-side rows: Purl.

Rows 2, 6, 10, 14, 18, 22, 26, and 30: Knit.

Rows 4, 8, 12, and 16: (K1, yo) 3 times, *ssk twice, slip 2 kwise, K1, p2sso, K2tog twice, (yo, K1) 5 times, yo; repeat from * to last 14 stitches, ssk twice, slip 2 kwise, K1, p2sso, K2tog twice, (yo, K1) 3 times.

Rows 20, 24, 28, and 32: K2tog 3 times, *(yo, K1) 5 times, yo, ssk twice, slip 2 kwise, K1, p2sso, K2tog twice; repeat from * to last 11 stitches, (yo, K1) 5 times, yo, ssk 3 times.

MEASUREMENTS	To fit an infant
YARN	Jaeger Cashmina, 80% cashmere/20% extra fine merino, 0.9 oz (25 g)/137 yds (125 m), 043 Sky
NEEDLES	US 3 (3.25 mm) and US 2 (3 mm) straight needles or size you need to obtain correct gauge
GAUGE	28 stitches = 4" on larger needle
OTHER SUPPLIES	Tapestry needle, 1 yard of 1/8" (3 mm) ribbon
ABBREVIATIONS	**kwise** knitwise **p2sso** pass two slipped stitches over **ssk** slip 1, slip 1, knit 2 slipped stitches together **yo** yarn over

Knitting the Bonnet

- With larger needles, cast on 83 stitches. Keeping first and last stitches (edge stitches) in stockinette throughout, work 32 rows of Ostrich Plume Lace pattern. Purl 1 row.

Ostrich Plume Baby Bonnet continued

Decreasing for Back of Bonnet

- Continue in stockinette stitch and bind off 4 stitches at the beginning of the next 14 rows. You now have 27 stitches. Decrease 1 stitch at the beginning and end of every 4th row 4 times. You now have 19 stitches.
- Work even on 19 stitches until back piece measures 3.5" (9 cm) from beginning of shaping. Bind off.

Knitting the Edging

- Lightly block the bonnet with steam. Sew bound off edges of backs to fronts. With smaller needles and right side facing, pick up and knit 53 stitches evenly spaced around bottom edge of bonnet.
- ROWS 1, 3, AND 5: *P1, K1; repeat from *.
- ROWS 2 AND 6: *K1, P1; repeat from *.
- ROW 4: *K2tog, yo; repeat from * to last stitch, K1.
- Bind off in pattern.

Finishing

- Weave in ends. Thread ribbon through eyelets.

Grampie's Tie

DESIGNED BY KELLY BRIDGES, photo on page 10

How cute is this? A tie for grampie made from granny squares. Each square measures about 2.5" (6 cm), and could use solid or variegated yarn.

MEASUREMENTS	Approximately 2.5" (6 cm) wide and 45" (114 cm) long
YARN	Tradewinds Knitwear Designs Celestial Merino, 100% merino wool, 3.5 oz (100 g)/350 yds (320 m), Fiesta
NEEDLES	One US C (2.5 mm) crochet hook or size you need to obtain correct gauge
GAUGE	Basic square = 2.5" (6 cm)
OTHER SUPPLIES	Tapestry needle

Crocheting the Squares (make 18)

- Ch 4, join with a slip stitch to form a ring.
- ROUND 1: Ch 3, 2 dc in ring, *ch 2, 3 dc in ring; repeat from * twice more, ch 2, join with a slip stitch to top of ch 3. Cut yarn and pull through last stitch.
- ROUND 2: Join to any ch 2 space. Ch 3, (2 dc, ch 2, 3 dc) into same space, *ch 1, (3 dc, ch 2, 3 dc) into next ch 2 space; repeat from * twice more, ch 1, join with a slip stitch to top of ch 3. Cut yarn and pull through last stitch.
- ROUND 3: Join to any ch 2 space. Ch 3, (2 dc, ch 2, 3 dc) into same space, *ch 1, 3 dc into next ch 1 space, ch 1, (3 dc, ch 2, 3 dc) into next ch 2 space; repeat from * twice more, ch 1, 3 dc into next ch 1 space, ch 1 join with a slip stitch to top of ch 3. Cut yarn and pull through last stitch.
- ROUND 4: Join to any ch 2 space. Ch 3, (2 dc, ch 2, 3 dc) into same space, *[ch 1, 3 dc into next ch 1 space] twice, ch 1, (3 dc, ch 2, 3 dc) into next ch 2 space; repeat from * twice more, [ch 1, 3 dc into next ch 1 space] twice, join with a slip stitch to top of ch 3. Cut yarn and pull through last stitch.

Joining the Squares

- With right sides of 2 squares together and stitches aligned, join one set of edges with slip stitch crochet. Join 18 squares together in a strip.
- With right sides facing, fold top 12 squares plus 1" (2.5 cm) of square 13 in half towards center. Join with slip stitch crochet. Weave in ends.

Finishing

- Turn tie right-side out. Work a row of sc through the back loop around unfolded section of tie, working 2 sc in the corners. Work a row of sc along bottom of folded section. Weave in remaining ends. Block.

Scrunchie Hand Warmers

Designed by Leah Oakley, photo on page 10

Why haven't we seen more of this? Of course all that wonderful self-patterning sock yarn makes wonderful mittens and hand warmers, too! These feature a nice long cuff adorned with scrunchie ruffles.

MEASUREMENTS	Approximately 7" (18 cm) circumference
YARN	Lana Grossa Meilenweit Magico, 80% wool/20% nylon, 3.5 oz (100 g)/457 yds (418 m), Color 2525
NEEDLES	Set of four US 1 (2.25 mm) double-point needles or size you need to obtain correct gauge
GAUGE	36 stitches = 4" (10 cm) in stockinette stitch
OTHER SUPPLIES	Stitch markers, tapestry needle
ABBREVIATIONS	**M1R** make 1 right leaning increase (see page 247) **M1L** make 1 left leaning increase (see page 247) **pm** place marker **sm** slip marker

stitch pattern

SCRUNCHIE

ROUNDS 1–3: *K3, P3; repeat from *.

ROUNDS 4–6: Purl.

ROUNDS 7–9: *P3, K3; repeat from *.

ROUNDS 10–12: Knit.

Repeat Rounds 1–12 for pattern.

Knitting the Cuff

- Cast on 72 stitches and distribute evenly onto 3 double-point needles. Join into a round, being careful not to twist stitches. Work K1, P1 rib until piece measures 1" (2.5 cm).
- Work Scrunchie pattern for five full repeats, 60 rounds total, ending on Round 12 of pattern.
- **DECREASE ROUND:** *K7, K2tog; repeat from *. You now have 64 stitches.
- Knit six rounds even.

Forming the Thumb Gusset

- **NEXT ROUND:** K32, pm, M1R, pm, K32. Increase for the thumb gusset as follows:
- **ROUNDS 1 AND 2:** Knit.
- **ROUND 3:** K32, sm, M1R, knit to next marker, M1L, sm, K32.
- Repeat Rounds 1–3 until you have 21 stitches between the gusset markers, 85 stitches total.

Knitting the Upper Hand

- **SET-UP ROUND:** Knit to 1 stitch before marker and slip it to right needle. Remove marker, place next 21 stitches on holder for thumb, remove second marker. Slip next stitch from left needle and hold it in front of work. Slip previously slipped stitch from right needle to left needle, then place the stitch held in front back to left needle. Knit these two stitches separately, knit to end of round.
- Continue even in stockinette stitch until piece measures 1.25" (3 cm) from top of gusset. Work K1, P1 rib for 1" (2.5 cm). Bind off loosely in pattern.

Knitting the Thumb

- Place 21 held thumb stitches on needles. Join yarn, and join into a round, knitting the first and last stitches together. You have 20 thumb stitches. Work stockinette stitch for 5 rounds. Work K1, P1 rib for 4 rounds. Bind off loosely in pattern.

Finishing

- Weave in ends.

Knitted Humbug Bag

Designed by Shelagh Smith, photo on page 9

This small carry-all is shaped like a popular English "sweetie" (candy) called the Humbug. Use this bag to carry small travel projects such as socks with 7" (18 cm) needles, yarn, and notions. Leave a small opening (shown in red) at the top of the bag through which to feed your yarn while knitting.

MEASUREMENTS	Approximately 7" (18 cm) wide and 6" (15 cm) tall when standing
YARN	Schachenmayr Nomotto Regia, 75% wool/25% acrylic, 1.75 oz (50 g)/ 230 yds (210 m), Jacquard Nordstern 5176
NEEDLES	US 3 (3.25 mm) straight needles or size you need to obtain correct gauge
GAUGE	28 stitches = 4" (10 cm) in pattern
OTHER SUPPLIES	Blocking pins, 10" (25 cm) zipper, tapestry needle, sewing needle and thread, 14" (36 cm) length of ribbon for wrist strap

stitch pattern

Knot Stitch

Purl 2 together and leave on left needle, knit same 2 together.

Knitting the Bag

- Cast on 71 stitches and purl one row.
- **ROW 1 (RIGHT SIDE):** Knit.
- **ROW 2:** K1, *Knot Stitch pattern; repeat from *.
- **ROW 3:** Knit.
- **ROW 4:** *Knot Stitch pattern; repeat from * to last stitch, K1.
- Repeat Rows 1–4 until piece measures 14" (36 cm). Knit 1 row, purl 1 row, bind off on right side.

Assembling the Bag

- Pin out piece to size (10" × 14" [25 × 36 cm]) and steam lightly. If necessary, cut bottom of zipper to fit the 10" (25 cm) opening. Sew across cut end of zipper several times. Pin zipper to cast-on and bind-off edges. Hand sew in place, keeping knit edges away from zipper teeth.
- Using drawing on facing page as a guide, fold corner D to E and stitch bottom seam with yarn. Fold corners A and B to center at C and stitch top seam leaving a .5" (12 mm) opening. Single crochet or blanket stitch around opening with same or scrap of contrasting yarn.

Finishing

- Weave in ends. Fold ribbon in half and sew with thread to inside of bag at C.

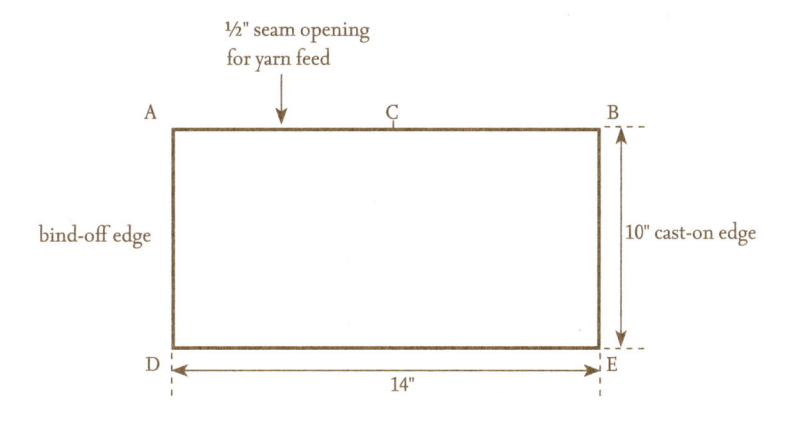

```
                    ½" seam opening
                      for yarn feed
                            ↓
         A                  C                    B
         ┌────────────────────────────────────────┐
         │                                        │
bind-off │                                        │ 10" cast-on edge
  edge   │                                        │
         │                                        │
         └────────────────────────────────────────┘
         D←──────────────14"─────────────────────→E
```

Megan's Ruffled Neck Warmer
Designed by Megan B. Wright, photo on page 7

This ruffled neck warmer buttons up for a nice snug fit. Wear it outdoors with your coat to keep you warm, then leave it on indoors with your sweater to keep you cool. Cool looking, that is.

MEASUREMENTS	Approximately 16" (41 cm) circumference
YARN	Collinette Jitterbug, 100% superwash merino, 3.5 oz (100 g)/ 293 yds (268 m), 48 Florentina
NEEDLES	US 4 (3.5 mm) straight needles or size you need to obtain correct gauge
GAUGE	22 stitches = 4" (10 cm) in garter stitch
OTHER SUPPLIES	Tapestry needle, 1⅜" (1 cm) button
ABBREVIATIONS	**Kfb** knit into front and back of stitch (one stitch increased) **RS** right side **WS** wrong side
NOTE	Yarn is used double throughout

Megan's Ruffled Neck Warmer continued

Knitting the Front

- Cast on 25 stitches. Work in garter stitch (knit every row) for 28 rows. Bind off.

Knitting the Neck Piece

- Pick up and knit 20 stitches along one short side of the front piece.
- **ROW 1 (WS):** K3, P14, K3.
- **ROW 2 (RS):** Knit.
- Repeat Rows 1 and 2 until neck piece measures 12" (30 cm), ending with a wrong-side row.

Working the Buttonhole

- **ROW A:** K8, bind off 5, K7.
- **ROW B:** K3, P4, cast on 5, P5, K3.
- Continue working Rows 1 and 2 for 1.5" (4 cm). Work garter stitch for 6 rows. Bind off.

Knitting the Ruffle

- With right side facing, pick up and knit 25 stitches along bottom of Front.
- **ROW 1 (WS):** Purl.
- **ROW 2 (RS):** *Kfb; repeat from *.
- Repeat Rows 1 and 2 two more times. You now have 200 stitches.
- Continue even in stockinette stitch until ruffle measures 2.75" (7 cm), ending with a right-side row. Work 2 rows of garter stitch. Bind off.

Finishing

- Weave in ends. Sew button to Front.

Wave Jumper
Designed by Leslie Barbazette, photo on page 7

While there are a lot of stitches in this jumper, once you find your rhythm with the wave pattern you'll surf right through it. The jumper is knitted in the round, then divided for front and back at armholes, and has buttons at the shoulders.

stitch pattern

Wave
Round 1: Knit.
Round 2: Knit.
Round 3: *K2tog 3 times, Kfb 6 times, K2tog 3 times; repeat from *.
Round 4: Purl.

MEASUREMENTS	To fit infant 0–3 (3–6, 6–12) months, approximately 13 (14.25, 15.5)" (33 [36, 39] cm) chest
YARN	Zitron Trekking XXL, 75% wool/25% nylon, 3.5 oz (100 g)/459 yds (420 m), Color 69
NEEDLES	One US 1 (2.5 mm) circular needle 16" (40 cm) long or size you need to obtain correct gauge
GAUGE	28 stitches = 4" (10 cm) in pattern
OTHER SUPPLIES	Stitch holder, two ⅝" (1.6 cm) buttons, tapestry needle
ABBREVIATIONS	**Kfb** knit into front and back of stitch (one stitch increased)

Knitting the Skirt

- Cast on 180 (204, 216) stitches loosely. Join into a round, being careful not to twist stitches. Work Wave pattern for 8 (10, 12)" (20 [25, 30] cm).
- **Next round:** *K2tog; repeat from *.
- **Next round:** Purl.
- Work evenly in stockinette stitch for 1" (2.5 cm).

Knitting the Front Yoke

- K45 (51, 54) stitches and place remaining 45 (51, 54) stitches on holder.

Shaping the Armholes

- Decrease 2 stitches at beginning of next 4 rows, then decrease 1 stitch at beginning and end of right-side rows 3 (4, 5) times. You now have 31 (35, 36) stitches.

Shaping the Neck

- K10 (11, 11) and place remaining 21 (24, 25) stitches on holder. Continue in stockinette stitch and decrease 1 stitch at neck edge every other row 4 times. You now have 6 (7, 7) stitches.

Wave Jumper continued

Working the Straps and Buttonholes

- Work even for 1" (2.5 cm), ending with a wrong-side row.
- **ROW 1:** K2 (3, 3) bind off 2, K2 (2, 2).
- **ROW 2:** P2 (2, 2), cast on 2, P2 (3, 3).
- Continue in stockinette stitch for .5" (1.3 cm). Bind off.
- Place held 21 (24, 25) front stitches on needles. Join yarn; bind off 11 (13, 14) stitches for neck edge. Repeat for other side, reversing shaping.

Knitting the Back Yoke

- Place held 45 (51, 54) back stitches on needles and work as for front, eliminating buttonholes.

Finishing

- Sew buttons to back straps. Weave in ends. Block.

Blue-Wave Baby Sweater

DESIGNED BY VALENTINA DEVINE, *photo on page 8*

This adorable little sweater is soft and light — perfect for baby.

MEASUREMENTS	Approximately 21" (53 cm) circumference and 10" (25 cm) length
YARN	Tess' Designer Yarns Baby Superwash Merino, 100% wool, 5 oz (142 g)/660 yds (604 m), Bahama Bay
NEEDLES	US 2 (2.75 mm) straight needles or size you need to obtain correct gauge
GAUGE	11 stitches = 1.5" (4 cm) in pattern
OTHER SUPPLIES	One US 4 (3.5 mm) crochet hook, tapestry needle, 4 or 5 decorative buttons

stitch pattern

WAVE

ROW 1: *K2tog twice, (yo, K1) 3 times, yo, K2tog twice; repeat from *.

ROW 2: Purl.

ROWS 3 AND 4: Knit.

Repeat Rows 1–4 for pattern.

Knitting the Front and Back

- Front and Back are worked the same. Cast on 77 stitches. Work 6 rows garter stitch, ending with wrong-side row. Work Rows 1–4 of Wave pattern 20 times. Bind off loosely.

Knitting the Sleeves (make two)

- Cast on 55 stitches. Work 6 rows garter stitch, ending with wrong-side row. Work Rows 1–4 of Wave pattern 11 times. Bind off loosely.

Crocheting the Collar

- Sew 22 stitches of right shoulder seam, leaving left shoulder open. Work 1 row of single crochet along 22 left front shoulder stitches, 33 front neck stitches, 33 back neck stitches and 22 left back shoulder stitches. Work another row of single crochet along left back shoulder stitches, making 4 evenly spaced buttonholes as follows: Work *3 sc, ch 5, skip 3 sc; repeat from * 3 more times, work 3 sc.
- **AT NECK EDGE, CROCHET A RUFFLE AS FOLLOWS:** *Ch 10, slip stitch into same stitch, slip stitch in next stitch; repeat from *. Continue ruffle around neck to left shoulder.

Finishing

- Sew tops of sleeves to arm hole edges, matching center of sleeves to shoulder seams. Sew side and sleeve seams. Weave in ends. Sew buttons opposite buttonholes on left shoulder.

Marialis End-to-End Scarf

DESIGNED BY MYRNA A.I. STAHMAN, photo on page 7

The beautiful undulating scallops of the lace pattern are maintained on both ends of the scarf with a clever combination of seed stitch borders and carefully placed decreases. Bison down is wonderfully soft!

MEASUREMENTS	Approximately 9" (23 cm) wide and 50" (127 cm) long
YARN	Buffalo Gold, 100% bison down, 2 oz (60 g)/288 yds (263 m), 8 Buffalo Gold
NEEDLES	US 3 (3.25 mm) straight needles or size you need to obtain correct gauge; US 10 (6 mm) straight needle for bind off
GAUGE	18 stitches = 3" (8 cm) in pattern blocked
OTHER SUPPLIES	Crochet hook, one US 10 (6 mm) straight needle for binding off, tapestry needle
ABBREVIATIONS	**B6** work six border stitches; see instructions below **pwise** as if to purl, inserting needle from back to front **wyif** with yarn in front

Marialis End-to-End Scarf continued

Casting On

- In order for the cast-on and bind-off edges to look the same, pull out one-yard tail of yarn and cast on with a provisional method (see page 248). After working 5 or more rows of the scarf, remove the provisional cast-on and use the tail to bind off in pattern. Bind off using a US 10 (6 mm) straight needle for the right needle.

Knitting the Beginning Border

- **CAST ON 41 STITCHES. WORK 8 ROWS OF SEED STITCH AS FOLLOWS:** Wyif, slip 1 pwise, move yarn to back between the needles, (K1, P1) 19 times, K2.
- The lace pattern is worked with 6 border stitches at the beginning and end of each row. These are designated B6.
- **BEGINNING OF ROW BORDER:** Wyif, slip 1 pwise, move yarn to back between the needles, K1, (P1, K1) twice.
- **END OF ROW BORDER:** (K1, P1) twice, K2.
- **SET-UP ROW 1:** B6, K1, K2tog, K1, (yo, K1) 6 times, (K2tog, K1) 3 times, (yo, K1) 6 times, K1, K2tog, K1, B6. You now have 48 stitches.

Knitting the Lace Pattern

- Beginning with Feather and Fan Lace pattern Row 2, work 6 border stitches at the beginning and end of every row as described above, and work 4-row pattern repeats until scarf is desired length.

Knitting the Ending Border

- Work Row 1 of pattern as usual.
- **ROW 2:** B6, K2tog, K14, (K2tog) twice, K14, K2tog, B6. You now have 44 stitches.
- **ROW 3:** Slip 1, (K1, P1) 10 times, K2tog, (P1, K1) 10 times, K1. You now have 43 stitches.
- **WORK 7 ROWS OF SEED STITCH AS FOLLOWS:** Wyif, slip 1 pwise, move yarn to back between the needles, (K1, P1) 20 times, K2. Bind off in pattern using the US 10 straight needle for the right needle.

Finishing

- Weave in ends. Block to desired size.

---

stitch pattern

FEATHER AND FAN LACE

ROW 1: (K2tog) 3 times, (yo, K1) 6 times, (K2tog) 6 times, (yo, K1) 6 times, (K2tog) 3 times.

ROWS 2 AND 4: Purl.

ROW 3: Knit.

Repeat Rows 1–4 for pattern.

Horseshoe Cable Socks

Designed by Judith Durant, *photo on page 10*

These lovely cabled socks are handsome and comfortable. The fine merino wool from Cherry Tree Hill is high quality and allows for plenty of stretch, meaning these socks will fit a range of sizes.

stitch pattern

1/1 Rib

Rounds 1: *K1, P1; repeat from *.

Repeat Round 1 for pattern.

Horseshoe Cable

Rounds 1, 2, and 4: *K6, P1, K2, P1; repeat from *.

Round 3: *Slip 2 stitches to cable needle and hold in back, K1, K2 from cable needle, slip 1 to cable needle and hold in front, K2, K1 from cable needle, P1, K2, P1; repeat from *.

Measurements	To fit a woman's foot, approximately 8" (20 cm) circumference
Yarn	Cherry Tree Hill Supersock, 100% superwash merino, 4 oz (113 g)/420 yds (384 m), Natural
Needles	Set of four US 3 (3.25 mm) double-point needles or size you need to obtain correct gauge
Gauge	21 stitches = 2" (5 cm) in pattern, unstretched
Other Supplies	Cable needle, tapestry needle
Abbreviations	**ssk** slip 1, slip 1, knit 2 slipped stitches together

Knitting the Leg

- Cast on 70 stitches and distribute over 3 needles so there are 20 stitches on needle 1, 26 stitches on needle 2, and 24 stitches on needle 3.
- **Note:** The "seam" is at the side of the leg, not the center back.
- Work 1/1 rib for 1.25" (3 cm). Work 18 repeats of Horseshoe Cable pattern or to desired length, ending on Row 4.

Knitting the Heel Flap

- **Adjust stitches as follows:** Move 16 stitches from needle 2 onto needle 1. Move remaining 10 stitches from needle 2 onto needle 3. You will work the heel flap back and forth on the 36 stitches now on needle 1 and hold the remaining 34 stitches for the instep. Slipping the first stitch of each row creates one chain stitch on the edges for every two rows worked.
- **Row 1:** *Slip 1, K1; repeat from *.
- **Row 2:** Slip 1, purl to end of row.
- Repeat Rows 1 and 2 seventeen times. You now have 18 chain stitches on each side of the heel flap.

Turning the Heel

- **Row 1:** K24, ssk, turn.

Horseshoe Cable Socks continued

- **ROW 2:** Slip 1, P12, P2tog, turn.
- **ROW 3:** Slip 1, K12, ssk, turn.
- **ROW 4:** Slip 1, P12, P2tog.
- Repeat Rows 3 and 4 until all heel stitches have been worked. You now have 14 heel stitches.

Knitting the Gussets

- Onto needle 1, knit 14 heel stitches and pick up 18 stitches along one side of the heel flap. Onto needle 2, work 34 instep stitches in pattern. Onto needle 3, pick up 18 stitches along the other side of the heel flap and knit 7 heel stitches from needle 1. The round now begins in the center of the heel, and you have 25 stitches on needle 1, 34 stitches on needle 2, and 25 stitches on needle 3.
- **ROUND 1:** Knit to last 2 stitches on needle 1, K2tog, work 34 instep stitches in pattern on needle 2, ssk at beginning of needle 3, knit to end of round.
- **ROUND 2:** Knit all stitches on needles 1 and 3 and work stitches on needle 2 in pattern as established.
- Repeat Rounds 2 and 3 until you have 17 stitches on needles 1 and 3 and 34 stitches on needle 2.

Knitting the Foot

- Continue working stockinette stitch on sole stitches (needles 1 and 3) and Horseshoe Cable pattern on instep stitches (needle 2) until foot measures 6.5" (17 cm) or desired length from back of heel.

Shaping the Toe

- Discontinue pattern stitch and knit all stitches.
- **ROUND 1:** Knit to last 3 stitches on needle 3, K2tog, K1. K1, ssk at beginning of needle 2, knit to last 3 stitches of needle 2, K2tog, K1. K1, ssk at beginning of needle 3, knit to end of round.
- **ROUND 2:** Knit.
- Repeat Rounds 1 and 2 until 6 stitches remain on needles 1 and 3 and 12 stitches remain on needle 2. Knit 6 stitches from needle 1 onto needle 3. Join toe stitches together with Kitchener stitch (see page 245).

Finishing

- Weave in ends. Block.

BlueBells Socks

Designed by Tamara Del Sonno, *photo on page 9*

These casual socks may be worn straight up or with the cuff folded down. Either way, they're trimmed with tiny ruffled "bells."

MEASUREMENTS	To fit women's small (medium, large) foot
YARN	Southwest Trading Company Tofutsies, 50% superwash wool/25% soysilk fibers/22.5% cotton/ 2.5% chitin (shrimp and crab shells), 3.5 oz (100 g)/465 yds (425 m), #720 Sweep You Off Your Feet
NEEDLES	Set of five US 0, 1, or 1.5 (2, 2.25 or 2.5 mm) double-point needles or size you need to obtain correct gauge
GAUGE	16 stitches = 2" (5 cm) in stockinette stitch
OTHER SUPPLIES	Stitch markers, tapestry needle
ABBREVIATIONS	**ssk** slip 1, slip 1, knit 2 slipped stitches together

Knitting the Ruffle

- Cast on 140 (150, 160) stitches and divide evenly onto double-point needles. Join into a round being careful not to twist stitches.
- ROUND 1: *K8, P2; repeat from *.
- ROUND 2: *Ssk, K4, K2tog, P2; repeat from *.
- ROUND 3: *K6, P2; repeat from *.
- ROUND 4: *Ssk, K2, K2tog, P2; repeat from *.
- ROUND 5: *Ssk, K2tog, P2; repeat from *.
- You now have 56 (60, 64) stitches.

Knitting the Leg

- Work K2, P2 rib until piece measures 8" (20 cm) or desired length to top of heel.

Knitting the Heel Flap

- K14 (15, 16), turn and P28 (30, 32). You will work the heel flap back and forth over these 28 (30, 32) stitches.
- ROW 1: *Slip 1, K1; repeat from *.
- ROW 2: Slip 1, purl to end of row.
- Repeat Rows 1 and 2 until heel flap is 2 (2, 2.5)" (5 [5, 6] cm) long.

BlueBells Socks continued

Turning the Heel

- ROW 1: Slip 1, K16 (17, 19), ssk, K1, turn.
- ROW 2: Slip 1, P5 (7, 9), P2tog, P1, turn.
- ROW 3: Slip 1, K6 (8, 10), ssk, K1, turn.
- ROW 4: Slip 1, P7 (9, 11), P2tog, P1, turn.
- ROW 5: Slip 1, K8 (10, 12), ssk, K1, turn.
- ROW 6: Slip 1, P9 (11, 13), ssk, P1, turn.
- ROW 7: Slip 1, K10 (12, 14), ssk, K1, turn.
- ROW 8: Slip 1, P11 (13, 15), P2tog, P1, turn.
- ROW 9: Slip 1, K12 (14, 16), ssk, K1, turn.
- ROW 10: Slip 1, P13 (15, 17), P2tog, P1, turn.
- ROW 11: Slip 1, K14 (16, 18), ssk, K1, turn.
- ROW 12: Slip 1, P14 (16, 18), P2tog, P1, turn.
- ROW 13: Knit all stitches.

Knitting the Gusset

- With right side facing, pick up 1 stitch in every slipped stitch along side of heel flap, place marker. Work instep stitches in rib pattern as established, place marker. Pick up same number of stitches along other side of heel flap, knit sole stitches. Place marker for end of round.
- ROUND 1: Knit to 2 stitches before 1st marker, K2tog; work ribbing on instep stitches; slip 2nd marker, ssk; knit to end of round.
- ROUND 2: Knit.
- Repeat Rounds 1 and 2 until you have 56 (60, 64) stitches.

Knitting the Foot

- Continue working K2, P2 rib on instep stitches and stockinette on sole stitches until foot measures 2" (5 cm) less than desired finished length. Knit 3 rounds stockinette stitch.

Shaping the Toe

- ROUND 1: Knit to 3 stitches before 1st marker, K2tog, K2, ssk, knit to 3 stitches before 2nd marker, K2tog, K2, ssk, knit to end of round.
- ROUND 2: Knit.
- Repeat Rounds 1 and 2 until you have 12 (14, 16) stitches.

Finishing

- Join top of toe to bottom of toe with Kitchener stitch (see page 245). Weave in ends. Block.

Picot Edge Socks

Designed by Betty Balcomb, photo on page 6

The picot edge at the top of this sock is worked into a hem, which is folded to the inside of the sock and stitched in place. While any type of sock yarn will work, we especially like the double-stripe effect shown here.

MEASUREMENT	Approximately 7.5" (19 cm) circumference, length as desired
YARN	Lana Grossa Meilenweit Wool 100g Fun, 80% wool/20% polymide, 3.5 oz (100 g)/462 yds (422 m), Color 311
NEEDLES	Set of four US 3 (3.25 mm) double-point needles or size you need to obtain correct gauge
GAUGE	28 stitches = 4" (10 cm) in stockinette stitch
OTHER SUPPLIES	Tapestry needle
ABBREVIATIONS	**K2tog tbl** knit two stitches together through the back loop **pwise** purlwise

Knitting the Picot Edge

- Cast on 52 stitches loosely leaving a 15" (38 cm) tail. Divide the stitches onto 3 double-point needles so you have 13 stitches on needle 1, 26 stitches on needle 2, and 13 stitches on needle 3. Join into a round being careful not to twist stitches. Knit 10 rounds.
- PICOT ROW: *K2tog, yo; repeat from *.

Knitting the Leg

- Work even in stockinette stitch until sock measures 7.5" (19 cm) from picot row.

Picot Edge Socks continued

Knitting the Heel Flap

- Knit 13 stitches from needle 1 onto needle 3. Turn and P26. The heel flap is worked back and forth on these 26 stitches. Leave the other 26 stitches on needle for instep.
- ROW 1: *Slip 1 pwise, K1; repeat from *.
- ROW 2: Slip 1 pwise, purl to end of row.
- Repeat Rows 1 and 2 until heel flap measures 2.5" (5 cm), ending with Row 2.

Turning the Heel

- ROW 1: Slip 1 pwise, K13, K2tog tbl, K1, turn.
- ROW 2: Slip 1 pwise, P3, P2tog, P1, turn.
- ROW 3: Slip 1 pwise, K4, K2tog tbl, K1, turn.
- ROW 4: Slip 1 pwise, P5, P2tog, P1, turn.
- ROW 5: Slip 1 pwise, K6, K2tog tbl, K1, turn.
- ROW 6: Slip 1 pwise, P7, P2tog, P1, turn.
- Continue in this manner, working 1 more stitch before the decrease on every row, until all stitches have been worked. You now have 14 heel stitches.

Knitting the Gusset

- Knit 14 heel stitches. Onto same needle, pick up 1 stitch between stitches on needle and slipped edge stitches, pick up 1 stitch in each slipped edge stitch, pick up 1 stitch between slipped edge stitches and instep stitches.
- Onto needle 2, knit 26 instep stitches.
- Onto needle 3, pick up 1 stitch between instep stitches and slipped edge stitches, pick up 1 stitch in each slipped edge stitch, pick up 1 stitch between slipped edge stitches on needle 1, knit 7 stitches from needle 1 to needle 3. The round begins in the middle of the heel.
- ROUND 1: Knit to last 3 stitches on needle 1, K2tog, K1; knit 26 stitches on needle 2; K1, K2tog tbl at beginning of needle 3 and knit to end of round.
- ROUND 2: Knit.
- Repeat Rounds 1 and 2 until you have 13 stitches on needles 1 and 3 and 26 stitches on needle 2.

Knitting the Foot

- Continue even in stockinette stitch until foot measures 1.5" (4 cm) less than desired finished length.

Shaping the Toe

- **ROUND 1:** Knit to last 3 stitches on needle 1, K2tog, K1; K1, K2tog tbl at beginning of needle 2, knit to last 3 stitches on needle 2, K2tog, K1; K1, K2tog tbl at beginning of needle 3, knit to end of round.
- **ROUND 2:** Knit.
- Repeat Rounds 1 and 2 until you have 8 stitches on needles 1 and 3 and 16 stitches on needle 2. Work Round 1 three more times. You now have 5 stitches on needles 1 and 3 and 10 stitches on needle 2. Knit 5 stitches from needle 1 onto needle 3. Cut the yarn leaving a 15" (38 cm) tail. Thread tail onto tapestry needle and graft toe stitches together with Kitchener stitch (see page 245).

Finishing

- Turn sock inside out. Fold cuff along picot row so that the stitches between the holes form little peaks. With the tail left from the cast on, sew hem in place to inside of sock. Weave in ends.

Catch-Me-If-You-Can Socks

DESIGNED BY SHIRLEY YOUNG, photo on page 6

These anklets are topped with a ribbed and ruffled cuff for a cute and comfortable fit. And if you start at the same place in the self-patterning yarn for both socks, the resulting patterns are very precise. The sock is knitted from the toe up.

MEASUREMENTS	Approximately 8" (20 cm) circumference and 8.5" (22 cm) length
YARN	Wisdom Yarns Marathon Socks–New York, 75% superwash wool/25% polyamide, 3.5 oz (100 g)/437 yds (400 m), Color 223
NEEDLES	Set of five US 1 (2.25 mm) double-point needles or size you need to obtain correct gauge
GAUGE	36 stitches = 4" (10 cm) in stockinette stitch
OTHER SUPPLIES	Stitch holders, tapestry needle
ABBREVIATIONS	**inc 1** increase 1 stitch by working into the row below kwise for a knit stitch and pwise for a purl stitch **M1** make 1 increase (see page 247) **RS** right side **WS** wrong side

Catch-Me-If-You-Can Socks continued

Knitting the Toe

- Holding two double-point needles together, wrap the yarn in a figure eight around the needles until there are 6 loops on each needle. Holding the tail down with your left thumb, use a third needle to knit the stitches off the top needle, leaving the loops on the bottom needle. Turn the knitting around and use an empty needle to knit the stitches off the bottom needle, knitting them through the back loop. Knit the stitches on these two needles once more. You now have a small rectangle of knitting with live stitches on two sides.

- With an empty needle, pick up 2 stitches along the first short side of the rectangle. With a new needle, knit the 4 stitches on the next needle. With an empty needle, pick up 2 stitches along the other short side. With a new needle, knit the 4 stitches on the next needle. You now have live stitches on all 4 sides of the rectangle.

- ROW 1: K2 on needle 1 (short side); inc 1, K4, inc 1 on needle 2; K2 on needle 3 (short side); inc 1, K4, inc 1 on needle 4.

- ROW 2: Knit.

- Repeat Rows 1 and 2 until you have 68 stitches.

Knitting the Foot

- Redistribute stitches 17 stitches on each needle, 34 sole stitches on needles 1 and 2 and 34 instep stitches on needles 3 and 4. Work even in stockinette stitch until foot is 2" (5 cm) less than desired finished measurement.

- NEXT ROUND: K1, M1, at beginning of needle 1, knit to end of needle. Knit to last stitch on needle 2, M1, K1. Work stitches even on needles 3 and 4.

- NEXT ROUND: Knit.

- Repeat these two rounds 3 more times. You now have 42 sole stitches and 34 instep stitches.

- Place first and last 14 sole stitches on holder. Working center 14 stitches only, knit bottom of heel as follows.

- ROW 1: *Slip 1, K1; repeat from *.

- ROW 2: Slip 1, P13.

- Repeat Rows 1 and 2 nineteen more times. You now have 10 slip stitches along each side of the heel.

- With WS facing, pick up and purl 10 stitches along one side of heel flap. Turn, slip 1, K1 along these 10 picked up stitches and the 14 heel stitches. Pick up and knit 10 stitches along other side of heel. You now have 34 heel stitches.

- NEXT ROW (WS): Purl to last stitch, P2tog (last stitch and 1 stitch from holder).

- **NEXT ROW (RS):** Slip 1, K1 to last stitch, ssk (last stitch and 1 stitch from holder).
- Repeat these 2 rows until all stitches from holders have been worked.

Knitting the Leg

- Begin working stockinette stitch in the round by knitting 34 instep stitches then knitting 34 back stitches. Work even in stockinette stitch for 2" (5 cm).

Knitting the Cuff

- Work K1, P1 rib for 1.5" (4 cm).
- **ROUND 1:** K1, inc 1, P1, inc 1; repeat from *. You now have 136 stitches.
- **ROUNDS 2–5:** K1, P3; repeat from *.
- **ROUND 6:** K1, inc 1, P3, inc 1; repeat from *. You now have 204 stitches.
- **ROUNDS 7 AND 8:** K1, P5; repeat from *.
- Bind off.

Finishing

- Weave in ends. Block.

Sport Weight

Guilty Pleasures Socks

Designed by Gabrielle Bolland, photo on page 12

Indulge yourself with luxurious hand-dyed alpaca socks. They are easy to knit and incredibly easy to wear.

MEASUREMENTS	Fits 7–9" (18–23 cm) circumference ankle
YARN	Frog Tree Hand-Dyed Sport, 100% alpaca, 3.5 oz (100 g)/260 yds (238 m), Poppy
NEEDLES	Set of five US 1 (2.25 mm) double-point needles or size you need to obtain correct gauge
GAUGE	28 stitches = 4" (10 cm) in stockinette stitch
OTHER SUPPLIES	Tapestry needle
ABBREVIATIONS	**SK2P** slip 1, K2tog, pass slipped stitch over **ssk** slip 1, slip 1, knit 2 slipped stitches together

stitch pattern

LACE

ROUND 1 AND ALL ODD-NUMBERED ROUNDS THROUGH 9: *K1, yo, K4, SK2P, K4, yo, K1; repeat from *.

ROUND 2 AND ALL EVEN-NUMBERED ROUNDS THROUGH 10: Knit.

ROUNDS 11 AND 12: Purl.

Repeat Rounds 1–12 for pattern.

Knitting the Top

- Cast on 52 stitches loosely and divide evenly over 4 needles. Join into a round, being careful not to twist stitches. The round begins in the center of the heel.
- Work Rounds 1–12 of Lace pattern twice.

Knitting the Heel Flap

- Knit 13 stitches from needle 1 onto needle 4. Turn, slip 1, P25. You will work the heel flap back and forth on these 26 stitches.
- **ROW 1:** *Slip 1, K1; repeat from *.
- **ROWS 2 AND 4:** Slip 1, P25.
- **ROW 3:** Slip 1, *slip 1, K1; repeat from * to last stitch, K1.
- Repeat Rows 1–4 until you have 26 heel flap rows, ending with a wrong-side row.

Turning the Heel

- **ROW 1:** Slip 1, K14, K2tog, K1, turn.
- **ROW 2:** Slip 1, P5, P2tog, P1, turn.
- **ROW 3:** Slip 1, K6, K2tog, K1, turn.
- **ROW 4:** Slip 1, P7, P2tog, P1, turn.
- Continue in this manner, working 1 more stitch before the decrease until all stitches have been worked, ending with a wrong-side row. You now have 16 heel stitches.

Knitting the Gussets

- Knit heel stitches. Onto same needle, pick up and knit 13 stitches along first side of heel flap and 1 stitch between heel flap and needle 2. Work instep stitches on needles 2 and 3 in lace pattern as established. With empty needle, pick up 1 stitch between needle 3 and heel flap and 13 stitches along second side of heel flap, then knit 8 heel stitches onto same needle.
- ROUND 1: Knit to last 3 stitches on needle 1, K2tog, K1; work even in Lace pattern on needles 2 and 3; K1, ssk at beginning of needle 4, knit to end of round.
- ROUND 2: Knit stitches on needles 1 and 4 and work even in Lace pattern on needles 2 and 3.
- Repeat Rounds 1 and 2 until you have 13 stitches remaining on needles 1 and 4. You now have 52 stitches.

Knitting the Foot

- Continue in patterns as established until foot measures approximately 2" (5 cm) from desired finished length.

Shaping the Toe

- ROUND 1: Knit to last 3 stitches on needle 1, K2tog, K1; K1, ssk at beginning of needle 2; knit to last 3 stitches on needle 3, K2tog, K1; K1, ssk at beginning of needle 4, knit to end of round.
- ROUND 2: Knit.
- Repeat Rounds 1 and 2 until you have 20 stitches remaining. Knit to the end of needle 1. Use Kitchener stitch (see page 245) to graft toe stitches together.

Finishing

- Weave in ends. Block.

Garter Stitch Loop-Through Scarf

Designed by Marci Richardson, photo on page 11

Here's a clever construction that will keep your scarf tidy at all times. Both ends of the scarf have a loop through which to pull the other end, so no matter which way you put it on, you can choose right through left or left through right. The shaping makes the ends stay where put.

MEASUREMENTS	Approximately 16" (41 cm) circumference
YARN	Lorna's Laces Shepherd Sport, 100% superwash wool, 2.5 oz (71 g)/200 yds (183 m), Tuscany
NEEDLES	US 4 (3.5 mm) straight needles and two US 4 (3.5 mm) double-point needles or size you need to obtain correct gauge
GAUGE	24 stitches = 4" (10 cm) in garter stitch
OTHER SUPPLIES	Tapestry needle
ABBREVIATIONS	**Kfb** knit into front and back of stitch (one stitch increased) **pwise** purlwise **wyif** with yarn in front **yo** yarn over

Getting Started

- Cast on 1 stitch.
- **ROW 1:** Kfb.
- **ROW 2:** Slip 1 pwise wyif, put yarn to back, Kfb.
- **ROW 3:** Slip 1 pwise wyif, put yarn to back, Kfb, K1.
- **ROW 4:** Slip 1 pwise wyif, put yarn to back, K1, yo, knit to end of row.
- Repeat Row 4 until you have 32 stitches.
- **NEXT ROW:** Slip 1 pwise wyif, put yarn to back, K1, yo, K2tog, knit to end of row.
- Repeat this last row until straight portion of scarf measures 2" (5 cm).

Dividing for the Loop

- Holding two empty double-point needles in your right hand and the knitting in your left hand, slip one stitch at a time from project needle to double-point needles, alternating one stitch on one double-point needle and the next on the other double-point needle. You now have 16 stitches on each of two double-point needles.
- Working each side of the loop separately, work K1, P1 rib for 2" (5 cm).

Rejoining the Loop

- Holding one empty needle in your right hand and the two needles with loop stitches in your left hand, slip one stitch at a time from left- to right-hand needle, alternating one stitch from one double-point needle and the next from the other double-point needle. You now have 32 stitches on one needle.

Knitting Around the Neck

- **NEXT ROW:** Slip 1 pwise wyif, put yarn to back, K1, yo, K2tog, knit to end of row.
- Repeat this last row until piece measures 16" (41 cm) from where you rejoined the loop.

Knitting the Second Side

- Form another loop following the instructions above through Rejoining the Loop.
- **NEXT ROW:** Slip 1 pwise wyif, put yarn to back, K1, yo, K2tog, knit to end of row.
- Repeat this last row until piece measures 2" (5 cm) from end of second loop.
- **NEXT ROW:** Slip 1 pwise wyif, put yarn to back, K1, yo, K2tog, knit to last 5 stitches, K2tog, K3.
- Repeat this last row until you have 8 stitches. Decrease for end of scarf as follows.
- **ROW 1:** Slip 1 pwise wyif, put yarn to back, K1, yo, K3tog, K3.
- **ROW 2:** Slip 1 pwise wyif, put yarn to back, K1, yo, K3tog, K2.
- **ROW 3:** Slip 1 pwise wyif, put yarn to back, K1, yo, K3tog, K1.
- **ROW 4:** Slip 1 pwise wyif, put yarn to back, K3tog, K1.
- **LAST ROW:** K3tog. Cut yarn and pull tail through remaining stitch.

Finishing

- Weave in ends. Block lightly if necessary.

Feather-and-Fan Baby Sweater

Designed by Kimberly Conterio, photo on page 12

This delightful baby sweater uses one of the most popular lace patterns: Feather and Fan. Because the lace works at a tighter gauge than stockinette, you will knit the lace pattern on a larger needle. The fronts and back are worked as one piece to the underarms, and all edges are finished with a neat garter-stitch border.

MEASUREMENTS	To fit 6–12 months, approximately 19" (48 cm) chest
YARN	Sheep Shop Yarn's Sheep Three, 70% wool/30% silk, 3.5 oz (100 g)/325 yds (297 m), Color F59
NEEDLES	US 4 (3.5 mm) straight and double-point needles and US 5 (3.75 mm) straight needles or size you need to obtain correct gauge
GAUGE	24 stitches = 4" (10 cm) in stockinette stitch on smaller needle
OTHER SUPPLIES	Stitch holder, three ⅜" (1 cm) buttons, tapestry needle
ABBREVIATIONS	**ssk** slip 1, slip 1, knit 2 slipped stitches together **yo** yarn over

stitch pattern

Feather and Fan

ROW 1 (WRONG SIDE): Knit.

ROW 2: Knit.

ROW 3: Purl.

ROW 4: *K2tog three times, (yo, K1) six times, K2tog three times; repeat from *.

Repeat Rows 1–4 for pattern.

Knitting the Body

- With larger needle, cast on 126 stitches. Begin Feather and Fan pattern and work until piece measures 4" (10 cm) from beginning, ending with Row 1 of pattern. With right side facing, change to smaller needle and knit 1 row, decreasing 14 stitches evenly spaced. You now have 112 stitches. Continue in stockinette stitch until piece measures 6" (15 cm) from beginning, ending having completed a wrong-side row.

Knitting the Right Front

- Knit 28 stitches for Right Front and place remaining 84 stitches on holder for Back and Left Front. Work stockinette stitch on 28 Right Front stitches until piece measures 8" (20 cm), ending having completed a wrong-side row.

Shaping the Neckline

- **ROW 1:** Bind off 6 stitches, knit to end of row.
- **ROW 2:** Purl.
- **ROW 3:** K2, ssk, knit to end of row.
- Repeat Rows 2 and 3 until 14 stitches remain. Continue even in stockinette stitch until piece measures 9.5" (24 cm) from the "up" end of the Feather and Fan pattern.

With larger needles, bind off remaining 14 stitches.

Knitting the Back

- With right side facing, join yarn and knit 56 stitches from holder. Work these 56 stitches in stockinette stitch until back measures same as Right Front. With larger needles, bind off.

Knitting the Left Front

- With right side facing, join yarn and work stockinette stitch on remaining 28 stitches until Left Front measures 8" (20 cm), ending having completed a right-side row.

Shaping the Neckline

- **ROW 1:** Bind off 6 stitches, purl to end of row.
- **ROW 2:** Knit.
- **ROW 3:** P2, P2tog, purl to end of row.
- Repeat Rows 2 and 3 until 14 stitches remain. Continue even in stockinette stitch until piece measures 9.5" (24 cm). With larger needles, bind off remaining 14 stitches.

Knitting the Sleeves

- Sew shoulder seams together. With right side facing and using double-point needles, pick up and knit 45 stitches around armhole and divide evenly onto 3 needles. Place marker for beginning of round.
- **ROUNDS 1–5:** Knit
- **ROUND 6:** K1, K2tog, knit to last 3 stitches, ssk, K1.
- **ROUND 7:** Knit.
- Repeat Rounds 1–7 six times. You now have 31 stitches. Work 5 rounds garter stitch (knit 1 round, purl 1 round). With larger needles, bind off. Repeat for 2nd sleeve.

Knitting the Collar

- With right side facing, pick up and knit 16 stitches along Right Front neck, 28 stitches along Back, and 16 stitches along Left Front neck. Knit 5 rows, bind off.

Knitting the Button Bands

- With right side facing, pick up and knit 49 stitches along Right Front edge. Knit 5 rows, bind off. With right side facing, pick up and knit 49 stitches along Left Front edge. Knit 3 rows.

Feather-and-Fan Baby Sweater continued

- **BUTTONHOLE ROW:** K25, K2tog, yo, K8, K2tog, yo, K8, K2tog, yo, K2.
- Knit 1 row. Bind off.

Finishing

- Weave in ends. Sew buttons opposite buttonholes. Block.

Lacy Beanie
Designed by Hélène Rush, *photo on page 11*

This lacy beanie is not only lovely to look at, it is a joy to wear. Knitted in a baby alpaca, silk, and cashmere blend, it is soft, soft, soft! Both the fiber and the weight of the yarn make this a good three-season hat. It is knitted back and forth and seamed up the back.

MEASUREMENTS	Approximately 18" (46 cm) circumference, unstretched
YARN	Knit One, Crochet Too Ambrosia, 70% baby alpaca/20% silk/10% cashmere, 1.75 oz (50 g)/137 yds (125 m), 510 Pale Moss
NEEDLES	US 3 (3.25 mm) straight needles or size you need to obtain correct gauge
GAUGE	24 stitches = 4" (10 cm) in stockinette stitch
OTHER SUPPLIES	Tapestry needle
ABBREVIATIONS	**psso** pass slipped stitch over **RS** right side **tbl** through the back loop **WS** wrong side **yo** yarn over

stitch pattern

LACE

ROWS 1 AND 3: Knit.

ROWS 2, 4, AND 6: Purl.

ROW 5: K3, *yo, slip 1 as to knit, K2tog, psso, yo, K4; repeat from *, ending last repeat K3.

Repeat Rows 1–6 for pattern.

Getting Started

- Cast on 117 stitches.
- **ROW 1:** P1, *K1 tbl, P1; repeat from *.
- **ROW 2:** K1, *P1 tbl, K1; repeat from *.
- Repeat Rows 1 and 2 two times more, increasing 4 stitches in last row. You now have 121 stitches.

- **NEXT ROW (RS):** Purl.
- **NEXT ROW:** Knit.

Knitting the Lace Pattern

- Work Rows 1–6 of Lace pattern until piece measures approximately 4" (10 cm) from beginning, ending with Row 4 of pattern.
- **NEXT ROW (RS):** Purl.
- **NEXT ROW:** Knit, decreasing 8 stitches. You now have 113 stitches.

Shaping the Top

- **ROW 1 (RS):** *K12, K2tog; repeat from * to last stitch, K1. You now have 105 stitches.
- **ROW 2 AND ALL WS ROWS:** Purl.
- **ROW 3:** Knit.
- **ROW 5:** *K11, K2tog; repeat from * to last stitch, K1. You now have 97 stitches.
- **ROW 7:** *K10, K2tog; repeat from * to last stitch, K1. You now have 89 stitches.
- **ROW 9:** Knit.
- **ROW 11:** *K9, K2tog; repeat from * to last stitch, K1. You now have 81 stitches.
- **ROW 13:** *K8, K2tog; repeat from * to last stitch, K1. You now have 73 stitches.
- **ROW 15:** Knit.
- **ROW 17:** *K7, K2tog; repeat from * to last stitch, K1. You now have 65 stitches.
- **ROW 19:** *K6, K2tog; repeat from * to last stitch, K1. You now have 57 stitches.
- **ROW 21:** Knit.
- **ROW 23:** *K5, K2tog; repeat from * to last stitch, K1. You now have 49 stitches.
- **ROW 25:** *K4, K2tog; repeat from * to last stitch, K1. You now have 41 stitches.
- **ROW 27:** *K3, K2tog; repeat from * to last stitch, K1. You now have 33 stitches.
- **ROW 29:** *K2, K2tog; repeat from * to last stitch, K1. You now have 25 stitches.
- **ROW 31:** *K1, K2tog; repeat from * to last stitch, K1. You now have 17 stitches.
- **ROW 33:** *K2tog; repeat from * to last stitch, K1. You now have 9 stitches.

Finishing

- Cut yarn leaving a tail long enough to sew back seam. Thread tail onto tapestry needle and pass through remaining 9 stitches twice. Fasten off on the inside. Sew back seam. Weave in all ends. Block.

Ring Bearer Pillow

DESIGNED BY SUSAN DIRK, photo on page 12

This elegant ring bearer pillow is knitted in luxurious silk yarn. Sized to fit a standard 8-inch pillow form, it is knitted from the center out to the edges and finished with a beaded fringe.

MEASUREMENTS	Approximately 8" (20 cm) square
YARN	Debbie Bliss Pure Silk, 100% silk, 1.75 oz (50 g)/137 yds (125 m), Ecru
NEEDLES	Set of five US 5 (3.75 mm) double-point needles or size you need to obtain correct gauge
GAUGE	22 stitches = 4" (10 cm) in stockinette stitch
OTHER SUPPLIES	Tapestry needle, 8-inch pillow form covered in fabric, sewing needle and thread, beading needle and thread, 204 size 8° seed beads, 156 size 8° cylinder beads, 24 charms

Knitting the Lace

- Cast on 8 stitches with the long tail method (see page 246), leaving a 10" (25 cm) tail. Place 2 stitches on each of 4 double-point needles. Join into a round, being careful not to twist the stitches.
- Following Ring Bearer Pillow chart (see page 98), work the repeat 8 times, twice on each needle. Continue through Row 36.

Binding Off

- *Using cable method (see page 244), cast on 3 stitches, then bind off 9 stitches. Move remaining stitch from right needle to left needle. Repeat from * until all stitches are bound off. Fasten off yarn.

Finishing the Lace Square

- Thread cast-on tail onto tapestry needle and draw through cast-on stitches twice. Pull up snug and fasten off on the back side. Weave in ends. Block lace into an 8-inch square.
- Position lace over pillow and use sewing needle and thread to sew into place along four sides of pillow.

Adding the Fringe

- With beading needle and thread, anchor the thread into the tip of a corner picot. *String 7 alternating 4 seed and 3 cylinder beads, string 1 charm and pass the thread through the loop of the charm again to hold it in place, string 7 beads alternating 4 seed and 3 cylinder beads, sew through tip of next picot. Repeat from * to 1 picot before next corner. String 7 beads alternating 4 seed and 3 cylinder beads, string charm as before. String 6 beads alternating 3 seed and 3 cylinder beads, and sew through pillow fabric right in the corner. Pass your needle back down through these 6 beads, then string 7 beads alternating 4 seed and 3 cylinder beads, and sew through next picot. Continue in this manner around the pillow. Fasten off the thread, hiding the tail.

Ring Bearer Pillow continued

Ring Bearer Pillow Chart

- ☐ knit
- ○ yarn over
- ╱ knit 2 together
- ⋏ slip 2 together as to knit, knit 1, pass the 2 slipped stitches over the knit stitch

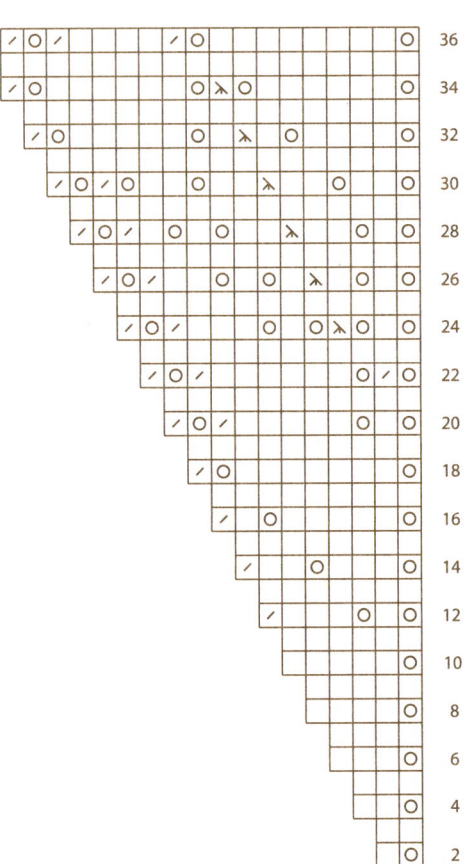

Plaited Cable Men's Belt

Designed by Anastasia Blaes, photo on page 11

This belt looks at home on a pair of blue jeans or khakis. We'd have to say it's more decorative than functional, but why shouldn't a man accessorize?

stitch pattern

Plaited Cable

Row 1: Slip 1, P1, K9, P1, K1.

Row 2 and all even-numbered rows through 8: Slip 1, K1, P9, K2.

Row 3: Slip 1, P1, C6F, K3, P1, K1.

Row 5: Repeat Row 1.

Row 7: Slip 1, P1, K3, C6B, P1, K1.

Repeat Rows 1–8 for pattern.

Note: Slip the first stitch of every row as if to purl.

Measurements	Approximately 1.25" (3 cm) wide and 42" (107 cm) long or desired length
Yarn	Kollage Yarns Delicious, 100% soybean, 1.5 oz (43 g)/121 yds (111 m), Tortugas
Needles	US 4 (3.5 mm) straight needles or size you need to obtain correct gauge
Gauge	24 stitches = 4" (10 cm) in stockinette stitch
Other Supplies	Cable needle, tapestry needle, 2" (5 cm) square belt buckle with two 1.5" (4 cm) openings,
Abbreviations	**C6F** slip 3 stitches to cable needle and hold in front, K3, K3 from cable needle **C6B** slip 3 stitches to cable needle and hold in back, K3, K3 from cable needle

Knitting the Belt

- Cast on 13 stitches. Work in Plaited Cable pattern until belt measures 4" (10 cm) more than desired waist circumference, ending with Row 7 of pattern.
- **Decrease row:** Slip 1, K1, (P2tog) twice, K1, (P2tog) twice, K2.
- Bind off.

Finishing

- Weave in ends. Insert bound off end of belt through first opening of buckle, then down through second opening. Fold about 2" (5 cm) over to wrong side and stitch the cast-on edge to the inside of the belt, being careful not to let stitches show on the right side.

DK/Light
Worsted Weight

Scallop-Edge Beaded Necklace
Designed by Carol Metzger, photo on page 14

Here's an easy yet satisfying project to learn how to knit with beads: You simply place beads between the stitches. The center is shaped with short rows.

MEASUREMENTS	Approximately 16" (41 cm) long
YARN	Tahki Cotton Classic, 100% cotton, 1.75 oz (50 g)/108 yds (100 m), Color 3912
NEEDLES	US 3 (3.25 mm) straight needles or size you need to obtain correct gauge
GAUGE	24 stitches = 4" (10 cm) in garter stitch
OTHER SUPPLIES	Approximately 178 size 6° seed beads, beading needle, sewing needle, toggle clasp, nylon thread, tapestry needle
ABBREVIATIONS	**B** slide bead up close to needle **CO** cast on **WT** wrap and turn (see Short Rows)

Getting Started

- Begin by stringing beads onto yarn. Using the backward loop method (see page 244) cast on stitches with beads between as follows.
- (CO2, 1B) 20 times, CO2, 2B, CO2, 3B, CO2, 4B, CO2, 5B, CO2, 6B, CO2, 7B, CO2, 6B, CO2, 5B, CO2, 4B, CO2, 3B, CO2, 2B, (CO2, 1B) 20 times.
- **ROW 1:** K42, 1B, K2, 2B, K2, 3B, K2, 4B, K2, 5B, K2, 6B, K2, 5B, K2, 4B, K2, 3B, K2, 2B, K2, 1B, K42.
- **ROW 2:** K44, 1B, K2, 2B, K2, 3B, K2, 4B, K2, 5B, K2, 4B, K2, 3B, K2, 2B, K2, 1B, K5, WT.
- **ROW 3:** K7, 1B, K2, 2B, K2, 3B, K2, 4B, K2, 3B, K2, 2B, K2, 1B, K5, WT.
- **ROW 4:** K7, 1B, K2, 2B, K2, 3B, K2, 2B, K2, 1B, K5, WT.
- **ROW 5:** K7, 1B, K2, 2B, K2, 1B, K5, WT.
- **ROW 6:** K7, 1B, K5, WT.
- **ROW 7:** K7, WT.
- **ROW 8:** Knit.
- Bind off.

Finishing

- Sew toggle clasp to ends with beading thread. Weave in ends.

Short Rows

Work the number of stitches specified, then wrap and turn (WT) as follows:

Bring yarn to front and slip next stitch onto right needle.

Bring yarn to back and slip stitch back to left needle.

Turn work to begin knitting in the opposite direction.

Simple Mistake Rib Vest
Designed by Karen J. Minott, photo on page 13

The Mistake Rib stitch results in a fabric that is elastic and lightweight, producing an attractive fit. Cast on at bottom back edge, divide at back neck edge, and knit up over shoulders and down fronts.

stitch pattern

Mistake Rib

Row 1: *K2, P2; repeat from * to last 3 stitches, K2, P1.

Repeat Row 1 for pattern.

Measurements	Approximately 34 (36, 38)" (86 [91, 97] cm) chest
Yarn	Great Adirondack Sierra, 100% alpaca, 7 oz (198 g)/600 yds (549 m), Painted Desert
Needles	US 7 (4.5 mm) straight needles or size you need to obtain correct gauge
Gauge	20 stitches = 4" (10 cm) in stockinette stitch
Other Supplies	Stitch holder, stitch markers, tapestry needle, US F/5 (3.75 mm) crochet hook, one ⅞" button

Knitting the Vest

- Cast on 87 (91, 99) stitches. Work in Mistake Rib pattern until piece measures 17 (17.5, 18)" (43 [44, 46] cm) ending on a wrong-side row.

Shaping the Back Neck and Dividing for Fronts

- Work in pattern for 31 (31, 35) stitches and place these stitches on holder. Bind off 25 (29, 29) stitches and continue in pattern on remaining 31 (31, 35) stitches. Continue until piece measures 3.5 (4, 4.25)" (9 [10, 11] cm) from back neck bind off. Mark midway for shoulder.

Increasing for the Front Neckline

- Continuing in pattern as established, increase 1 stitch at the neck edge every 3rd row 3 times, every other row 2 times, then every row until you have 43 (45, 47) stitches. Be sure to continue the pattern into the new stitches. Continue until front, when folded at the shoulder marker, matches the back in length. Bind off loosely.

- Return stitches on holder to needles and work as for first side of front reversing shaping. Do not cut yarn.

Finishing

- Sew side seams together with mattress stitch (see page 248) to desired armhole opening. Beginning at lower right front edge, place last bind-off loop on crochet hook and work single crochet around to lower left front edge, working a loop for a buttonhole on the right front. Weave in ends. Block lightly. Sew button on left front.

Elegant-and-Easy Garter Stitch Tie

Designed by Marci Richardson, photo on page 14

This easy wardrobe basic makes a great gift for the man in your life. Knitted with DK-weight yarn, the slipped stitch beginning of each row creates a nice clean edge. Directions are given in parentheses for worsted-weight yarn.

MEASUREMENTS	Approximately 54" (137 cm) long and 4" (10 cm) wide at widest point
YARN	Rowan Tapestry, 70% wool/30% soy protein, 1.75 oz (50 g)/131 yds (120 m), Color 175
NEEDLES	US 4 (3.5 mm) (5 [3.75 mm]) straight needles or size you need to obtain correct gauge
GAUGE	24 (22) stitches = 4" (10 cm) in garter stitch
OTHER SUPPLIES	Tapestry needle
ABBREVIATIONS	**ssk** slip 1, slip 1, knit 2 slipped stitches together

Getting Started

- Cast on 20 (18) stitches.
- **ROW 1:** Slip the first stitch as if to purl with yarn in front. Bring yarn to back and K19 (17).
- Repeat Row 1 until piece measures 6" (15 cm).
- **DECREASE ROW:** Slip the first stitch as if to purl with yarn in front. Bring yarn to back. K1, ssk, K to last 4 stitches, K2tog, K2. You now have 18 (16) stitches.
- *Work Row 1 for 3" (7.5 cm), then work Decrease Row. Repeat from * three more times. Piece measures 18" (46 cm) and you have 10 (8) stitches.
- Work Row 1 until piece measures 54" (137 cm).

Finishing

- Weave in ends and block lightly. If desired, make a small "tuck-in" tab for the back of the tie by casting on 6 stitches and knitting for 2" (5 cm). Tack to inside front of tie approximately 6" (15 cm) from bottom of tie.

Pink Tweed for Baby

Designed by Lorna Miser, photo on page 13

The color name of this yarn says it all: "It's a Girl." Knitted in stockinette stitch with garter stitch edgings, the girly look is completed with three sweet heart-shaped buttons.

MEASUREMENTS	To fit infant 0–3 months, approximately 18" (46 cm) chest
YARN	Kraemer Yarns Little Lehigh Pebbles, 45% cotton/55% acrylic, 3.5 oz (100 g) /250 yds (229 m), It's a Girl
NEEDLES	US 5 (3.75 mm) straight needles or size you need to obtain correct gauge
GAUGE	20 stitches = 4" (10 cm) in stockinette stitch
OTHER SUPPLIES	Stitch holder, tapestry needle, three .75" (2 cm) buttons
ABBREVIATIONS	**RS** right side **WS** wrong side **yo** yarn over

Knitting the Bottom Edging

- Cast on 6 stitches.
- ROW 1 (WS): Knit.
- ROW 2 (RS): K1, yo, K2tog, K3.
- Repeat Rows 1 and 2 until edging has 90 ridges (180 rows). Bind off. Do not cut yarn.

Knitting the Body

- Turn edging sideways with eyelet at bottom edge. Pick up and knit 90 stitches along the K3 side of edging. Work in stockinette stitch for 4" (10 cm).

Divide for Fronts and Back

- Knit 22 stitches and place them on holder for Right Front. Knit 46 stitches for back and place remaining 22 stitches on holder for Left Front. Continue in stockinette stitch on back stitches for 4.5" (11 cm). Place stitches on holder.

Knitting the Fronts

- Working each front separately, place 22 stitches on needles and work 4 rows even. Decrease 1 stitch at neck edge (work this decrease one-stitch in from the edge) every other row 10 times. Work even until front length matches back and place 12 shoulder stitches on holder.

Pink Tweed for Baby continued

Joining Fronts and Back

- Join front shoulder stitches to back shoulder stitches with the 3-needle bind-off (see page 251), leaving center 22 back stitches on holder for neck.

Knitting the Front and Neck Edging

- Beginning at lower right front edge, just above the edging, pick up and knit 39 stitches along right front edge to shoulder, knit 22 back neck stitches, pick up and knit 39 stitches along left front edge to just above the edging. Knit 3 rows. Beginning at lower right front edge, make three buttonholes as follows:
- **BUTTONHOLE ROW:** K2, yo, K2tog, K6, yo, K2tog, K6, yo, K2tog, knit to end of row.
- Knit 3 rows, bind off loosely.

Sleeves *(make two)*

- Work edging same as for body for 4" (10 cm). Pick up and knit 25 stitches along K3 edge. Work in stockinette stitch, increasing 1 stitch at the beginning and end of every 4th row seven times. Work even until sleeve measures 4" (10 cm). Bind off.

Finishing

- Sew sleeve seam. Sew sleeves to body. Weave in all ends. Sew buttons to button band opposite buttonholes. Block.

DK/Light Worsted Weight

Sachets and Keepsake Pouches

Designed by Dorothy T. Ratigan, photo on page 14

Here's an opportunity to practice various pattern stitches and make something useful at the same time. Fill them with your favorite scent and place them in your lingerie drawer. Use them to hold jewelry while traveling. Jazz them up with beads or embroidery. Make them for family and friends. The pouches are worked in variations of knit 2, purl 2. They are worked on 38 stitches and 40 rows, but the sizes vary slightly depending on take-up of the patterns.

MEASUREMENTS	Approximately 6" (15 cm) tall and 7" (18 cm) circumference
YARN	The Fibre Company Savannah DK, 50% merino wool/20% organic cotton/15% linen/15% soya fiber, 1.75 oz (50 g)/160 yds (146 m), Blue Sky
NEEDLES	US 6 (4 mm) straight needles or size you need to obtain correct gauge
GAUGE	24 stitches = 4" (10 cm) in stockinette stitch
OTHER SUPPLIES	Tapestry needle, 2 yd thin silver cord, various beads for trim
ABBREVIATIONS	**WS** wrong side

Working the Eyelet Row

Each pouch has an eyelet row to accommodate a drawstring. When the 40-row pattern is complete, with wrong-side facing work P2, P2tog, yo to end of row. Knit one row. Bind off.

Knitting the Pouches

- Cast on 38 stitches leaving a 12-inch tail. The first and last stitches are edge stitches and are knitted on right-side rows and purled on wrong-side rows. Work each pattern for 40 rows and then work the Eyelet Row (see at left). Finally, follow the finishing instructions.

Pattern 1

- **SET-UP ROW (WS):** *P2 (the first of these stitches is your edge stitch), K2; repeat from *, ending P2 (the last of these stitches is your edge stitch).
- **ROW 1:** K1 (edge stitch), *P2, knit the second stitch on the needle and lift it over the first stitch, knit the first stitch; repeat from *, ending K1 (edge stitch).
- **ROW 2:** P1 (edge stitch), K1, *P2, K2; repeat from *, ending K1, P1 (edge stitch).
- **ROW 3:** K1 (edge stitch), *knit the second stitch on the needle and lift it over the first stitch, knit the first stitch, P2; repeat from *, ending K1 (edge stitch).

Sachets and Keepsake Pouches continued

- **ROW 4:** *P2 (the first of these stitches is your edge stitch), K2; repeat from *, ending P2 (the last of these stitches is your edge stitch).

Pattern 2

- **SET-UP ROW (WS):** *P2 (the first of these stitches is your edge stitch), K2; repeat from *, ending P2 (the last of these stitches is your edge stitch).
- **ROW 1:** K1 (edge stitch), *K2, P2; repeat from *, ending K1 (edge stitch).
- **ROWS 2, 4, 6, AND 8:** Knit the knit stitches and purl the purl stitches.
- **ROW 3:** K1 (edge stitch), P1, *K2, P2; repeat from *, ending P1, K1 (edge stitch).
- **ROW 5:** K1 (edge stitch), *P2, K2; repeat from *, ending K3 (the last of these stitches is your edge stitch).
- **ROW 7:** *K2, (the first of these stitches is your edge stitch), P2; repeat from *, ending K2 (the last of these stitches is your edge stitch).

Pattern 3

- **SET-UP ROW (WS):** *P2 (the first of these stitches is your edge stitch), K2; repeat from * ending K1, P1 (edge stitch).
- **ROW 1:** K3 (the first of these stitches is your edge stitch), *P2, K2; repeat from *, ending K3 (the last of these stitches is your edge stitch).
- **ROWS 2 AND 4:** Knit the knits and purl the purls.
- **ROW 3:** K1 (edge stitch), P1, *K2, P2; repeat from *, ending K2 (the last of these stitches is your edge stitch).

Pattern 4

- **SET-UP ROW (WS):** P3 (the first of these stitches is your edge stitch), *K2, P2; repeat from * ending P3 (the last of these stitches is your edge stitch).
- **ROW 1:** K1 (edge stitch), *P2, K2; repeat from *, ending P2, K1 (edge stitch).
- **ROWS 2 AND 4:** Knit the knits and purl the purls.
- **ROW 3:** K1 (edge stitch), *K2, P2; repeat from *, ending K1 (edge stitch).

Finishing

- Thread the 12-inch (30 cm) tail onto tapestry needle and sew side edges together. Turn inside out. Center seam at back of pouch and stitch cast-on edge closed. Turn right-side out.
- Weave in ends. Cut a length of silver cord for a drawstring and weave it in and out of the eyelet round. Embellish with beads as desired.

Between-Seasons Cap

Designed by Cathy Campbell, *photo on page 13*

This delightful cap is 50/50 cotton/wool and is a perfect weight for wearing on either side of winter. The twisted-stitch cable band at the bottom is knitted back and forth and then joined with a seam at the back; you'll then pick up stitches for the crown and knit it in the round.

stitch pattern

Twisted-Stitch Cable

Row 1 and all wrong-side rows: P4, K2, P8, K2, P3.

Rows 2 and 4: K1, RT, P2, K8, P2, LT, K2.

Row 6: K1, RT, P2, slip 4 stitches onto cable needle and hold in front, K4, K4 from cable needle, P2, LT, K2.

Rows 8 and 10: Repeat Rows 2 and 4.

Repeat Rows 1–10 for pattern.

Measurements	Approximately 20" (51 cm) circumference
Yarn	O-Wool Balance, 50% organic merino/50% organic cotton, 1.75 oz (50 g)/130 yds (119 m), 2026 Opal
Needles	One US 6 (4 mm) circular needle 16" (40 cm) long and set of five US 6 (4 mm) double-point needles or size you need to obtain correct gauge
Gauge	20 stitches = 4" (10 cm) in stockinette stitch
Other Supplies	Cable needle, tapestry needle
Abbreviations	**LT** left twist. Insert needle into back of second stitch of left needle and knit it, then knit the first stitch and drop both stitches from left needle. **RT** right twist. Insert needle into front of second stitch of left needle and knit it, then knit the first stitch and drop both stitches from left needle. **ssk** slip 1, slip 1, knit 2 slipped stitches together

Knitting the Bottom Band

- Cast on 19 stitches and work 13 repeats of Twisted-Stitch Cable pattern until piece measures 20" (51 cm). Work Row 1 once more. Bind off and sew center back seam.

Knitting the Body

- With circular needle, pick up 100 stitches from left edge of band (you'll be picking up approximately 3 of every 4 stitches). Join and knit one round.
- **Round 1:** *K9, P1, LT, P1, RT, P1, K9; repeat from * 3 more times.
- **Round 2:** *K9, P1, K2, P1, K2, P1, K9; repeat from * 3 more times.
- Repeat Rounds 1 and 2 until piece measures 3" (8 cm) from the top of the cable band.

Between-Seasons Cap continued

Decreasing for the Crown

- Change to double-point needles when necessary.
- ROUND 1: *K7, K2tog, P1, LT, P1, RT, P1, ssk, K7; repeat from * 3 more times.
- ROUNDS 2, 4, AND 6: Knit the knits and purl the purls.
- ROUND 3: *K8, P1, LT, P1, RT, P1, K8; repeat from * 3 more times.
- ROUND 5: *K6, K2tog, P1, LT, P1, RT, P1, ssk, K6; repeat from * 3 more times.
- ROUND 7: *K7, P1, LT, P1, RT, P1, K7; repeat from * 3 more times.
- ROUND 8: *K5, K2tog, P1, K2, P1, K2, P1, ssk, K5; repeat from * 3 more times.
- ROUND 9: *K6, P1, LT, P1, RT, P1, K6; repeat from * 3 more times.
- Repeat Rounds 8 and 9, working one fewer stitch at the beginning and end of the rounds and decreasing on the first round and twisting the stitches on the next until you have 52 stitches remaining (13 on each of 4 needles).
- NOW YOU WILL DECREASE EVERY ROUND AS FOLLOWS:
- ROUND 1: *K1, K2tog, P1, LT, P1, RT, P1, ssk, K1; repeat from * 3 more times.
- ROUND 2: *K2tog, P1, K2, P1, K2, P1, ssk; repeat from * 3 more times.
- ROUND 3: *K2tog twice, P1, K2tog twice; repeat from * 3 more times.
- ROUND 4: *K2tog, P1, K2tog; repeat from * 3 more times.
- Cut yarn leaving a 10" (25 cm) tail. Thread tail onto tapestry needle, draw through remaining 12 stitches. Pull up snug and fasten off on the inside.

Finishing

- Weave in ends.

Child's Hat with Pompom

Designed by Nancy Abel, photo on page 14

This cute little hat features a self-rolling brim, a simple knit and purl pattern, and is topped with a pompom. You may begin on circular needles and change to double-point needles when you decrease for the crown or work on double-point needles throughout.

MEASUREMENTS	Approximately 17" (43 cm) circumference
YARN	Steadfast Fibers Wonderful Wool, 85% wool/15% mohair, 4 oz (113 g)/190 yds (174 m), 3259 Hot Lips
NEEDLES	One US 7 (4.5 mm) circular needle 12" (30 cm) long and set of four US 7 (4.5 mm) double-point needles or size you need to obtain correct gauge
GAUGE	22 stitches = 4" (10 cm) in stockinette stitch
OTHER SUPPLIES	Stitch marker, tapestry needle

Knitting the Brim

- Cast on 80 stitches. Join into a round, being careful not to twist stitches. Place a marker for the beginning of the round.
- Work stockinette stitch (knit every round) for 2" (5 cm).

Working the Pattern

- **ROUNDS 1 AND 2:** Purl.
- **ROUNDS 3–6:** *K4, P4; repeat from *.
- **ROUNDS 7 AND 8:** Purl.
- **ROUNDS 9–12:** *K4, P4; repeat from *.
- **ROUNDS 13 AND 14:** Purl.
- Continue in stockinette stitch (knit every round) until piece measures 2.5" (6 cm) from end of pattern.

Decreasing for the Crown

- Change to double-point needles when necessary.
- **ROUND 1:** *K8, K2tog; repeat from *.
- **ROUND 2 AND ALL EVEN-NUMBERED ROUNDS:** Knit.

Child's Hat with Pompom continued

- ROUND 3: *K7, K2tog; repeat from *.
- ROUND 5: *K6, K2tog; repeat form *.
- Continue in this manner, working one fewer stitch between decreases and knitting one round even between decrease rounds until you have 16 stitches.
- NEXT ROUND: *K2tog; repeat from *. You now have 8 stitches.
- Cut yarn, leaving a 10" (25 cm) tail. Thread tail onto tapestry needle, draw through remaining 8 stitches twice. Pull up snug and fasten off on the inside.

Finishing

- Make a pompom (see page 248) and attach to top of crown. Weave in ends.

Baby Squash Hat

DESIGNED BY TAMARA DEL SONNO, photo on page 13

This cute little hat is shaped like a gourd, but knitted in natural-colored yarn, it's just plain cute. The I-cord that finishes the hat has a slight curl.

MEASUREMENTS	To fit infant
YARN	Treliske Organic Merino DK, 100% merino wool, 1.75 oz (50 g)/110 yds (100 m), Cream
NEEDLES	One US 6 (4 mm) circular needle 16" (40 cm) long and set of four US 6 (4 mm) double-point needles or size you need to obtain correct gauge
GAUGE	20 stitches = 4" (10 cm) in stockinette stitch
OTHER SUPPLIES	Stitch markers, tapestry needle

Knitting the Hat

- With circular needle, cast on 64 stitches. Knit 2 rows (back and forth). Join into a round, being careful not to twist stitches. Place marker for beginning of round.
- ROUND 1: *K8, P8; repeat from *.
- Repeat Round 1 until piece measures 4.5" (11 cm).

Decreasing for the Top

- Change to double-point needles when necessary.
- **ROUND 1:** *K6, K2tog, P6, P2tog; repeat from *.
- **ROUND 2:** Knit the knits and purl the purls.
- **ROUND 3:** *K5, K2tog, P5, P2tog; repeat from *.
- **ROUND 4:** Knit the knits and purl the purls.
- Continue in this manner, working 1 fewer stitch between decreases and working 1 round even between decrease rounds until you have 16 stitches.
- **NEXT ROUND:** *K2tog, P2tog; repeat from *. You now have 8 stitches.
- **NEXT ROUND:** *K2tog; repeat from *. You now have 4 stitches.

Knitting the I-Cord

- Place remaining 4 stitches on one double-point needle. Work I-cord as follows:
- **ROW 1:** Knit, then slide stitches back to right end of needle. Do not turn.
- **ROW 2:** K3, slip 1, then slide stitches back to right end of needle. Do not turn.
- **NOTE:** Slipping the last stitch every other row will make the I-cord curl slightly.
- Repeat these two rows to desired length.

Finishing

- Cut yarn, leaving a 8" (20 cm) tail. Thread tail onto tapestry needle. Draw through remaining 4 stitches twice. Pull up snug and fasten off. Weave in ends.

Mohair Yarn

Lace Kid Merino Cowl

Designed by Dawn Leeseman, photo on page 15

This light and lofty cowl can be worn around the neck as a warmer or, better yet, up over the head — the scalloped edge frames your face when you wear it this way. The bottom is bound off with a picot edge, and the large size needle produces the lovely open lacework.

MEASUREMENTS	Approximately 12" (30 cm) wide and 16" (40 cm) tall
YARN	Crystal Palace Kid Merino, 28% kid mohair/28% kid merino/44% micro nylon, .9 oz (25 g)/240 yds (219 m), Color 4676
NEEDLES	One US 10.5 (6.5 mm) circular needle 24" (60 cm) long or size you need to obtain correct gauge
GAUGE	17 stitches = 4" (10 cm) in pattern before blocking, 16 stitches = 4" (10 cm) after blocking
OTHER SUPPLIES	Tapestry needle, blocking pins
ABBREVIATIONS	**SK2P** slip 1 as to knit, K2tog, pass slipped stitch over **yo** yarn over

stitch pattern

QUILL EYELET LACE

Worked over a multiple of 6 stitches.

ROUND 1: Knit.

ROUND 2: *K1, yo, K1, SK2P, K1, yo; repeat from *.

Repeat Rounds 1 and 2 for pattern.

Getting Started

- Cast on 90 stitches. Join into a round, being careful not to twist stitches.
- Work Quill Eyelet Lace pattern until piece measures 16" (40 cm) or desired length.

Working the Picot Bind-off

- The picot bind-off will make the bottom (shoulder) edge flare slightly.
- Bind off 1 stitch, *slip stitch from right needle back to left needle, cable cast on 2 stitches, bind off 4 stitches; repeat from *.

Finishing

- Weave in ends. Block by pinning out the upper edge scallops and body, leaving the flared picot edge unpinned.

Chicly Chevroned "Broadway" Hat
Designed by Lily M. Chin, photo on page 15

This hat is knitted from beginning to end on a 16" (40 cm) circular needle — no need for double-points! The subtle shading in the yarn provides the chicness, the stitch forms chevrons, and the fiber combination makes the hat a joy to wear.

stitch pattern

Chevron Lace

Round 1: *K1, yo, K4, SK2P, K4, yo; repeat from *, forming 6 chevrons.

Round 2: Purl or knit (see directions below).

Repeat Rounds 1 and 2 for pattern.

Measurements	Approximately 21" (53 cm) circumference
Yarn	Lily Chin Signature Collection "Broadway", 38% mohair/38% wool/15% nylon/9% rayon, 1.75 oz (50 g)/153 yds (140 m), Color 3520
Needles	One US 10.5 (6.5 mm) circular needle 16" (40 cm) long or size you need to obtain correct gauge
Gauge	14 stitches = 4" (10 cm) in chevron pattern
Other Supplies	Stitch markers, tapestry needle
Abbreviations	**SK2P** slip 1 knitwise, K2tog, pass slipped stitch over **yo** yarn over

Getting Started

- Cast on 72 stitches. Join into a round, being careful not to twist stitches. Place marker for beginning of round.
- Work Chevron Lace pattern with purled even-numbered rounds for 10 rounds.
- Change to Chevron Lace pattern with knitted even-numbered rounds and continue until piece measures 8.5" (22 cm) from beginning, ending on Round 1. Bind off loosely.

Finishing

- Sew sides of each chevron to each other to form crown. Weave in ends.

Tiers-of-Waves Beaded Scarf

Designed by Kristin Omdahl, photo on page 15

Adding just a few beads turns this lovely lacy scarf into an extraordinarily lovely lacy scarf. Be sure that you buy beads with holes large enough to allow the beads to slide easily along the yarn.

MEASUREMENTS	Approximately 8" (20 cm) wide and 64" (163 cm) long
YARN	Wagtail Yarns Mohair, 100% fine kid mohair, 3.5 oz (100 g)/410 yds (375 m), Medium Violet
NEEDLES	Two US 6 (4 mm) circular needles 24" (60 cm) long or size you need to obtain correct gauge
GAUGE	14 stitches = 4" (10 cm) in garter stitch, blocked
OTHER SUPPLIES	288 size 6° silver hex beads, sewing needle and thread, tapestry needle
ABBREVIATIONS	**BKfb** beaded kfb: insert needle into front next stitch, slide bead up close to needle, finish stitch; insert needle into back of same stitch, slide bead up close to needle, finish stitch **BK2tog** beaded K2tog: insert needle into next 2 stitches, slide bead up close to needle, finish knitting the 2 stitches together **Kfb** knit into front and back of stitch (one stitch increased) **WS** wrong side

stitch pattern

Modified Chevron

ROW 1 (WS): Knit.

ROW 2: Knit.

ROW 3: *(K2tog) 4 times, (Kfb) 8 times, (K2tog) 4 times; repeat from *.

ROW 4: Knit.

3-needle Joining Row

This is worked like the 3-needle bind off (see page 251) except that you do not bind off the stitches, you just knit them together across the row.

Preparing the Yarn

- Wind the yarn into two 50-gram balls.

Knitting the First Half of the Scarf

- **Thread 48 beads onto one ball of yarn. Cast on 48 stitches loosely.
- **ROWS 1 AND 2:** Knit.
- **ROW 3:** *(BK2tog) 4 times, (BKfb) 8 times, (BK2tog) 4 times; repeat from *.
- **ROW 4:** Knit.**
- **ROWS 5–20:** Work Rows 1–4 of Modified Chevron pattern 4 times.
- Break yarn but leave stitches on needle. Set aside.
- Repeat from ** to **.

- **NEXT ROWS:** Work Rows 1–4 of Modified Chevron pattern 2 times.
- **JOINING ROW:** Holding the pieces together with the right side of the longer piece (the first one knitted) facing wrong side of shorter piece, join the pieces with the 3-needle joining row (see at left).
- **NEXT 12 ROWS:** Repeat Rows 1–4 of Modified Chevron pattern 3 times.
- Break yarn but leave stitches on needle. Set aside.
- Repeat from ** to **.
- **NEXT ROWS:** Work Rows 1–4 of Modified Chevron pattern 2 times.
- Work joining row as described above.
- Continue working Modified Chevron pattern until you have approximately 1 yard (91 cm) of yarn left on first 50-gram ball.

Knitting the Second Half of the Scarf

- Repeat as for first scarf half, making sure that you've worked the same number of rows from beginning to end.

Joining the Halves

- With right sides together, join with 3-needle bind off (see page 251).

Finishing

- Weave in ends. Block to finished measurements.

Lace Spiral Scarf

Designed by Gail Owens, photo on page 15

Short rows are used to shape this spiral scarf, and it is worked with lace at the outside edge. Fuzzy mohair gives the scarf plenty of loft, and it will keep you warm and chic at the same time.

MEASUREMENTS	Approximately 64" (163 cm) long
YARN	Crystal Palace Kid Merino, 28% kid mohair/28% merino wool/44% micro nylon, .88 oz (25 g)/240 yds (219 m), 436 Chocolate Almond
NEEDLES	US 6 (4 mm) straight needles or size you need to obtain correct gauge
GAUGE	16 stitches = 4" (10 cm) in garter stitch
OTHER SUPPLIES	Tapestry needle
ABBREVIATIONS	**WT** wrap and turn for short row (see page 249) **yo** yarn over

Knitting the Scarf

- Cast on 10 stitches.
- NOTE: The stitches in brackets [ ] indicate the lace edging.
- ROW 1: [K1, yo twice, K1], K7, WT.
- ROW 2: Slip 1, K7, [K2, P1, K1].
- ROW 3: [K4], K6, WT.
- ROW 4: Slip 1, K6, [K2tog twice, loosely].
- ROW 5: [K1, yo twice, K1], K5, WT.
- ROW 6: Slip 1, K5, [K2, P1, K1].
- ROW 7: [K4], K4, WT.
- ROW 8: Slip 1, K4, [K2tog twice, loosely].
- ROW 9: [K1, yo twice, K1], K3, WT.
- ROW 10: Slip 1, K3, [K2, P1, K1].
- ROW 11: [K4], K2, WT.
- ROW 12: Slip 1, K2, [K2tog twice, loosely].

- **ROW 13:** [K1, yo twice, K1], K1, WT.
- **ROW 14:** Slip 1, K1, [K2, P1, K1].
- **ROW 15:** [K4], K8.
- **ROW 16:** Slip 1, K7, [K2tog twice, loosely].
- Repeat Rows 1–16 until piece measures 64" (163 cm) or desired length.

Finishing
- Bind off. Weave in ends.

Worsted Weight

Kat's Hat

Designed by Diana Foster, photo on page 23

This hat was knitted for Katrina, Diana's tenth grandchild. Not only does she have the right name, she loves cats!

MEASUREMENTS	To fit a child, approximately 18" (46 cm) circumference
YARN	Peace Fleece, 70% wool/30% mohair, 4 oz (113 g)/200 yds (183 m), Ukranian Red
NEEDLES	One US 5 (3.75 mm) circular needle 16" (40 cm) long and set of four US 5 (3.75 mm) double-point needles or size you need to obtain correct gauge
GAUGE	16 stitches = 4" (10 cm) in stockinette stitch
OTHER SUPPLIES	Stitch markers, tapestry needle, eye and nose buttons, small amount of black embroidery thread
ABBREVIATIONS	**ssk** slip 1, slip 1, knit 2 slipped stiches together

Knitting the Body

- With circular needle, cast on 90 stitches. Join into a round, being careful not to twist stitches, place marker. Work garter stitch for 1.5" (4 cm). Knit even for 6" (15 cm).

Decreasing for the Crown

- ROUND 1: *K7, K2tog, repeat from *.
- ROUND 2 AND ALL EVEN-NUMBERED ROUNDS: Knit.
- ROUND 3: *K6, K2tog; repeat from *.
- ROUND 5: *K5, K2tog; repeat from *.
- Continue in this manner, knitting 1 fewer stitch between decreases and knitting 1 round even between decrease rounds until you have 20 stitches.
- NEXT ROUND: *K2tog; repeat from *. You now have 10 stitches.
- Cut yarn leaving a 10" (25 cm) tail. Thread tail onto tapestry needle and draw through remaining stitches twice. Pull up snug and fasten off on the inside.

Knitting the Ears

- Fold hat in half with marker at center back. On top of one side, pick up 9 stitches. Knit 3 rows and decrease as follows.
- ROW 1: Ssk, K5, K2tog. You now have 7 stitches.

- **ROW 2 AND ALL EVEN-NUMBERED ROWS:** Knit.
- **ROW 3:** Ssk, K3, K2tog. You now have 5 stitches.
- **ROW 5:** Ssk, K1, K2tog. You now have 3 stitches.
- **ROW 7:** K3tog.
- Fasten off yarn. Weave in tail. Repeat for second ear.

Knitting the Earflaps

- With right side facing, measure 2" (5 cm) from center back. Pick up and purl 17 stitches from row above cast-on row. Decrease as follows.
- **ROW 1 AND ALL ODD-NUMBERED ROWS:** Knit.
- **ROW 2:** Ssk, K13, K2tog. You now have 15 stitches.
- **ROW 4:** Ssk, K11, K2tog. You now have 13 stitches.
- **ROW 6:** Ssk, K9, K2tog. You now have 11 stitches.
- Continue in this manner, working 2 fewer stitches between the decreases and knitting one row even between decrease rows until you have 3 stitches.
- Following the instructions on page 245, work 3-stitch I-cord for 10" (25 cm).
- Repeat for second earflap.

Finishing

- Weave in ends. Sew on eye and nose buttons and embroider mouth and whiskers.

Taos Slippers
Designed by Dawn Leeseman, photo on page 25

These colorful little slippers are great for padding around the house in. The instructions are given for three sizes, and the tying ribbon allows for fine-tuning the fit.

MEASUREMENTS	To fit shoe size 6.5–7 (7.5–8, 8.5–9)
YARN	Crystal Palace Taos, 100% wool, 1.75 oz (50g)/128 yds (117 m), Color 02
NEEDLES	US 9 (5.5 mm) straight needles or size you need to obtain correct gauge
GAUGE	18 stitches = 4" (10 cm) in stockinette stitch
OTHER SUPPLIES	Stitch markers, US F/5 (3.75 mm) crochet hook, tapestry needle, 2 split ring markers, 2 yds ribbon
ABBREVIATIONS	**Kfb** knit into front and back of stitch (one stitch increased) **ssk** slip 1, slip 1, knit 2 slipped stitches together

Knitting the Sole

- Cast on 10 (11, 12) stitches. Knit 1 row, purl 1 row. Increase as follows.
- **ROW 1:** Kfb, knit to last stitch, Kfb.
- **ROW 2:** Purl.
- Repeat Rows 1 and 2 until you have 18 (19, 22) stitches.
- Work even in stockinette stitch until piece measures 6 (7, 8)" (15 [18, 20] cm). Decrease as follows.
- **ROW 1:** Ssk, knit to last 2 stitches, K2tog.
- **ROW 2:** Purl.
- Repeat Rows 1 and 2 until you have 10 (11, 12) stitches and piece measures 8 (9, 10)" (20 [23, 25] cm). Purl 1 row. Bind off.

Knitting the Uppers

- Cast on 10 (11, 12) stitches. Knit 1 row, purl 1 row. Increase as follows.
- **ROW 1:** Kfb, knit to last stitch, Kfb.
- **ROW 2:** Purl.
- Repeat Rows 1 and 2 until you have 18 (19, 22) stitches.

- Purl 1 row. Mark this as heel end of slipper.

Divide for Foot Opening

- With right side facing, K6 (6, 7). Join new yarn, bind off 6 (7, 8), K6 (6, 7). Working two sides at the same time, continue in stockinette stitch until piece measures 5.5 (6, 6.5)" (14 [15, 17] cm), ending with a wrong-side row.

Joining for Toe

- K6 (6, 7), cast on 6 (7, 8), K6 (6, 7). You now have 18 (19, 22) stitches. Work even in stockinette stitch until piece measures 6 (7, 8)" (15 [18, 20] cm), ending with a wrong-side row. Decrease as follows.
- ROW 1: Ssk, knit to last 2 stitches, K2tog.
- ROW 2: Purl.
- Repeat Rows 1 and 2 until you have 12 stitches and piece measures 8 (9, 10)" (20 [23, 25] cm). Purl 1 row. Bind off.

Finishing

- Sew uppers to soles around outside edge.

Crocheting the Trim

- Join yarn with slip stitch at lower edge of center opening.
- ROUND 1: Single crochet around opening.
- ROUND 2: *sc4, skip 1 sc; repeat from * to form eyelets.
- Fasten off yarn. Weave in tails. Cut ribbon in half and thread one through the eyelets of each slipper. Tie in a bow.

His 'n' Hers Shower Soap Holders

Designed by Cathy Carron, photo on page 18

These drawstring soap holders are designed to hang in the shower. They also can function as a washcloth. His and Hers are distinguished by the different stitch patterns.

MEASUREMENTS	Approximately 4" (10 cm) wide and 5.5" (14 cm) tall
YARN	Classic Elite Provence, 100% Egyptian cotton, 3.5 oz (100 g)/205 yds (188 m), 2616 Natural
NEEDLES	US 6 (4 mm) double-point needles or size you need to obtain correct gauge
GAUGE	20 stitches = 4" (10 cm) in stockinette stitch
OTHER SUPPLIES	Tapestry needle
ABBREVIATIONS	yo yarn over

stitch pattern

His — Raised Rib

ROUNDS 1–3: Knit.

ROUND 4: Purl.

Repeat Rounds 1–4 for pattern.

Hers — Seed Stitch

ROUND 1: *K1, P1; repeat from *.

ROUND 2: *P1, K1; repeat from *.

Repeat Rounds 1 and 2 for pattern.

Getting Started

- Cast on 40 stitches leaving a 12" (30 cm) tail for sewing bottom seam and divide the stitches onto 3 double-point needles. Join into a round, being careful not to twist stitches. Work 36 rounds in chosen pattern.

Knitting the Top Band

- **ROUNDS 1–3:** Knit.
- **ROUND 4:** *K2, yo, K2tog; repeat from *.
- **ROUNDS 5–7:** Knit.
- Bind off all stitches.

Knitting the Cord

- Following the instructions on page 245, knit a 13" (33 cm) 4-stitch I-cord. Bind off, leaving an 8" (20 cm) tail.

Finishing

- Thread the cast-on tail onto tapestry needle and sew bottom seam of bag. Weave the I-cord through the holes in the Top Band of the bag. Thread the tail of the I-cord onto tapestry needle and sew ends of I-cord together. Weave in ends.

Ribbed Headband

Designed by Marlaine DesChamps, photo on page 18

This headband is sure to keep your ears warm! Knitted in sport-weight yarn the headband is worked in a double layer of ribbing.

MEASUREMENTS	Approximately 3" (8 cm) wide and 19" (48 cm) circumference
YARN	Plymouth Boku, 95% wool/5% silk, 1.75 oz (50 g)/99 yds (90 m), Color 2
NEEDLES	One US 4 (3.5 mm) circular needle 16" (40 cm) long or size you need to obtain correct gauge
GAUGE	26 stitches = 4" (10 cm) in K1, P1 rib
OTHER SUPPLIES	Tapestry needle

Knitting the Headband

- Cast on 104 stitches loosely. Join into a round, being careful not to twist stitches.
- ROUND 1: *K1, P1; repeat from *.
- Repeat Round 1 until piece measures 6" (15 cm). Bind off loosely. Cut yarn leaving a 24" (61 cm) tail.

Finishing

- Thread tail onto tapestry needle. With wrong sides together, fold headband in half matching cast-on edge to bind-off edge. Sew edges together loosely, allowing the headband to stretch. Weave in ends.

Knitted Notebook Cover

Designed by Marlaine DesChamps, *photo on page 22*

Sized to fit a 5" by 7" (13 × 18 cm) notebook, this knitted cover turns a regular old notebook into a personal journal. All you need to do now is write something!

MEASUREMENTS	To fit a 5" (13 cm) by 7" (18 cm) notebook
YARN	Lion Brand Wool Prints, 100% wool, 2.75 oz (78 g)/143 yds (131 m), Blue
NEEDLES	US 6 (4 mm) straight needles or size you need to obtain correct gauge
GAUGE	20 stitches = 4" (10 cm) in stockinette stitch
OTHER SUPPLIES	Tapestry needle
ABBREVIATIONS	**RS** right side **WS** wrong side

Getting Started

- Cast on 37 stitches.
- **ROW 1 (WS)**: *K1, P1; repeat from * to last stitch, K1.
- **ROW 2 (RS)**: *P1, K1; repeat from * to last stitch, P1.
- **ROW 3**: Repeat Row 1.
- Beginning with a knit row, work stockinette stitch (knit on RS, purl on WS) until piece measures 3.75" (9.5 cm) from beginning, ending with a right-side row.
- **NEXT ROW**: Knit. This shows as a purl row on right side and creates a turning ridge.
- Continue in stockinette stitch until piece measures 3.75" (9.5 cm) from turning ridge. Work garter stitch (knit every row) for 3" (7.5 cm). Return to stockinette stitch and work for 3.75" (9.5 cm) ending with a right-side row. Work a turning ridge and then continue with stockinette stitch for 3.75" (9.5 cm). Repeat rows 1-3. Bind off loosely.

Finishing

- Fold end flaps to inside along turning ridges and sew in place. Weave in all ends. To make a bookmark, cut a piece of yarn 30" (76 cm) long and fold in half. Pull folded loop through edge of notebook cover at the center of one edge of the garter stitch section. Pull yarn ends through the loop and tighten. Tie overhand knots with both strands at 1" (2.5 cm) intervals.

Garterlac Bath Rug

Designed by Sarah Keller, photo on page 19

This rug is at once practical and attractive. Knitted with three strands of cotton held together, the rug is thick and cushiony. The cotton is very absorbent, and easy to care for, too.

MEASUREMENTS	Approximately 16.5" (42 cm) wide and 30" (76 cm) long
YARN	Peaches & Crème 4-Ply Worsted Cotton, 100% cotton, 16 oz (454 g)/840 yds (768 m), 04 Ecru
NEEDLES	One US 15 (10 mm) circular needle 24" (60 cm) long or size you need to obtain correct gauge
GAUGE	8 stitches = 4" (10 cm) in garter stitch
OTHER SUPPLIES	US M or N crochet hook, tapestry needle
ABBREVIATIONS	**Kfb** knit into front and back of stitch (one stitch increased) **SKP** slip 1 purlwise, knit 1, pass slipped stitch over **sc** single crochet

Getting Started

- Divide the one-pound cone of yarn into three equal balls weighing 5.3 oz (151 g) each.

Knitting the Rug

- With 3 strands held together, cast on 48 stitches.

Knitting the Bottom Triangles

- **ROW 1:** K1, turn, K1, turn.
- **ROW 2:** K2, turn, K2, turn.
- **ROW 3:** K3, turn, K3, turn.
- **ROW 4:** K4, turn, K4, turn.
- **ROW 5:** K5, turn, K5, turn.
- **ROW 6:** K6, turn, K6, turn.
- **ROW 7:** K7, turn, K7, turn.
- **ROW 8:** K8, do not turn.
- Repeat Rows 1–8 five more times.
- Turn after knitting the 6th triangle.

Garterlac Bath Rug continued

Knitting the Increasing Side Triangle

- **ROW 1:** K1, turn, Kfb, turn.
- **ROW 2:** K1, K2tog, turn, Kfb, K1, turn.
- **ROW 3:** K2, K2tog, turn, K1, Kfb, K1, turn.
- **ROW 4:** K3, K2tog, turn, K2, Kfb, K1, turn.
- **ROW 5:** K4, K2tog, turn, K3, Kfb, K1, turn.
- **ROW 6:** K5, K2tog, turn, K4, Kfb, K1, turn.
- **ROW 7:** K6, K2tog, turn, K5, Kfb, K1, turn.
- **ROW 8:** K7, K2tog, do not turn.

Knitting the Squares

- Pick up 8 stitches from side of next triangle. Slip last stitch to left needle, K2tog, turn.
- **ROW 1:** K8, turn, K7, K2tog, turn.
- Repeat Row 1 six more times. Do not turn on last row.
- Repeat the Square sequence 4 more times.

Knitting the Decreasing Side Triangle

- **ROW 1:** Pick up 8 stitches from first triangle, turn, K8, turn.
- **ROW 2:** K6, K2tog, turn, K7, turn.
- **ROW 3:** K5, K2tog, turn, K6, turn.
- **ROW 4:** K4, K2tog, turn, K5, turn.
- **ROW 5:** K3, K2tog, turn, K4, turn.
- **ROW 6:** K2, K2tog, turn, K3, turn.
- **ROW 7:** K1, K2tog, turn, K2, turn.
- **ROW 8:** K2tog, turn.
- Slip last stitch to right needle and count it as the first stitch of the next square.
- Using the instructions above, knit squares and triangles in the following sequence:
- Knit 6 Squares.
- Knit 1 Increasing Side Triangle.
- Knit 5 Squares.
- Knit 1 Decreasing Side Triangle.
- Knit 6 Squares.
- Knit 1 Increasing Side Triangle.
- Knit 5 Squares.
- Knit 1 Decreasing Side Triangle.

Knitting the Top Triangles

- **ROW 1:** Counting stitch on needle as first stitch, pick up 7 more stitches from edge of the Decreasing Side Triangle, turn.
- **ROW 2:** K6, K2tog, turn, K6, SKP, turn.
- **ROW 3:** K5, K2tog, turn, K5, SKP, turn.
- **ROW 4:** K4, K2tog, turn, K4, SKP, turn.
- **ROW 5:** K3, K2tog, turn, K3, SKP, turn.
- **ROW 6:** K2, K2tog, turn, K2, SKP, turn.
- **ROW 7:** K1, K2tog, turn, K1, SKP, turn.
- **ROW 8:** K2tog, turn, SKP.
- K1, pass last stitch over.
- Repeat 5 more times.

Finishing

- Transfer last stitch to crochet hook. Turn. Work a single crochet border around rug as follows:
- 47 sc across top, 3 sc in corner, 23 sc along left side, 3 sc in corner, 47 sc across bottom, 3 sc in corner, 23 sc along right side. Fasten off, weave in ends.

New Directions Hat

DESIGNED BY MARGARET RADCLIFFE, photo on page 17

This hat starts with a horizontal garter stitch band, then you'll pick up stitches and knit the rest vertically. Designed for quick knitting and an easy fit, you'll want to knit these for all your friends.

MEASUREMENTS	Approximately 21" (53 cm) circumference and 9.25" (21 cm) depth
YARN	Noro Kureyon, 100% wool, 1.75 oz (50 g)/109 yds (100 m), Color 154
NEEDLES	One US 10 (6 mm) circular needle 16" (40 cm) long and set of four US 10 (6 mm) double-point needles or size you need to obtain correct gauge
GAUGE	15 stitches = 4" (10 cm) in stockinette stitch
OTHER SUPPLIES	Tapestry needle
ABBREVIATIONS	**kwise** knitwise

New Directions Hat continued

Knitting the Bottom Band
- Using 2 double-point needles, cast on 6 stitches leaving an 8" (20 cm) tail.
- **ROW 1:** Slip 1 kwise, K4, P1.
- Repeat Row 1 until band measures 21" (53 cm) or smaller desired length. Bind off but do not cut yarn. Use cast-on tail to sew ends of band together.

Knitting the Body
- Using working yarn still attached and circular needle, pick up and knit 1 stitch into each slipped edge stitch along one side of the band. When picking up stitches, insert the needle into the center of the edge stitch so that the strand of the stitch closest to you shows on the right side of the fabric. You should have half as many stitches as there are rows around the band, plus perhaps 1 or 2 extras at the seam. Work in stockinette stitch until the length above the band is one-third the circumference of the band, or 7" (18 cm).

Decreasing for the Crown
- **ROUND 1:** *K2tog; repeat from *. If you have one extra stitch, just knit it.
- **ROUND 2:** Knit.
- Repeat Rounds 1 and 2 until you have 4 stitches.

Finishing
- Place 4 remaining stitches onto a double-point needle. Following the instructions on page 245, work a 4-stitch I-cord for 4 rounds. Cut yarn leaving a 6" (15 cm) tail. Thread tail onto tapestry needle and draw through remaining stitches twice. Pull snug, then pass down through I-cord to inside of hat and fasten off. Weave in ends.

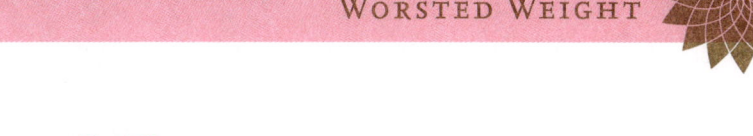

Boy-O-Boy

Designed by Carol Scott, photo on page 16

This little sweater is as handsome as it is easy to knit. A slipped stitch on the wrong side defines the pattern, and it is flanked by reverse stockinette stitch.

MEASUREMENTS	To fit infant 6–9 months, approximately 20" (51 cm) chest and 10" (25 cm) length
YARN	Dream in Color Handpainted Yarn, 100% merino superwash wool, 4 oz (113 g)/250 yds (231m), Deep Seaflower
NEEDLES	US 8 (5 mm) straight needles or size you need to obtain correct gauge
GAUGE	20 stitches = 4" (10 cm) in pattern
OTHER SUPPLIES	Stitch markers, stitch holders, tapestry needle, four ⅝" (15 mm) buttons
ABBREVIATIONS	**pwise** purlwise **WS** wrong side **wyif** with yarn in front **yo** yarn over

Knitting the Back

- Cast on 52 stitches. Knit 2 rows. Begin slip stitch pattern as follows.
- **ROW 1 (WS):** K3, *slip 1 pwise wyif, K4; repeat from * to last 4 stitches, slip 1, K3.
- **ROW 2:** P3, *K1, P4; repeat from * to last 4 stitches, K1, P3.
- Repeat Rows 1 and 2 for pattern.
- Work in slip stitch pattern until piece measures 5.5" (14 cm). Place markers at the beginning and end of this row to mark underarms. Continue in pattern until piece measures 10" (25 cm). Place stitches on 3 holders: 18 stitches for each shoulder and 16 stitches for the neck.

Knitting the Right Front

- Cast on 27 stitches. Knit 2 rows.
- Work in slip stitch pattern, maintaining a 3-stitch garter edge at the center front as follows.
- **ROW 1 (WS):** K3, *slip 1 pwise wyif, K4; repeat from * to last 4 stitches, slip 1, K3.

Boy-O-Boy continued

- **ROW 2:** K3, *K1, P4; repeat from * to last 4 stitches, K1, P3.
- Repeat Rows 1 and 2 for pattern.
- Work in pattern until piece measures 5.5" (14 cm). Place a marker at the side to mark underarm. Continue in pattern until piece measures 8.5" (22 cm), ending with Row 1.
- **NEXT ROW:** K3, place these 3 stitches on holder, continue in pattern to end of row.
- Beginning with this next row, decrease 1 stitch at neck edge every row 4 times and every other row 2 times. You now have 18 stitches.
- Continue in pattern until piece measures 10" (25 cm). Place 18 stitches on holder for shoulder.
- Mark center front garter band for 4 buttons.

Knitting the Left Front

- Work as for Right Front, maintaining a 3-stitch garter edge at the center front as follows.
- **ROW 1 (WS):** K3, *slip 1 pwise wyif, K4; repeat from * to last 4 stitches, slip 1, K3.
- **ROW 2:** P3, *K1, P4; repeat from * to last 4 stitches, K4.
- Repeat Rows 1 and 2 for pattern and at the same time make buttonholes in center front garter band to correspond with markings on Right Front band as follows:
- **BUTTONHOLE:** K1, yo, K2tog.
- Continue in pattern until piece measures 8.5" (22 cm), ending with Row 1.
- **NEXT ROW:** Work in pattern to last 3 stitches, place these stitches on holder.
- Beginning with this next row, decrease 1 stitch at neck edge every row 4 times and every other row 2 times. You now have 18 stitches.
- Continue in pattern until piece measures 10" (25 cm). Place 18 stitches on hold for shoulder.

Knitting the Sleeves (make two)

- Cast on 32 stitches. Knit 2 rows.
- Work in pattern as for Back and at the same time beginning with Row 6 (Row 2 of pattern) increase 1 stitch at each end of every 6 rows 6 times. You now have 44 stitches. Continue even in pattern until sleeve measures 7" (18 cm). Bind off.

Joining the Pieces

- Join shoulders together with a 3-needle bind off (see page 251). Sew sleeves to garment between armhole markers. Sew underarm seams.

Knitting the Neckband

- With right side of Right Front facing, knit 3 stitches from holder onto needle, pick up and knit 11 stitches along neckline, knit 16 back neck stitches, pick up and knit 11 stitches along Left Front neckline, knit 3 stitches from holder. You now have 44 stitches. Knit 2 rows. Bind off.

Finishing

- Weave in ends. Sew buttons at markings. Steam lightly or wash and lay flat to dry.

Tweed Silk Scarf

Designed by Katherine Eng, photo on page 20

Designed for warm-weather wearing, this cool pastel scarf will look great in the summer sun. The scarf is worked in lengthwise rows, and the crocheted design can be completed in about two hours.

MEASUREMENTS	Approximately 4.5" (11 cm) wide and 34.5" (88 cm) long
YARN	N. Y. Yarns Tropical Silk, 60% cotton/30% viscose/5% silk/5% acrylic, 1.75 oz (50 g) /81 yds (74 m), Color 07
NEEDLES	US K/10.5 (7 mm) crochet hook or size you need to obtain correct gauge
GAUGE	3 sc and 2 ch 2 = 2" (5 cm)
OTHER SUPPLIES	US I/9 (5.5 mm) crochet hook for final border, tapestry needle
ABBREVIATIONS	**RS** right side

Getting Started

- **NOTES:** Row 2 establishes the right side of the scarf. At the end of wrong-side rows, you will work a chain 5, turn — this counts as first double crochet and chain-2 space of the next row.
- With larger hook, chain 110.
- **ROW 1:** Sc in 2nd ch from hook, *ch 2, skip 2, sc in next ch; repeat from *, ch 5, turn. You now have 37 single crochets and 36 chain-2 spaces.
- **ROW 2 (RS):** Skip 1st sc and ch-2 space, dc in next sc, *ch 2, skip next ch-2 space, dc in next sc; repeat from *, ch 1, turn.

Tweed Silk Scarf continued

- **ROW 3:** Sc in 1st dc, *ch 2, skip next ch-2 space, sc in next dc; repeat from *, ending with ch 2, skip 2 chs, sc in 3rd ch of turning ch 5. Ch 5, turn.
- **ROWS 4–7:** Repeat Rows 2 and 3 twice. At the end of Row 7, ch 1, turn.

Crocheting the Border

- Change to smaller hook. Working on the right side of one long edge, skip over the single crochets and work (sc, ch 3, sc) in each ch-2 space.
- **FIRST SHORT END:** (Sc, ch 3, sc) in corner sc. Working over posts at end of dc rows only, *(sc, ch 3, sc) in post, ch 1; repeat from * once, (sc, ch 3, sc) in last post. (Sc, ch3, sc) in corner sc.
- Work second long and short edges as first. Join to beginning sc with a slip stitch. Fasten off.

Finishing

- Weave in ends.

Broken Rib Socks

DESIGNED BY KATHLEEN TAYLOR, photo on page 16

These adult-size socks can be knitted in a flash in worsted weight yarn. They'll be toasty warm, too!

MEASUREMENTS	To fit adult small (medium, large) Note: All sizes are worked on same number of stitches. The difference is in the length of the foot.
YARN	Decadent Fibers Cookie Dough, 80% merino blend wool/ 20% mohair, 8 oz (227 g)/490 yds (448 m), Nutmeg Note: There is enough yarn on one skein for two pairs of socks.
NEEDLES	Set of four US 5 (3.75 mm) double-point needles or size you need to obtain correct gauge
GAUGE	24 stitches = 4" (10 cm) in stockinette stitch
OTHER SUPPLIES	Tapestry needle
ABBREVIATIONS	**pwise** purlwise

stitch pattern

BROKEN RIB

ROUNDS 1 AND 2: Knit.

ROUNDS 3 AND 4: *K2, P2; repeat from *.

Repeat Rounds 1–4 for pattern.

Knitting the Leg

- Cast on 48 stitches and divide evenly onto 3 double-point needles. Join into a round, being careful not to twist stitches.
- Work K2, P2 ribbing for 14 rounds.
- Work Broken Rib pattern until sock measures 6.5" (17 cm) from beginning or desired length to top of heel, ending on Round 4.

Knitting the Heel Flap

- Knit 11 stitches from needle 1 in pattern. Put next 24 stitches on holder for instep. Slide 13 stitches from needle 3 to needle 1. You will work the heel flap back and forth on these 24 stitches.
- ROW 1: Slip 1 pwise, P23.
- ROW 2: Slip 1 pwise, K22, turn.
- ROW 3: Slip 1, P21, turn.
- ROW 4: Slip 1, K20, turn.
- Continue in this manner, working one fewer stitch each row, until there are 9 stitches between the turning points, ending with a right-side row.

Turning the Heel

- ROW 1: Slip 1, P8, slip 1, pick up and purl 1 stitch in the gap, slide that stitch and the slipped stitch back onto left needle and purl them together, turn.
- ROW 2: Slip 1, K9, slip 1, pick up and knit 1 stitch in the gap, pass slipped stitch over picked up stitch, turn.
- ROW 3: Slip 1, P10, slip 1, pick up and knit 1 stitch in the gap, pass slipped stitch over picked up stitch, turn.
- Continue in this manner, increasing the number of stitches before picking up and turning, until all heel stitches have been worked.

Knitting the Foot

- Return instep stitches to needles. Working instep stitches in Broken Rib pattern and sole stitches in stockinette, work even until foot measures 5 (5.5, 6)" (13 [14, 15] cm).

Decreasing for the Toe

- ROUND 1: *K6, K2tog; repeat from *.
- ROUND 2 AND ALL EVEN-NUMBERED ROUNDS: Knit.

Broken Rib Socks continued

- **ROUND 3:** *K5, K2tog; repeat from *.
- **ROUND 5:** *K4, K2tog; repeat from *.
- Continue in this manner, knitting 1 fewer stitch between decreases and working one round even between decrease rounds until 12 stitches remain.

Finishing

- Cut yarn leaving a 10" (25 cm) tail. Thread tail onto tapestry needle and draw through remaining stitches twice. Pull up snug and fasten off on the inside. Weave in ends. Block.

Elegant-and-Easy Cable Mittens for the Family

Designed by Marci Richardson, photo on page 19

These mittens are sized to fit a small child, a large child, a small adult, and a large adult. Sorry, nothing for the dog. Instructions are given for a right and left mitten.

MEASUREMENTS	Approximately 6 (7, 8, 9)" (15 [18, 20, 23] cm) circumference
YARN	Mountain Colors Mountain Goat, 55% mohair/45% wool, 3.5 oz (100 g)/230 yds (210 m), Painted Rocks
NEEDLES	Set of four US 4 (3.5 mm) double-point needles or size you need to obtain correct gauge
GAUGE	24 stitches = 4" (10 cm) in stockinette stitch
OTHER SUPPLIES	Cable needle, stitch markers, tapestry needle
ABBREVIATIONS	**cn** cable needle **M1L** make 1 with left slant (see page 247) **M1R** make 1 with right slant (see page 247) **pm** place marker **sm** slip marker

Knitting the Cuff

- Cast on 36 (40, 44, 48) stitches loosely. Divide stitches onto 3 double-point needles so you have 12 (12, 16, 16) stitches on needle 1, 12 (16, 12, 16) stitches on needle 2, and 12 (12, 16, 16) stitches on needle 3. Join into a round, being careful not to twist stitches.

stitch pattern

Twisted Rib

ROUNDS 1–3: *K2, P2; repeat from *.

ROUND 4: *Knit into 2nd stitch on left needle, knit into first stitch on left needle, slip both stitches from needle.

Repeat Rounds 1–4 for pattern.

Cable

ROUNDS 1–3: P2, K6, P2.

ROUND 4: P2, place 3 stitches onto cn and hold in back, K3, K3 from cn, P2.

ROUNDS 5–6: P2, K6, P2.

- **SET-UP ROUND:** Beginning with Row 1 of patterns, work 14 (14, 18, 18) stitches in Twisted Rib pattern (ending K2), pm, work 10 stitches in Cable pattern, pm, work 12 (16, 16, 20) stitches in Twisted Rib pattern.
- Work patterns as established until cuff measures 2 (2.5, 2.75, 3)" (5 [6, 7, 8] cm).
- **NEXT ROUND:** Discontinuing Twisted Rib but maintaining Cable pattern, increase 2 stitches evenly spaced on needles 1 and 3. You now have 40 (44, 48, 52) stitches.
- Work 1 round in pattern.

Knitting the Thumb Gussets

Right Hand
- **ROUND 1:** Work 33 (34, 39, 40) stitches in pattern, pm M1L, K1, M1R, knit to end of round.

Left Hand
- **ROUND 1:** K8 (7, 10, 9), pm, M1L, K1, M1R, pm, work in pattern to end of round.

Both Hands
- **ROUND 2:** Work even in pattern as established.
- **ROUND 3:** Work in pattern to thumb gusset, sm, M1L, knit to next marker, M1R, sm, work in pattern to end of round.
- **ROUNDS 4 AND 5:** Work even in pattern as established.
- Repeat Rounds 3–5 until you have 13 (15, 17, 19) thumb gusset stitches between the markers, ending with Round 3.
- **NEXT ROUND:** Work even in pattern as established to thumb gusset, remove markers and place thumb gusset stitches on holder, cast on 1 stitch, continue in pattern to end of round.
- Continue even in pattern as established until mitten measures 4.5 (5.5, 6.5, 7)" (11 [14, 17, 18] cm) from ribbing.

Shaping the Top
- Discontinue Cable pattern and work all stitches in stockinette stitch.
- **ROUND 1:** *K2, K2tog; repeat from *.
- **ROUNDS 2–4:** Knit.
- **ROUND 5:** *K1, K2tog; repeat from *.
- **ROUNDS 6–8:** Knit.
- **ROUND 9:** *K2tog; repeat from *.
- Cut yarn leaving a 8" (20 cm) tail. Thread tail onto tapestry needle and draw through remaining stitches twice. Pull up snug and fasten off on the inside.

Elegant-and-Easy Cable Mittens for the Family continued

Knitting the Thumb

- Place thumb stitches onto 3 double-point needles, picking up 1 extra stitch on both sides of the cast-on stitch. Work in stockinette stitch until thumb measures 1.5 (1.75, 2, 2.25)" (3 [4, 5, 6] cm).
- **NEXT ROUND:** *K2tog; repeat from *.
- Cut yarn leaving an 8" (20 cm) tail. Thread tail onto tapestry needle and draw through remaining stitches twice. Pull up snug and fasten off on the inside.

Finishing

- Weave in ends. Block.

Four Egg-Cozy Hats

DESIGNED BY MIRIAM G. BRIGGS, photo on page 20

These little hats were inspired by Kristin Nicholas' egg cozies in the book *Weekend Knitting* (Kristin made sweaters). Whether you use them to keep your eggs warm, decorate your Christmas tree, or dress a medium-sized doll, they're fun to knit!

MEASUREMENTS	Approximately 7" (18 cm) circumference
YARN	Classic Elite Skye Tweed, 100% wool, 1.75 oz (50 g)/110 yds (101 m), Color 1253
NEEDLES	Sets of four US 6 (4 mm) and US 4 (3.5 mm) double-point needles or size you need to obtain correct gauge
GAUGE	18 stitches = 4" (10 cm) in stockinette stitch on larger needles
OTHER SUPPLIES	Tapestry needle, crochet hook, stitch markers
ABBREVIATIONS	**Kfb** knit into front and back of stitch (one stitch increased) **M1** make 1 increase **RT** right twist: knit second stitch on left needle, knit first stitch, drop both stitches from left needle **SKP** slip 1, K1, pass slipped stitch over **sm** slip marker

stitch pattern

ARAN TWIST

ROUNDS 1, 2 AND 4: *K1, P1, K4, P1; repeat from *.

ROUND 3: *K1, P1, RT twice, P1; repeat from *.

Knitting the Roll Brim Hat

- With smaller needles, cast on 36 stitches. Join in round being careful not to twist stitches. Knit 4 rows. Change to larger needles and knit 22 rows or until piece measures 3⅝" (9 cm).

Decreasing for the Crown

- **ROUND 1:** *K4, SKP; repeat from *. You now have 30 stitches.
- **ROUND 2:** *K3, SKP; repeat from *. You now have 24 stitches.
- **ROUND 3:** *K2, SKP; repeat from *. You now have 18 stitches.
- **ROUND 4:** *K1, SKP; repeat from *. You now have 12 stitches.
- **ROUND 5:** *K1, SKP; repeat from *. You now have 8 stitches.
- **ROUND 6:** *SKP; repeat from *. You now have 4 stitches.
- Following the instructions on page 245, knit a 3-row, 4-stitch I-cord.

Finishing

- Cut yarn leaving a 10" (25 cm) tail. Thread tail onto tapestry needle and draw through remaining stitches twice. Pull up snug and fasten off on the inside. Weave in ends.

Knitting the Beret

- With smaller needles, cast on 36 stitches. Join in round being careful not to twist stitches. Work K1, P1 rib for 5 rounds. Change to larger needles and increase as follows.
- **ROUND 1:** *K2, M1; repeat from *. You now have 54 stitches.
- **ROUNDS 2 AND 4:** Knit.
- **ROUND 3:** *K6, M1; repeat from *. You now have 63 stitches.
- **ROUND 5:** *K7, M1; repeat from *. You now have 72 stitches.
- Knit 4 rounds even.

Decreasing for the Crown

- **ROUND 1:** *K7, SKP; repeat from *. You now have 64 stitches.
- **ROUND 2 AND ALL EVEN-NUMBERED ROUNDS:** Knit.
- **ROUND 3:** *K6, SKP; repeat from *. You now have 56 stitches.
- **ROUND 5:** *K5, SKP; repeat from *. You now have 48 stitches.
- Continue in this manner, knitting 1 fewer stitch between decreases and working 1 round even between decrease rounds until you have 16 stitches.
- **NEXT ROUND:** *SKP; repeat from *. You now have 8 stitches.

Four Egg-Cozy Hats continued

Finishing

- Cut yarn leaving a 10" (25 cm) tail. Thread tail onto tapestry needle and draw through remaining stitches twice. Pull up snug and make a 4-stitch crochet chain. Thread the tail back onto tapestry needle and weave through crochet chain. Bring yarn to inside, pull to curl the chain, and fasten off. Weave in ends.

Knitting the Chullo

Knitting the Flaps (make two)

- With crochet hook, chain 4. Slip last chain onto knitting needle.
- **ROW 1:** Kfb.
- **ROW 2:** K1, Kfb.
- **ROW 3:** K2, Kfb.
- **ROW 4:** K3, Kfb.
- **ROW 5:** K2, P2, Kfb.
- **ROW 6:** K5, Kfb.
- **ROW 7:** K2, P4, Kfb.
- **ROW 8:** K7, Kfb.
- **ROW 9:** K2, P5, K2.
- When you finish 2nd earflap, do not break yarn.

Knitting the Body

- With attached yarn, knit 9 stitches of second earflap, cast on 6 stitches, pick up and knit 9 stitches from 1st earflap, cast on 12 stitches. You now have 36 stitches. Join into a round, being careful not to twist stitches.
- Place marker, K35, P1.
- **NEXT ROUND:** sm, P1, K7, P8, K7, P12, K1.
- **NEXT ROUND:** sm, knit to end of round.
- **NEXT ROUND:** sm, K10, P6, K10, P10.
- Work even in stockinette stitch until piece measures 2" (5 cm).

Decreasing for the Crown

- **ROUND 1:** *K4, SKP; repeat from *. You now have 30 stitches.
- **ROUNDS 2 AND 3:** Knit.
- **ROUND 4:** *K3, SKP; repeat from *. You now have 24 stitches.
- **ROUNDS 5 AND 6:** Knit.
- Continue in this manner, knitting 1 fewer stitch between decreases and knitting 2 rounds even between decrease rounds until you have 12 stitches.
- **NEXT ROUND:** *SKP; repeat from *. You now have 6 stitches.
- Knit 2 rounds.

Finishing

- Cut yarn leaving an 8" (20 cm) tail. Thread tail onto tapestry needle and draw through remaining stitches twice. Pull up snug. With crochet hook chain 4. Fasten off yarn. Weave in ends.

Knitting the Aran

- With smaller needles, cast on 42 stitches. Divide stitches onto 3 double-point needles. Join into a round, being careful not to twist stitches.
- Work 3 rounds of Aran Twist pattern, beginning with Round 4.
- Change to larger needles and continue Aran Twist pattern until you have worked 19 rounds, ending with pattern Round 2.

Decreasing for the Crown

- **ROUND 1:** *K1, P1, K2tog twice, P1; you now have 30 stitches.
- **ROUNDS 2 AND 3:** *K1, P1, K2, P1; repeat from *.
- **ROUND 4:** *K1, P1, K2tog, P1; repeat from *. You now have 24 stitches.
- **ROUNDS 5 AND 6:** *K1, P1; repeat from *.
- **ROUND 7:** *SKP, P2tog; repeat from *. You now have 12 stitches.

Finishing

- Make a .5" (1.25 cm) pompom (see page 248). Cut yarn leaving an 8" (20 cm) tail. Thread tail onto tapestry needle and draw through remaining stitches twice. Attach pompom. Fasten off yarn on inside. Weave in ends.

Indian Cross Scarf

Designed by Marci Richardson, photo on page 19

For this scarf you'll cast on stitches for the entire length. That's a lot of stitches, but you won't have too many rows to work. You'll need a long circular needle to hold all those stitches.

MEASUREMENTS	Approximately 5" (13 cm) wide and 53" (135 cm) long
YARN	Mountain Colors Merino Ribbon, 80% super fine merino/20% nylon, 3.5 oz (100 g)/245 yds (224 m), Ruby River
NEEDLES	One US 9 (5.5 mm) circular needle 32" (80 cm) long or size you need to obtain correct gauge
GAUGE	16 stitches = 4" (10 cm) in stockinette stitch
OTHER SUPPLIES	Tapestry needle, crochet hook for fringe

Getting Started

- Cast on 216 stitches loosely. Knit four rows.
- **ROW 1:** K1, *insert needle in next stitch knitwise, wrap the yarn around needle 3 times and finish the stitch, leaving all 3 wraps on needle; repeat from * to last stitch, K1.
- **ROW 2:** *With yarn in back, slip next 8 stitches to right needle, dropping the extra wraps. You now have 8 elongated stitches on right needle. Slip the first 4 stitches over the second 4 stitches but do not drop them from the needle. Return all 8 stitches to left needle and knit them, keeping the crossed order. Repeat from *.
- **ROWS 3–6:** Knit.
- **ROW 7:** Repeat Row 1.
- **ROW 8:** With yarn in back, slip next 4 stitches to right needle, dropping the extra wraps. Slip the first 2 stitches over the second 2 stitches but do not drop them from the needle. Return all 4 stitches to left needle and knit them, keeping the crossed order. Continue as for Row 2, crossing 8 stitches and knitting them, to the last 4 stitches. Work last 4 stitches as first 4 stitches in this row.
- **ROWS 9–12:** Knit.
- Repeat Rows 1–12 once more. Bind off loosely.

Finishing

- Weave in ends. Add fringe if desired.

Hugs-and-Kisses-with-Love Hand Warmers

Designed by Nancy Bowron, photo on page 22

These super-soft hand warmers feature the classic XOX (kiss, hug, kiss) cable pattern on the back of the hand. The palm has a heart motif. Worked back and forth then seamed, these warmers are knitted with love in angora and wool.

stitch pattern

XOX Cable
Row 1: P2, K8, P2.
Row 2 and all even-numbered rows through 16: K2, P8, K2.
Row 3: P2, C4F, C4B, P2.
Row 5: Repeat Row 1.
Row 7: P2, C4B, C4F, P2.
Row 9: Repeat Row 1.
Row 11: P2, C4B, C4F, P2.
Row 13: Repeat Row 1.
Row 15: P2, C4F, C4B, P2.

Measurements	Approximately 7" (18 cm) around and 8" (20 cm) long
Yarn	Classic Elite Lush, 50% angora/50% wool, 1.75 oz (50 g)/ 123 yds (112 m), 4419 Pink Icing
Needles	US 7 (4.5 mm) straight needles or size you need to obtain correct gauge
Gauge	18 stitches = 4" (10 cm) in stockinette stitch
Other Supplies	Stitch markers, cable needle, tapestry needle
Abbreviations	**C4B** place 2 stitches on cable needle and hold in back, knit 2, knit 2 from cable needle **C4F** place 2 stitches on cable needle and hold in front, knit 2, knit 2 from cable needle **Kfb** knit into front and back of stitch (one stitch increased)

Knitting the Cuff

- Cast on 40 stitches. Place a marker after the 6th and before the 18th stitches for the right warmer and after the 22nd and before the 34th stitch for the left warmer. Work K2, P2 rib to first marker, work XOX Cable pattern over stitches between the markers, work K2, P2 rib to end of row. Repeat through Row 8 of XOX Cable pattern.

Beginning the Body

- Continuing XOX Cable pattern as established, work stockinette stitch over all stitches outside the markers until you have completed 20 rows from beginning.

Knitting the Heart Motif and Thumb Gusset

Right Warmer

- **Row 21:** Work as established to 4 stitches after cable marker, place marker for gusset, Kfb twice, place 2nd gusset marker, K7, P1, K8.

Hugs-and-Kisses-with-Love Hand Warmers continued

- **ROW 22 AND ALL EVEN-NUMBERED ROWS THROUGH ROW 36:** Knit the knits and purl the purls.
- **ROW 23:** Work as established to gusset marker, slip marker, Kfb, knit to 2nd gusset marker, Kfb, slip marker, K6, P3, K7.
- Continue as established in stockinette and XOX Cable pattern, increasing 1 stitch after 1st gusset marker and 1 stitch before 2nd gusset marker and at the same time working heart motif over last 16 stitches as follows:
- **ROW 25:** K5, P5, K6.
- **ROW 27:** K4, P7, K5.
- **ROW 29:** K4, P7, K5.
- **ROW 31:** K4, P3, K1, P3, K5.
- **ROW 33:** K5, P1, K3, P1, K6.
- **ROW 35:** K16.

Left Warmer

- **ROW 21:** K8, P1, K7, place marker for gusset, Kfb twice, place 2nd gusset marker, K4, work pattern as established to end of row.
- **ROW 22 AND ALL EVEN-NUMBERED ROWS THROUGH ROW 36:** Knit the knits and purl the purls.
- **ROW 23:** K7, P3, K6, slip gusset marker, Kfb, knit to 2nd gusset marker, Kfb, slip marker, K4, work pattern as established to end of row.
- Continue as established in stockinette and XOX Cable pattern, increasing 1 stitch after 1st gusset marker and 1 stitch before 2nd gusset marker and at the same time working heart motif over first 16 stitches as follows:
- **ROW 25:** K6, P5, K5.
- **ROW 27:** K5, P7, K4.
- **ROW 29:** K5, P7, K4.
- **ROW 31:** K5, P3, K1, P3, K4.
- **ROW 33:** K6, P1, K3, P1, K5.
- **ROW 35:** K16.
- You now have 18 stitches between the gusset markers and have completed 36 rows and finished the heart motif on the palm.

Finishing Body of Warmer

Right Warmer

- Work stockinette stitch and XOX Cable pattern as established to 1st gusset marker. Remove marker, K1, place 16 thumb stitches on holder, K1, remove 2nd gusset marker, knit to end of row.

Left Warmer

- Knit to 1st gusset marker. Remove marker, K1, place 16 thumb stitches on holder, K1, remove 2nd gusset marker, work XOX Cable pattern and stockinette stitch as established to end of row.
- You now have 40 stitches on needle and 16 stitches held for thumb.
- Continue stockinette stitch and XOX Cable pattern on 40 stitches as established until you have completed 48 rows.
- Work 4 rows with K2, P2 rib on either side of the cable pattern. Bind off loosely and cut yarn, leaving a tail long enough to sew side seam.

Knitting the Thumb

- Return 16 thumb stitches to needle. Work 4 to 6 rows of stockinette stitch. Bind off loosely and cut yarn, leaving a tail long enough to sew thumb seam.

Finishing

- Sew side and thumb seams. Weave in ends.

Hugs-and-Kisses with Love Headband

Designed by Nancy Bowron, photo on page 22

Like the lovely Hand Warmers on page 147, this headband is knitted with the classic XOX (kiss, hug, kiss) cable and has hearts hidden inside the band.

MEASUREMENTS	To fit head up to 22" (56 cm), approximately 18" (46 cm) circumference, unstretched
YARN	Classic Elite Lush, 50% angora/50% wool, 1.75 oz (50 g)/123 yds (112 m), 4419 Pink Icing
NEEDLES	US 7 (4.5 mm) straight needles or size you need to obtain correct gauge
GAUGE	18 stitches = 4" (10 cm) in stockinette stitch
OTHER SUPPLIES	Cable needle, tapestry needle
ABBREVIATIONS	**C4B** place 2 stitches on cable needle and hold in back, knit 2, knit 2 from cable needle **C4F** place 2 stitches on cable needle and hold in front, knit 2, knit 2 from cable needle **Kfb** knit into front and back of stitch (one stitch increased)

stitch pattern

XOX Cable

Row 1: P2, K8, P2.
Row 2 and all even-numbered rows through 16: K2, P8, K2.
Row 3: P2, C4F, C4B, P2.
Row 5: Repeat Row 1.
Row 7: P2, C4B, C4F, P2.
Row 9: Repeat Row 1.
Row 11: P2, C4B, C4F, P2.
Row 13: Repeat Row 1.
Row 15: P2, C4F, C4B, P2.

Getting Started

- Cast on 34 stitches.
- **Row 1:** K17, K2, work XOX Cable pattern over next 12 stitches, K3.
- **Row 2:** P3, work XOX Cable pattern over next 12 stitches, P2, K17.
- Repeat 16-row cable pattern sequence as established 7 times or to desired length and at the same time work heart motifs over last 17 stitches of even-numbered (wrong side) rows as follows:
- **Row 6:** K8, P1, K8.
- **Row 8:** K7, P3, K7.
- **Row 10:** K6, P5, K6.
- **Row 12:** K5, P7, K5.
- **Row 14:** K5, P3, K1, P3, K5.
- **Row 16:** K6, P1, K3, P1, K6.

Finishing

- Bind off loosely. Sew cast-on to bind-off edge. Sew side seam. Bury tails inside headband.

Mini Messenger Bag

Designed by Lori Law, photo on page 17

Whether you knit this bag flat or circularly, it's a winner. Designed to lay flat against your body when you wear it, there's plenty of room to hold essentials without adding bulk to your silhouette. The felted strap is strong, and the extra-long flap will keep things inside where they belong.

MEASUREMENTS	Approximately 7" (18 cm) wide and 7.5" (19 cm) tall after felting
YARN	Cascade 220, 100% Peruvian Highland Wool, 3.5 oz (100 g)/220 yds (201 m), 8404 Teal or 8415 Cranberry
NEEDLES	Circular version: One US 10.5 (6.5 mm) circular needle 16" (40 cm) long; Flat version: US 10.5 (6.5 mm) straight needles or size you need to obtain correct gauge
GAUGE	14 stitches = 4" (10 cm) in stockinette stitch
OTHER SUPPLIES	Stitch markers, cable needle, tapestry needle
ABBREVIATIONS	**2/2LC** slip 2 stitches to cable needle and hold in front, K2, K2 from cable needle **C3F** slip 2 stitches to cable needle and hold in front, P1, K2 from cable needle **C3B** slip 1 stitch to cable needle and hold in back, K2, P1 from cable needle **C4F** slip 2 stitches to cable needle and hold in front, P2, K2 from cable needle **C4B** slip 2 stitches to cable needle and hold in back, K2, P2 from cable needle **K3tog tbl** knit 3 stitches together through the back loop **WS** wrong side

stitch pattern

CABLE

ROW 1: P2, K2, P6, K2, P2.
ROW 2: K2, P2, K6, P2, K2.
ROW 3: P2, C3F, P4, C3B, P2.
ROW 4: K3, P2, K4, P2, K3.
ROW 5: P3, C4F, C4B, P3.
ROW 6: K5, P4, K5.
ROW 7: P5, 2/2LC, P5.
ROW 8: Repeat Row 6.
ROW 9: P3, C4B, C4F, P3.
ROW 10: Repeat Row 4.
ROW 11: P2, C3B, P4, C3F, P2.
ROWS 12 AND 14: Repeat Row 2.
ROW 13: Repeat Row 1.

Mini Messenger Bag continued

Knitting the Bag in the Round

- Cast on 30 stitches. Beginning with a wrong-side row, knit 6 rows back and forth. On last row, do not turn work. Pick up and knit 3 stitches along short edge, 30 stitches along long edge, and 3 stitches on other short edge. Place a marker for beginning of round (right front). You will now work in the round on these 66 stitches.

Knitting the Body

- Work in stockinette stitch until piece measures 9.5" (24 cm). Work 4 rounds of garter stitch beginning with a purl round, and end 3 stitches before marker on last round. Bring yarn to front, slip next stitch, return yarn to back, return slipped stitch to left needle.

Binding Off for Top Edge

- **BIND OFF 3 STITCHES FOR SIDE OF BAG. BIND OFF NEXT 30 STITCHES AS FOLLOWS:** *Slip stitch on right needle to left needle and K3tog tbl; repeat from * 14 times. Bring yarn to front, slip next stitch from left needle to right needle, return yarn to back, return slipped stitch to left needle. Bind off 3 stitches for other side of bag. Knit 30 front flap stitches.

Knitting the Flap

- Flap is worked back and forth on 30 stitches.
- **SET UP ROW (WS):** K2, P6, K2, P2, K6, P2, K2, P6, K2.
- **ROW 1:** K8, work center 14 stitches in Cable pattern, K8.
- **ROW 2:** K2, P6, work center 14 stitches in Cable pattern, P6, K2.
- Repeat Rows 1 and 2, following chart or written instructions for cable, until you have completed 4 repeats of the 14-row Cable pattern. Bind off in knit with wrong side facing.

Knitting the Handles

- Following the instructions on page 245, make a 4-stitch I-cord 55"–72" (140–183 cm) long or desired length × 1.25.

Finishing

- Weave in ends. Insert one end of handle through side of bag, going in about 4 rows below garter band and coming out 6 rows below that. Repeat for other side. Knot the ends.

Felting the Bag

- Place bag inside pillowcase or other cloth bag and tie closed. Set the washing machine for the lowest water level, longest washing cycle, and hottest temperature. Place bag in machine with a pair of jeans or other heavy garment. Add a tiny amount of liquid soap. Start the washer and check the felting progress frequently. You want a dense fabric with cable definition. If necessary, reset the machine and run again. When desired size is reached, remove the bag and rinse in cold water. Blot excess water with a towel. Shape the bag and allow it to dry.

Knitting the Bag Flat

- Cast on 30 stitches. Knit 6 rows garter stitch. At the end of the last row, cast on 1 stitch (selvedge stitch). Turn, K30, cast on 37 stitches (includes another selvedge stitch).

Knitting the Body

- Work back and forth in stockinette stitch until piece measures 9.5" (24 cm). Work 4 rows garter stitch.

Binding Off for Top Edge

- Bind off 1 stitch, K29, bind off 3. Bind off next 30 stitches as follows: Slip stitch on right needle to left and K3tog tbl. Bind off 3 stitches. Break yarn, leaving a tail for seaming. Rejoin yarn to beginning of remaining 30 stitches with right side facing.

Finishing

- Work the flap as for circular version. Sew side and bottom seams using selvedge stitches. Make and attach the handles, weave in ends, and felt as for circular version.

Baby Basket Hat

Designed by Patti Ghezzi, photo on page 18

This hat has a dual purpose: When not in use as a hat, simply turn it upside-down and use it as a basket to store ribbons or other small items. Smaller needles are used for the crown (or basket bottom) for a slightly tighter and firmer fabric.

MEASUREMENTS	To fit infant 9–12 months
YARN	Plymouth Yarn Company Royal Cashmere, 100% cashmere, 75 oz (50 g)/125 yds (114 m), Color 2581
NEEDLES	US 5 (3.75 mm) and US 4 (3.5 mm) straight and two US 5 (3.75 mm) double-point needles or size you need to obtain correct gauge
GAUGE	16 stitches = 4" (10 cm) in pattern
OTHER SUPPLIES	Tapestry needle

Knitting the Hat

- Using larger needle, cast on 72 stitches. Work even in Woven Stitch pattern for 6 rows.
- **NEXT ROW:** Work 17 stitches in pattern as established, yo, K2tog, work 34 stitches in pattern as established, yo, K2tog, work in pattern to end of row. You have made eyelet holes that will be used later for the chin strap.
- Continue in Woven Stitch pattern as established until piece measures 4" (10 cm) from beginning, ending on Row 2 of pattern.

Decreasing for the Crown

- Change to smaller needles.
- **ROW 1:** *K6, K2tog; repeat from *.
- **ROW 2 AND ALL EVEN-NUMBERED ROWS:** Purl.
- **ROW 3:** Knit.
- **ROW 5:** *K5, K2tog; repeat from *.
- Continue in this manner, knitting one fewer stitch between decreases but working only one row even between decrease rows until you have 9 stitches. Cut yarn leaving a 16" (41 cm) tail. Thread tail onto tapestry needle and draw through remaining stitches twice. Pull up snug, and use remaining tail to sew center back seam.

stitch pattern

WOVEN STITCH

ROWS 1, 3, 5, AND 7: *K2, P2, K2, K6 for garter block *.

ROW 2 AND ALL EVEN-NUMBERED ROWS THROUGH 8: *K6 for garter block, P2, K2, P2; repeat from *.

ROWS 9, 11, 13, AND 15: *K6 for garter block, K2, P2, K2; repeat from *.

ROW 10 AND ALL EVEN-NUMBERED ROWS THROUGH 16: *P2, K2, P2, K6 for garter block.

Repeat Rows 1–16 for pattern.

Knitting the Chin Strap

- Following the instructions on page 245, knit a 3-stitch I-cord about 21" (53 cm) long. Thread one strap end through each eyelet hole and tie into a loop, adjusting the length as needed to fit your baby.

Finishing

- Weave in ends. Block lightly by spritzing with water and allowing to dry on a cylinder-shaped object overnight.

Little Monster Bear

Designed by Wendy Gross, *photo on page 25*

Wendy has knitted a virtual ark-full of little monsters, and here we have the Little Monster Bear. This felted creature is sure to please everyone he meets — young and old alike. Please note that Little Monsters should not be given to children under three unless the plastic eyes are omitted.

MEASUREMENTS	Approximately 5.5" (14 cm) body length
YARN	Malabrigo Merino Worsted, 100% merino wool, 3.5 oz (100 g)/ 215 yds (198 m), Oceanos
NEEDLES	US 10 (6 mm) straight needles and two US 10 (6 mm) double-point needles or size you need to obtain correct gauge
GAUGE	16 stitches = 4" (10 cm) in stockinette stitch
OTHER SUPPLIES	Polyfil, plastic doll safety eyes, tapestry needle
ABBREVIATIONS	**Kfb** knit into front and back of stitch (one stitch increased)

Knitting the Body

- Cast on 8 stitches using the long tail method (see page 246), leaving a 10" (25 cm) tail.
- ROW 1: *K1, Kfb; repeat from *. You now have 12 stitches.
- ROW 2 AND ALL EVEN-NUMBERED ROWS THROUGH 10: Purl.
- ROW 3: *K2, Kfb; repeat from *. You now have 16 stitches.
- ROW 5: *K2, Kfb; repeat from * to last stitch, K1. You now have 21 stitches.

Little Monster Bear continued

- ROW 7: *K3, Kfb; repeat from * to last stitch, K1. You now have 26 stitches.
- ROW 9: *K3, Kfb; repeat from * to last 2 stitches, K2. You now have 32 stitches.
- Work even in stockinette stitch until piece measures 3.5" (9 cm).

Shaping the Neck

- ROW 1: *K4, K2tog; repeat from * to last 2 stitches, K2. You now have 27 stitches.
- ROW 2: *P3, P2tog; repeat from * to last 2 stitches, P2. You now have 22 stitches.
- ROW 3: Knit.
- ROW 4: Purl.
- ROW 5: *K6, Kfb; repeat from * to last stitch, K1. You now have 25 stitches.
- Work even in stockinette stitch until piece measures 5.5" (14 cm).

Shaping the Head

- ROW 1: *K2, K2tog; repeat from * to last stitch, K1. You now have 19 stitches.
- ROW 2: *Purl.
- ROW 3: *K1, K2tog; repeat from * to last stitch, K1. You now have 13 stitches.
- ROW 4: *P1, P2tog; repeat from * to last stitch, P1. You now have 9 stitches.
- Bind off, leaving a 24" (61 cm) tail.

Knitting the Legs *(make two)*

- Cast on 9 stitches with the long tail method (see page 246), leaving a 10" (25 cm) tail.
- ROWS 1 AND 3: Knit.
- ROW 2: Purl.
- ROW 4: P2, P2tog, P1, P2tog, P2.
- ROW 5: K1, K2tog, K1, K2tog, K1.
- Following the instructions on page 245, work 10 rows of 5-stitch I-cord. Bind off leaving a 10" (25 cm) tail.

Knitting the Arms *(make two)*

- Cast on 7 stitches with the long tail method, leaving a 10" (25 cm) tail.
- ROW 1: Knit.
- ROW 2: Purl.
- ROW 3: K1, K2tog, K1, K2tog, K1.
- ROW 4: P1, P2tog, P2.

- Following the instructions on page 245, work 8 rows of 4-stitch I-cord. Bind off leaving a 10" (25 cm) tail.

Knitting the Ears *(make two)*

- Cast on 6 stitches with the long tail method, leaving a 10" (25 cm) tail.
- **ROWS 1–4:** Knit.
- **ROW 5:** K2, K2tog, K2.
- **ROW 6:** K1, K2tog, K2.
- Bind off leaving a 10" (25 cm) tail. Thread the tail onto a tapestry needle and weave it along the side of the ear toward the cast-on row.

Assembling the Bear

- Turn the body inside-out. Line up the edges and stitch together from top to bottom, leaving 1" (2.5 cm) openings at top and bottom. Turn right-side-out and stuff with polyfil, being careful not to overstuff. Finish stitching the bottom and pull up the extra tail through the body and out the opening in the head.
- Partially stitch up the feet and hands along the heel and wrist edges, creating pockets. Stuff with a small amount of polyfil. Finish stitching the feet and hands.
- Using the tails left from casting on and binding off, attach the legs and arms to the body. Keep the seams in the center back of each piece to guide the positions. Attach the plastic eyes. Stitch up the head opening. Stitch the ears to the top of the head, stitching first in one direction with one tail and then in the other direction with the second tail. Weave in all ends.

Felting the Bear

- Place bear inside a pillowcase or other cloth bag and tie closed. Set the washing machine for the lowest water level, longest washing cycle, and hottest temperature. Place the pillowcase in the machine with a pair of jeans or other heavy garment. Add a tiny amount of liquid soap. Start the washer and check the felting progress frequently. If necessary, reset the machine and run again. When desired size is reached, remove the bear and rinse in cold water. Blot excess water with a towel. Shape the bear and allow it to dry.

Essentials Mini-Purse

Designed by Lorna Miser, photo on page 23

This purse is just big enough for your cell phone, lipstick, and cab fare. Oh, you could probably fit another one or two small items in there too. A cotton fabric lining gives the purse plenty of body.

MEASUREMENTS	Approximately 4" (10 cm) wide and 6" (15 cm) tall
YARN	Steinbach Wolle Inka, 50% alpaca/50% wool, 1.75 oz (50 g)/110 yds (100 m), 008 Cranberry
NEEDLES	Two US 8 (5 mm) double-point needles 8" (20 cm) long or size you need to obtain correct gauge
GAUGE	18 stitches = 4" (10 cm)
OTHER SUPPLIES	Tapestry needle, 5" × 13" (13 × 30 cm) piece of cotton fabric, one 1" (2.5 cm) button
ABBREVIATIONS	**psso** pass slipped stitch over **ssk** slip 1, slip 1, knit 2 slipped stitches together **WS** wrong side **yo** yarn over

Knitting the Purse Flap

- Following instructions on page 245, work 3-stitch I-cord for 2" (5 cm). K3tog. Place needle through 3 stitches at beginning of I-cord and K3tog. You now have 2 stitches and a loop of I-cord.
- ROW 1 (WS): P2.
- ROW 2: K1, yo, K1.
- ROW 3: P3.
- ROW 4: *Yo, K1; repeat from *. You now have 6 stitches.
- ROW 5: Yo, P5, K1.
- ROW 6: Yo, P1, K2, yo, K1, yo, K2, P1. You now have 10 stitches.
- ROW 7: Yo, K1, P7, K2.
- ROW 8: Yo, P2, K3, yo, K1, yo, K3, P2. You now have 14 stitches.
- ROW 9: Yo, K2, P9, K3.
- ROW 10: Yo, P3, K4, yo, K1, yo, K4, P3. You now have 18 stitches.
- ROW 11: Yo, K3, P11, K4.
- ROW 12: Yo, P4, ssk, K7, K2tog, P4.
- ROW 13: Yo, K4, P9, K5.

- **ROW 14:** Yo, P5, ssk, K5, K2tog, P5.
- **ROW 15:** Yo, K5, P7, K6.
- **ROW 16:** Yo, P6, ssk, K3, K2tog, P6.
- **ROW 17:** Yo, K6, P5, K7.
- **ROW 18:** Yo, P7, ssk, K1, K2tog, P7.
- **ROW 19:** Yo, K7, P3, K8.
- **ROW 20:** Yo, P8, slip 1, K2tog, psso, P8.
- **ROW 21:** Yo, K18.

Knitting the Body of the Purse

- Change to stockinette stitch (knit on right side, purl on wrong side) and work even until stockinette section measures 12" (30 cm). Bind off. Stitch side seams. Block.

Knitting the Handle

- Following the instructions on page 245, work 5-stitch I-cord for 36" (91 cm). Bind off.

Lining the Purse

- With right sides together fold lining in half and stitch side seams with .5" (1.25 cm) seam allowances. Slip lining inside bag, fold under .5" (1.25 cm) along top and neatly slip stitch lining to inside top of bag.

Finishing

- Beginning at bottom of bag, sew one end of handle to each side seam of bag. Sew button to front where loop falls.

Lavender Lace Beanie

DESIGNED BY LORNA MISER, photo on page 21

Cute and comfortable, the openwork design makes this hat perfect for spring and fall, indoors and out! The hat is knitted in the round, and you can work on circulars for the beginning or work with double-point needles throughout.

MEASUREMENTS	Approximately 18" (46 cm) circumference, unstretched
YARN	Fiber Trends Naturally Sensation, 70% merino/30% angora, 1.75 oz (50 g)/131 yds (120 m), 304 Dusty Purple
NEEDLES	One US 9 (5.5 mm) circular needle 16" (40 cm) long and set of four US 9 (5.5 mm) double-point needles or size you need to obtain correct gauge
GAUGE	14 stitches = 4" (10 cm) in lace pattern
OTHER SUPPLIES	Stitch markers, tapestry needle
ABBREVIATIONS	**psso** pass slipped stitch over

Knitting the Lace

- Cast on 60 stitches loosely and join into a round, being careful not to twist stitches. Place marker for beginning of round. Work 4 rounds of garter stitch (purl 1 round, knit 1 round). Begin Lavender Lace pattern and work even until piece measures approximately 5" (13 cm).

Shaping the Crown

- **ROUND 1:** *K8, K2tog; repeat from *.
- **ROUND 2 AND ALL EVEN-NUMBERED ROUNDS:** Knit.
- **ROUND 3:** *K7, K2tog; repeat from *.
- **ROUND 5:** *K6, K2tog; repeat from *.
- Continue as established, working one fewer stitch between decreases and knitting one round even between decrease rounds, until you have 8 stitches.

Finishing

- Cut yarn, leaving a 10" (25 cm) tail. Thread tail onto tapestry needle and pass through remaining 8 stitches twice. Pull up snug and fasten off on the inside. Weave in ends.

stitch pattern

LAVENDER LACE

WORKED ON A MULTIPLE OF 6 STITCHES.

ROUND 1: *Yo, K1, yo, P1, P3tog, P1; repeat from *.

ROUNDS 2, 4, AND 6: Knit.

ROUND 3: *K3, yo, slip 1 as to knit, K2tog, psso, yo; repeat from *.

ROUND 5: *P3tog, P1, yo, K1, yo, P1; repeat from *.

ROUND 7: Remove beginning of round marker, slip last stitch worked to left needle, replace marker. *Slip 1 as to knit, K2tog, psso, yo, K3, yo; repeat from *.

ROUND 8: Knit to marker, remove marker, K1, replace marker.

Repeat Rounds 1–8 for pattern.

Crochet Ruffle Scarf

Designed by Barry Klein, photo on page 16

It's amazing how many different things come in this one ball of yarn. This yarn is at once fuzzy, smooth, metallic, and above all, colorful. This crocheted scarf accented with a ruffle of corkscrew fringe shows off every attribute to the max.

MEASUREMENTS	Approximately 4" (10 cm) wide and 66" (168 cm) long with fringe
YARN	Trendsetter Venus, 47% acrylic/30% polyamide/21% new wool/2% polyester, 3.5 oz (100 g)/200 yds (183 m), 3434 Garden of Eden
NEEDLES	US G/6 (4 mm) crochet hook or size you need to obtain correct gauge
GAUGE	2 stitches = 4" (10 cm)
OTHER SUPPLIES	Tapestry needle
ABBREVIATIONS	**sc** single crochet Note: Work into both loops of sc.

Crocheting the Scarf

- **ROW 1:** Chain 8, turn. Make 1 sc in the 2nd chain from the hook and again into each remaining chain. At the end of the row, make a fringe as follows:
- *Chain 10, turn. Work 2 sc into each of the 10 chains.*
- **ROWS 2 AND 3:** Work 1 sc into each stitch of scarf base. At the end of each row, chain 1 and turn. Work single crochet into each stitch of base. Repeat between * and * for ruffle.
- Continue as established to desired length.

Finishing

- Weave in ends.

Little Green Wristlets

Designed by Therese Chynoweth, photo on page 24

These wristlets are knitted in a three-season silk/cotton blend. Knitted from the finger opening to the cuff, they are trimmed with yarn-over eyelet rounds and there is subtle shaping for the right and left hands.

MEASUREMENTS	Approximately 7.5" (19 cm) long
YARN	Cascade Yarns Pima Silk, 85% pima cotton/15% silk, 1.75 oz (50 g)/ 109 yds (100 m), Color 5144
NEEDLES	Set of four US 7 (4.5 mm) double-point needles or size you need to obtain correct gauge
GAUGE	17 stitches = 4" (10 cm) in stockinette stitch
OTHER SUPPLIES	Stitch marker, tapestry needle
ABBREVIATIONS	**pwise** purlwise **ssk** slip 1, slip 1, knit 2 slipped stitches together **yo** yarn over

Knitting the Left Wristlet

- Cast on 32 stitches and knit 1 row flat. Divide stitches onto 3 double-point needles and join the purl side of the first row on the right side. Place marker for beginning of round.
- **ROUND 1:** Purl.
- **ROUND 2:** *K2tog, yo; repeat from *.
- **ROUND 3:** Knit.
- **ROUND 4:** Purl.
- **ROUNDS 5 AND 6:** Knit.

Knitting the Thumb Opening

- **ROUND 1:** K2tog, yo 4 times, ssk, knit to end of round. You now have 34 stitches.
- **ROUND 2:** Knit, working (K1, P1, K1, P1) into yo.
- **ROUNDS 3–8:** Knit.

Shaping the Thumb Gusset

- **ROUND 1:** K1, K2tog, ssk, knit to end of round.
- **ROUND 2:** Knit.
- **ROUND 3:** K2tog, ssk, knit to end of round.
- **ROUND 4:** Knit.
- **ROUND 5:** Slip first stitch of round onto last needle, ssk, knit to last 2 stitches, K2tog.
- **ROUNDS 6–8:** Knit.

Knitting the Cuffs

- **ROUND 1:** Purl.
- **ROUND 2:** Knit.
- **ROUND 3:** Purl.
- **ROUND 4:** *K2tog, yo; repeat from *.
- **ROUNDS 5–8:** Repeat Rounds 2 and 3 twice.
- **ROUNDS 9–11:** Knit.
- Repeat Rounds 1–11 once, then work Rounds 1–8.
- Bind off pwise.

Knitting the Thumb

- Pick up 12 stitches around thumb opening. Join into a round.
- **ROUND 1:** Purl.
- **ROUND 2:** *K2tog, yo; repeat from *.
- **ROUND 3:** Knit.
- **ROUND 4:** Purl.
- **ROUND 5:** Knit.
- Bind off pwise.

Knitting the Right Wristlet

- Work as for Left Wristlet, working thumb opening round as follows:
- Knit to last 4 stitches, K2tog, yo 4 times, ssk.

Finishing

- Weave in ends.

Spiral Hat

Designed by Marci Blank, photo on page 22

The spiral patterning in this hat offsets the natural stripe of the yarn. You may choose another type of self-striping yarn, or try it with a plain yarn to emphasize the spiral. This hat used exactly one skein — no leftovers!

MEASUREMENTS	Approximately 20" (51 cm) circumference
YARN	Trendsetter Tonalita, 52% wool/48% acrylic, 1.75 oz (50 g)/100 yds (91 m), Color 2354
NEEDLES	One US 8 (5 mm) circular needle 16" (40 cm) long and set of four US 8 (5 mm) double-point needles or size you need to obtain correct gauge
GAUGE	16 stitches = 4" (10 cm) in stockinette stitch
OTHER SUPPLIES	Stitch marker, tapestry needle

Knitting the Brim

- Cast on 79 stitches. Join into a round, being careful not to twist stitches.
- Knit 7 rows. These rows form the self-rolling brim.

Beginning Spiral Pattern

- *Knit 6, purl 4; repeat from *. That's it! Because you have 79 stitches, this 10-stitch repeat will form a continuing spiral pattern. Continue until piece measures 5" (13 cm). End with purl 4 and place a marker to mark the beginning of subsequent rounds.

Decreasing for the Crown

- Change to double-point needles when necessary.
- ROUND 1: *K2tog, K4, P4; repeat from *.
- ROUND 2: *K5, P4; repeat from *.
- ROUND 3: Continue in pattern, ending with a P4. Move marker here.
- ROUND 4: *K5, P2tog, P2; repeat from *.
- ROUND 5: *K5, P3; repeat from *, ending with a P3. Move marker here.
- ROUND 6: *K2tog, K3, P3; repeat from *.

- ROUND 7: *K4, P3; repeat from *, ending with a P3. Move marker here.
- ROUND 8: *K2tog, K2, P3; repeat from *.
- ROUND 9: *K3, P3; repeat from *, ending with a P3. Move marker here.
- ROUND 10: *K3, P2tog, P1; repeat from *.
- ROUND 11: *K3, P2; repeat from *, ending with a P2. Move marker here.
- ROUND 12: *K2tog, K1, P2; repeat from *.
- ROUND 13: Purl.
- ROUND 14: *P2tog, P2; repeat from *.
- ROUND 15: Purl.
- ROUND 16: *P2tog, P1; repeat from *.

Finishing

- Cut yarn, leaving a 10" (25 cm) tail. Thread tail onto tapestry needle and draw through remaining stitches twice. Pull up snug and fasten off on the inside. Weave in ends.

The Edge-of-Lace Hat and Cuffs
Designed by Cheryl Oberle, photo on page 20

The lace edging on this set is feminine and flattering. The hat is given in three sizes, and the cuffs are sized as "one size fits most." You may enlarge either the hat or the cuffs in two-inch increments by adding one lace repeat.

MEASUREMENTS	Hat approximately 16 (18, 20)" (41 [46, 51] cm) circumference; cuffs approximately 6" (15 cm) circumference
YARN	Cheryl Oberle Designs Hand-Dyed Hoseki, 50% silk/50% merino wool, 3.5 oz (100 g)/219 yds (200 m), Cherry
NEEDLES	One US 8 (5 mm) circular needle 16" (40 cm) long, US 8 (5 mm) straight needles, and set of four US 8 (5 mm) double-point needles or size you need to obtain correct gauge
GAUGE	20 stitches = 4" (10 cm) in stockinette stitch
OTHER SUPPLIES	Tapestry needle, blocking pins
ABBREVIATIONS	**SK2P** slip 1, k2tog, pass slipped stitch over **yo** yarn over

Knitting the Hat

- With circular needle, cast on 80 (90, 100) stitches. Join into a round, being careful not to twist stitches. Work Rounds 1–8 of Edge-of-Lace pattern twice.
- **ROUND 17:** Purl.
- **ROUNDS 18 AND 19:** Knit.
- **ROUND 20:** Purl.
- **ROUND 21:** Knit.
- **ROUND 22:** Purl.
- Work even in stockinette stitch until piece measures 5.5 (5.75, 6)" (14 [15, 16] cm) above lace border or 8" (20 cm) from cast-on edge.
- Divide stitches onto two straight needles, centering beginning of round on one needle. With wrong sides together, join seam with 3-needle bind off (see page 251).

Finishing

- Weave in ends. Thread tapestry needle with 18" (45 cm) of yarn. Fold corners of top to center of crown and join together, then tack down to center of hat. Block, pinning out lace points.

Knitting the Cuffs

- With double-point needles, cast on 30 stitches loosely. Join into a round, being careful not to twist stitches. Work Rounds 1–8 of Edge-of-Lace pattern twice.
- Work Rounds 17–22 as for Hat.
- Work even in stockinette stitch for 1" (2.5 cm). Purl 1 row, and bind off loosely in purl.

The Edge-of-Lace Hat and Cuffs Chart

- ☐ knit
- ⊙ yarn over
- − purl
- ⋏ slip 1, knit 2 together, pass the slipped stitch over

    Row 2 and all even-numbered rows: Knit.

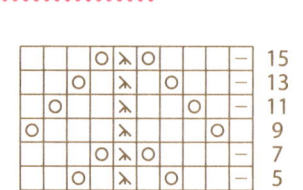

stitch pattern

EDGE-OF-LACE

ROUND 1: *K1, yo, K3, SK2P, K3, yo; repeat from *.

ROUND 2 AND ALL EVEN-NUMBERED ROUNDS THROUGH 8: Knit.

ROUND 3: *P1, K1, yo, K2, SK2P, K2, yo, K1; repeat from *.

ROUND 5: *P1, K2, yo, K1, SK2P, K1, yo, K2; repeat from *.

ROUND 7: *P1, K3, yo, SK2P, yo, K3; repeat from *.

Repeat Rounds 1–8 for pattern.

Basket Lattice Cap
Designed by Cathy Campbell, photo on page 16

This lovely red hat will keep you warm and stylish at the same time. The band is knitted flat and seamed up the back. You'll then pick up stitches around the top of the band and work circularly to the center.

stitch pattern

Basket Lattice

row 1 (WS): P3, K2, *P4, K2; repeat from * to last 2 stitches, P2.

row 2: K2, P2, *C4B, P2; repeat from * to last 3 stitches, K3.

row 3: P3, K2, *P4, K2; repeat from * to last 2 stitches, P2.

row 4: K2, P1, *C3B, C3F; repeat from * to last 4 stitches, P1, K3.

row 5: P3, K1, P2, K2, *P4, K2; repeat from * to last 5 stitches, P2, K1, P2.

row 6: K2, P1, K2, P2, *C4F, P2; repeat from * to last 6 stitches, K2, P1, K3.

row 7: P3, K1, P2, K2, *P4, K2; repeat from * to last 5 stitches, P2, K1, P2.

row 8: K2, P1, *C3F, C3B; repeat from * to last 4 stitches, P1, K3.

Repeat Rows 1–8 for pattern.

Measurements	Approximately 20" (51 cm) circumference, unstretched
Yarn	O-Wool Classic, 100% organic merino, 3.5 oz (100 g)/198 yds (181 m), 4400 Sumac
Needles	One US 8 (5 mm) circular needle 16" (40 cm) long and set of four US 8 (5 mm) double-point needles or size you need to obtain correct gauge
Gauge	18 stitches = 4" (10 cm) in stockinette stitch, 26 stitches = 4" (10 cm) in pattern
Other Supplies	Cable needle, tapestry needle
Abbreviations	**C3B** slip 1 stitch onto cable needle and hold in back, K2, P1 from cable needle **C4B** slip 2 stitches onto cable needle and hold in back, K2, K2 from cable needle **C3F** slip 2 stitches onto cable needle and hold in front, P1, K2 from cable needle **C4F** slip 2 stitches onto cable needle and hold in front, K2, K2 from cable needle **ssk** slip 1, slip 1, knit 2 slipped stitches together **WS** wrong side

Knitting the Band

- Using 2 double-point needles as if they were single-point needles, cast on 31 stitches and knit one row. Work Rows 1–8 of Basket Lattice pattern for 15 full repeats (120 rows, approximately 20" [51 cm]), ending with Row 8. Purl one row. Bind off and sew back seam.

Picking Up for the Crown

- With right side facing and using circular needle, pick up 90 stitches along left edge of band (this is the edge with 3 knit stitches). You will pick up 3 stitches for every 4 rows. Work stockinette stitch (knit every round) for 1" (2.5 cm).

Basket Lattice Cap continued

Decreasing for the Crown

- Decrease the top of the crown as follows, changing to double-point needles when necessary.
- ROUND 1: *Ssk, K14, K2tog; repeat from *.
- ROUNDS 2–4: Knit.
- ROUND 5: *Ssk, K12, K2tog; repeat from *.
- ROUNDS 6 AND 7: Knit.
- ROUND 8: *Ssk, K10, K2tog; repeat from *.
- ROUND 9: Knit.
- ROUND 10: *Ssk, K8, K2tog; repeat from *.
- ROUND 11: Knit.
- ROUND 12: *Ssk, K6, K2tog; repeat from *.
- ROUND 13: Knit.
- ROUND 14: *Ssk, K4, K2tog; repeat from *.
- ROUND 15: *Ssk, K2, K2tog; repeat from *.
- ROUND 16: *Ssk, K2tog; repeat from *.
- Cut yarn leaving a 10" (25 cm) tail. Thread tail onto tapestry needle and draw through remaining 10 stitches twice. Pull up snug and fasten off on the inside.

Finishing

- Weave in ends.

Cabled Baglet

Designed by Chrissy Gardiner, *photo on page 23*

First you have a small project on which to practice your cables, then you have a lovely little gift or tote bag. The bottom is knitted back and forth on straight needles, then you pick up stitches and knit in the round for the body of the bag.

Measurements	Approximately 14" (36 cm) around and 9" (23 cm) tall
Yarn	Lorna's Laces Shepherd Worsted, 100% superwash wool, 4 oz (114 g)/225 yds (206 m), 45 Cranberry
Needles	US 7 (4.5 mm) straight needles and set of five US 7 (4.5 mm) double-point needles or size you need to obtain gauge
Gauge	20 stitches = 4" (10 cm) in stockinette stitch
Other Supplies	Cable needle, stitch markers, tapestry needle
Abbreviations	**C4F** slip 2 stitches to cable needle and hold in front, K2, K2 from cable needle **C4B** slip 2 stitches to cable needle and hold in back, K2, K2 from cable needle **C6F** slip 3 stitches to cable needle and hold in front, K3, K3 from cable needle **C6B** slip 3 stitches to cable needle and hold in back, K3, K3 from cable needle **C3F** slip 2 stitches to cable needle and hold in front, P1, K2 from cable needle **C3B** slip 1 stitch to cable needle and hold in back, K2, P1 from cable needle **C4FP** slip 2 stitches to cable needle and hold in front, P2, K2 from cable needle **C4BP** slip 2 stitches to cable needle and hold in back, K2, P2 from cable needle **Kfb** knit into front and back of stitch (one stitch increased) **yo** yarn over

stitch pattern

XO Cable Panel (worked in the round)

Rounds 1 and 2: P1, K4, P2, K12, P2, K4, P1.
Round 3: P1, C4F, P2, C6F, C6B, P2, C4B, P1.
Rounds 4–6: Repeat Round 1.

Cabled Baglet continued

ROUND 7: P1, C4F, P2, C6B, C6F, P2, C4B, P1.
ROUNDS 8–10: Repeat Round 1.
ROUND 11: Repeat Round 7.
ROUNDS 12–14: Repeat Round 1.
ROUND 15: Repeat Round 3.
ROUND 16: Repeat Round 1.

Repeat Rounds 1–16 for pattern.

Celtic Braid

ROUND 1: P3, C4B, (P4, C4B) twice, P3.
ROUND 2 AND ALL EVEN-NUMBERED ROUNDS THROUGH 16: Knit the knits and purl the purls.
ROUND 3: P2, C3B, (C4FP, C4BP) twice, C3F, P2.
ROUND 5: P1, C3B, P3, C4F, P4, C4F, P3, C3F, P1.
ROUND 7: P1, K2, P3, C3B, C4FP, C4BP, C3F, P3, K2, P1.
ROUND 9: P1, (K2, P3) twice, C4B, (P3, K2) twice, P1.
ROUND 11: P1, K2, P3, C3F, C4BP, C4FP, C3B, P3, K2, P1.
ROUND 13: P1, C3F, P3, C4F, P4, C4F, P3, C3B, P1.
ROUND 15: P2, C3F, (C4BP, C4FP) twice, C3B, P2.

Repeat Rounds 1–16 for pattern.

Knitting the Base

- With straight needles, cast on 20 stitches. Work garter stitch (knit every row) for 5" (13 cm). With 3 double-point needles, pick up 20 stitches along each edge of the rectangle that does not have live stitches. Transfer 20 stitches from straight needle to 4th double-point needle. You now have 80 stitches, 20 on each of 4 needles. Place a marker for beginning of round.
- **ROUND 1:** Purl.
- **ROUND 2:** Knit.
- **ROUND 3:** Purl.
- **ROUND 4:** *(K2, Kfb) six times, K2; repeat from *. You now have 104 stitches, 26 on each needle.

Knitting the Body

- Work XO Cable on stitches 1–26 and 53–78 (needles 1 and 3) and work Celtic Braid on stitches 27–52 and 79–104 (needles 2 and 4). Work two full repeats of the patterns

(32 rounds total), then work Round 1 of the patterns once more. Decrease for the top of the bag as follows:

- **ROUND 1:** *(K2, K2tog) six times, K2; repeat from *. You now have 80 stitches, 20 on each needle.
- **ROUND 2:** Purl.
- **ROUND 3:** Knit.
- **ROUND 4:** Purl.

Knitting the Top of the Bag

- Work even in stockinette stitch for 1" (2.5 cm).
- **EYELET ROUND:** *K2tog, yo; repeat from *.
- Work even in stockinette stitch for 1" (2.5 cm).
- **NEXT ROUND:** Purl.
- **NEXT ROUND:** Knit.
- **NEXT ROUND:** Purl.
- Bind off in knit.

Making the Drawstrings

- Cut two pieces of yarn about 4 yards (3.5 m) long. Working one at a time, fold in half, tie one end over a doorknob and slide a double-point needle through the opposing loop. Turn the needle clockwise until the yarn is lightly twisted. Keeping the yarn taut, fold it in half so it twists onto itself. Remove from doorknob and needle and tie a knot about 1" (2.5 cm) from each end.

Finishing

- Weave in ends and block. Fold one cord in half and thread it through the eyelets, beginning at the center of an XO Cable Panel. Pull through so that the ends meet and knot approximately 2" (5 cm) from the end. Remove the knots near the end and cut even for a 1"–1.5" (2.5–4 cm) fringe. Repeat with second cord, beginning at the center of the other XO Cable Panel and threading in the opposite direction.

Not-Your-Average Washcloths

Designed by Elizabeth Prusiewicz, *photo on page 17*

All it takes is some brilliant color to turn the ordinary into the extraordinary. These simple cotton washcloths can be used in the kitchen or in the bath. The first stitch of every row is slipped for a nice neat edge. One skein will produce two cloths.

MEASUREMENTS	Approximately 7" (18 cm) square
YARN	Rowan Cotton Handknit, 100% cotton, 1.75 oz (50 g)/93 yds (85 m), 219 Green/254 Orange
NEEDLES	US 7 (4.5 mm) straight needles or size you need to obtain correct gauge
GAUGE	20 stitches = 4" (10 cm) in stockinette stitch
OTHER SUPPLIES	Crochet hook, tapestry needle

Knitting the Washcloth

- Cast on 36 stitches.
- **ROW 1:** Slip 1, K35.
- **ROW 2:** Slip 1, P35.
- **ROW 3:** Slip 1, P32, K3.
- **ROW 4:** Slip 1, P2, K15, P15, K3.
- Repeat Row 4 eighteen times.
- **NEXT ROW:** Slip 1, K2, P15, K15, P3.
- Repeat this row 18 times.
- Knit 1 row.
- Purl 1 row.

Finishing

- Bind off loosely. Cut yarn, leaving a 10" (25 cm) tail. Use a crochet hook to make a 2" (5 cm) chain with tail. Form a loop and attach end of chain to washcloth. Weave in ends.

La Cancion Amulet Purse and Flower Brooch

Designed by Jenny Dowde, *photo on page 19*

These two pieces are crocheted with one skein. The flower may be pinned to a knitted chain and worn as a necklace or pinned to your clothing and worn as a brooch.

MEASUREMENTS	Amulet purse approximately 3.5" (9 cm) wide and 4" (10 cm) tall; flower approximately 5" (13 cm) by 5" (13 cm)
YARN	La Lana Wools Forever Random Fines, 60% wool/40% mohair, 2 oz (60 g)/118 yds (108 m), La Cancion
NEEDLES	US G/6 (4.5 mm) crochet hook
OTHER SUPPLIES	Beads for purse: 25 olive size 11°, 28 small red bicone, 20 silver-lined clear size 8°, 14 silver-lined clear size 11°, 1 green oval 13mm, 2 green ovals 6mm; beads for flower: mix of bugles, size 11° and 8° seed beads, and 4 or 5 oval accent beads; beading thread, beading needle, 1" (2.5 cm) pin back

Flower Brooch

Crocheting the Petals

- Chain 6, join with slip stitch to form a circle.
- **ROUND 1:** Ch 3, 2 dc into circle, [ch 7, 3 dc into circle] 4 times, ch 7, slip stitch to top of ch 3.
- **ROUND 2:** Ch 3, [skip 1 dc, dc into next dc, 15 tr into ch 7 loop, dc into next dc] 4 times, skip 1 dc, dc in next dc, 15 tr into ch 7 loop, slip stitch to top of ch 3. Fasten off.

Crocheting the Flower Center

- Chain 4, join with slip stitch to form a circle.
- **ROUND 1:** Work 8 sc into circle, join with slip stitch to first sc.
- **ROUND 2:** Ch 3, 4 dc into first sc, 5 dc into each sc around circle, slip stitch to top of ch 3. Fasten off and stitch to center of larger piece.

Beading the Tassel

- Attach beading thread to center of flower and randomly string mixture of beads ending with a size 11° bead. Pass back through all beads except this last size 11° bead. Repeat 3 or 4 times as desired, making each strand a different length. Fasten off securely.

La Cancion Amulet Purse and Flower Brooch continued

Crocheting the Strap (optional)

- Chain 4.
- **ROW 1:** Skip ch closest to hook, 1 sc into front loop of next ch, 1 sc into back loop of next ch, sc into front loop of next ch, ch 1, turn.
- **ROW 2:** Sc into front loop of first sc, sc into back loop of next sc, sc into front loop of next sc, ch 1, turn.
- Repeat Row 2 until piece measures 45" (114 cm) or desired length. Sew edges of strap together for about 1" (2.5 cm) approximately 6" (15 cm) from ends.

Finishing

- Weave in ends. Sew pin back to flower at center back.

Amulet Purse

Crocheting the Purse (make two pieces)

- **BASE ROW:** Ch 3, skip first ch, sc in next 2 ch, ch 1, turn.
- **ROW 1:** 2 sc in each sc, ch 1, turn, [4sc].
- **ROW 2:** 2 sc in first sc, sc in each of next 2 sc, 2 sc in last sc, ch 1, turn [6 sc].
- **ROW 3:** Sc in each sc to end, ch 1, turn.
- **ROW 4:** 2 sc in first sc, sc in each of next 2 sc to last sc, 2 sc in last sc, ch 1, turn [8 sc].
- Repeat Rows 3 and 4 until you have 12 sc.
- Work 3 rows without increasing.
- **ROW 12:** Dec 1 at each end of row [10 sc].
- **ROW 13:** Sc in each sc to end, 1 ch, turn.
- **ROW 14:** Dec 1 at each end of row [8 sc].
- Work 2 rows without decreasing.

Joining Front to Back

- Begin with wrong-sides facing and start at top left corner. Join yarn to corner, ch 3, sc through both pieces at .5" (1.25 cm) intervals along first side, bottom, and second side making 7 stitches on the sides and 2 on the bottom. Do not fasten off yarn.

Crocheting the Neck Strap

- *Ch 2, sc in both loops of second ch from hook; repeat from * until strap measures 24" (60 cm) or desired length. Attach to other side of pouch with a sc. Fasten off.

Beading the Fringe

- Thread needle with beading thread and attach to top at outside edge, close to neck strap.

- **FRINGE 1:** 3 olive, 2 red, 1 silver lined 8°, 2 red, 1 silver lined 8°, 1 olive, 1 silver lined 11°, 1 olive, 1 silver lined 11°. Skip last 3 beads added and pass back through remaining beads to top.
- **FRINGE 2:** 3 olive, 2 red, 2 silver lined 8°, 2 red, 1 silver lined 8°, 2 olive, 1 silver lined 11°, 1 olive, 1 silver lined 11°. Skip last 3 beads added and pass back through remaining beads to top.
- **FRINGE 3:** 3 olive, 2 red, 1 silver lined 8°, 1 small oval, 1 silver lined 8°, 2 red, 1 silver lined 8°, 2 olive, 1 silver lined 11°, 1 olive, 1 silver lined 11°. Skip last 3 beads added and pass back through remaining beads to top.
- **FRINGE 4 (CENTER):** 3 olive, 2 red, 1 silver lined 8°, 1 large oval, 1 silver lined 8°, 2 red, 1 silver lined 8°, 2 olive, 1 silver lined 11°, 1 olive, 1 silver lined 11°. Skip last 3 beads added and pass back through remaining beads to top.
- **FRINGE 5:** Repeat Fringe 3.
- **FRINGE 6:** Repeat Fringe 2.
- **FRINGE 7:** Repeat Fringe 1.

Elizabeth's Perfect Hat

DESIGNED BY ELIZABETH PRUSIEWICZ, photo on page 20

This simple hat is knitted in one wide strip, which is then sewn together for the body of the hat. The seam is at the back, and you'll pick up stitches along the top edge of the body to knit the crown. Top it all off with knotted I-cord. Perfect!

MEASUREMENTS	Approximately 20" (51 cm) circumference
YARN	Noro Silk Garden, 45% silk/45% kid mohair/10% lambs wool, 1.75 oz (50 g)/109 yds (100 m), Color 87
NEEDLES	US 8 (5 mm) straight needles and set of five US 8 (5 mm) double-point needles or size you need to obtain correct gauge
GAUGE	19 stitches = 4" (10 cm) in stockinette stitch
OTHER SUPPLIES	Crochet hook, tapestry needle

Elizabeth's Perfect Hat continued

Knitting the Body

- NOTE: For smooth edges, slip the first stitch on all rows.
- With straight needles, cast on 35 stitches using a provisional method (see page 248).
- ROW 1: K1, (K1, P1) 4 times, K26.
- ROW 2: Slip 1, P25, (K1, P1) 4 times, P1.
- ROW 3: Slip 1, (K1, P1) 4 times, K26.
- Repeat Rows 2 and 3 until piece measures 20" (50 cm) or desired length. Join to cast-on edge with 3-needle bind off (see page 251).

Knitting the Crown

- Pick up 56 stitches along top edge of hat and place 14 stitches onto each of 4 double-point needles. Knit one round.
- ROUND 1: *K2tog, K5; repeat from *.
- ROUND 2 AND ALL EVEN-NUMBERED ROUNDS: Knit.
- ROUND 3: *K2tog, K4; repeat from *.
- ROUND 5: *K2tog, K3; repeat from *.
- Continue in this manner, knitting one fewer stitch between decreases and working one round even between decrease rounds until you have 16 stitches remaining.
- NEXT ROUND: *K2tog; repeat from *. You now have 8 stitches.
- Cut yarn leaving a 10" (25 cm) tail. Thread tail onto tapestry needle, draw through remaining 8 stitches twice. Pull up snug and fasten off on the inside.

Finishing

- Knit 3 pieces of 3-stitch I-cord (see page 245) approximately 4" (10 cm) long. Make a knot at one end of each I-cord and attach the unknotted ends to the center of the crown. Weave in ends.

Poems Easy Headband

Designed by Shirley Young, photo on page 25

This headband is so easy you'll want to knit one in every color. And using one skein of Poems or another multicolored yarn, you can get more than one look from the same skein. The I-cord at the back makes this headband very comfortable to wear.

MEASUREMENTS	Approximately 15 (17, 19.5)" (38 [43, 50] cm) circumference, unstretched
YARN	Wisdom Yarns Poems, 100% wool, 1.75 oz (50 g)/109 yds (100 m), Color 564
NEEDLES	US 11 (8 mm) straight needles and two US 11 (8 mm) double-point needles or size you need to obtain correct gauge
GAUGE	14 stitches = 4" (10 cm) in garter stitch
OTHER SUPPLIES	Tapestry needle
ABBREVIATIONS	**Kfb** knit into the front, then the back of 1 stitch **RS** right side **WS** wrong side

Knitting the Headband

- Cast on 5 stitches onto a double-point needle. Following the instructions on page 245, work a 5-stitch I-cord for 2 (2.5, 3)" (5 [6, 8] cm). Change to straight needles.
- **INCREASE ROW (RS):** *Kfb; repeat from *. You now have 10 stitches.
- Work even in stockinette stitch for 1.5" (4 cm).
- Change to garter stitch and work even for 8 (9, 10.5)" (20 [23, 27] cm).
- Work even in stockinette stitch for 1.5" (4 cm).
- **DECREASE ROW (WS):** *P2tog; repeat from *. You now have 5 stitches.
- Change to double-point needles and work I-cord (see page 245) for 2 (2.5, 3)" (5 [6, 8] cm).

Finishing

- Cut yarn leaving a 10" (25 cm) tail. Thread tail onto tapestry needle and use it to graft the two ends of the I-cord together. Weave in ends.

Blossom Belt

Designed by Jenny Dowde, photo on page 18

This project involves both knitting and crochet — knit the belt and crochet the flowers. Then use another popular technique and add beads to the flower centers. The best of three worlds.

MEASUREMENTS	Approximately 31" (78 cm) long
YARN	La Lana Wools Phat Silk Phat, 50% silk/50% fine wool, 2 oz (57 g)/98 yds (90 m), Grape
NEEDLES	US 10 (6.5 mm) straight needles or size you need to obtain correct gauge
GAUGE	22 stitches = 4" (10 cm) in pattern
OTHER SUPPLIES	US F/5 (4 mm) crochet hook, 24 round 6mm beads, sewing needle and thread, tapestry needle
ABBREVIATIONS	**ch** chain **sc** single crochet

Knitting the Belt

- Cast on 12 stitches and purl 1 row.
- Work Cross pattern stitch until piece measures 31" (79 cm). Bind off but do not cut yarn.

Making the Closure

- With crochet hook, work 9 sc along short end, turn. *Ch 2, skip 1 sc, sc in next sc; repeat from * 3 more times. Cut yarn. Join yarn to other end of belt and repeat.
- Leaving an 8" (20 cm) tail at both ends, make a crochet chain 40" (102 cm) long. Weave chain criss-cross fashion through loops at end of belt.
- Insert hook into last chain, *count back 12 chains, insert hook, pull yarn through both loops. Repeat from * twice more. Fasten off. Repeat for other side.

Crocheting the Flowers (make 2)

- Ch 4, join with a slip stitch to form a ring.
- **ROUND 1:** Sc 8 in circle, join with slip stitch to 1st sc.
- **ROUND 2:** *Ch 3, sc 1 in next sc; repeat from * 7 times, join with slip stitch to ch 3 loop.

stitch pattern

Cross

ROW 1: *Knit the 2nd stitch without removing it from the needle by reaching behind and inserting needle between 1st and 2nd stitch, knit the first stitch and take both stitches off left needle; repeat from *.

ROW 2: P1, *purl the 2nd stitch without removing it from the needle, purl the 1st stitch and take both stitches off left needle; repeat from * to last stitch, P1.

Repeat Rows 1 and 2 for pattern.

- **ROUND 3:** *Ch 4, slip stitch in same ch 3 loop, slip stitch in next ch 3 loop; repeat from * 6 times, ch 4, slip stitch in same ch 3 loop. Fasten off.

Finishing

- Weave in ends. Sew 12 beads to the center of each flower. Sew flowers to either side of closure.

Eyelet Shruglet

DESIGNED BY MARY C. GILDERSLEEVE, *photo on page 25*

These little shrugs are all the rage, and at one skein each, they could become the next big fashion accessory. Imagine having one in every color to go with your little black dress. This shrug will fit a small adult — it's meant to be close-fitting.

MEASUREMENTS	Approximately 35" (89 cm) chest
YARN	Coats and Clark Red Heart Soft, 100% acrylic, 5 oz (140 g)/256 yds (234 m), 9522 Leaf
NEEDLES	US 7 (4.5 mm) circular needle 24" (60 cm) long and set of four US 7 (4.5 mm) double-point needles or size you need to obtain correct gauge
GAUGE	17 stitches = 4" (10 cm) in stockinette stitch
OTHER SUPPLIES	Stitch markers, stitch holder, tapestry needle, one ¾" (19 mm) button
ABBREVIATIONS	**pm** place marker **RS** right side **sm** slip marker **ssk** slip 1, slip 1, knit 2 slipped stitches together **WS** wrong side **yo** yarn over

stitch pattern

SIMPLE EYELET LACE

NOTE: Add an extra K1 between the lace pattern and the 3-st garter borders on all RS rows.

ROW 1: *K2tog, yo, K2; repeat from * over all sets of 4 sts, then knit any remaining sts to the marker.

ROWS 2, 4, 6, AND 8: Purl.

ROWS 3 AND 7: Knit.

ROW 5: *K2, yo, ssk; repeat from * over all sets of 4 sts, then knit any remaining sts to the marker.

Maintain pattern as established in the first 8-row repeat and work increased stitches into pattern when you have enough of them.

Knitting the Collar

- The shrug is worked from the neck down, back and forth on a circular needle. Cast on 69 stitches.
- **ROW 1:** K3, *K1, P1; repeat from * to last 4 stitches, K4.
- **ROW 2:** K3, *P1, K1; repeat from * to last 4 stitches, P1, K3.

Eyelet Shruglet continued

- Repeat Rows 1 and 2 through Row 12, keeping 3 stitches on each end in garter stitch and working 1/1 rib between and at the same time on Row 7 make a buttonhole by working to last 4 stitches, yo, ssk, K2; on Row 12, increase 1 stitch. You now have 70 stitches.

Setting Up for the Body

- **SET-UP ROW 1:** K3, (K10, pm, K1,) twice, K20, (pm, K11,) twice, K3.
- **SET-UP ROWS 2 AND 4:** K3, purl to last 3 stitches, K3.
- **SET-UP ROW 3:** Knit to marker, * yo, slip marker, K1, yo, knit to next marker; repeat from *, to last marker, yo, slip marker, K1, yo, knit to end of row.

Begin Eyelet Pattern

- **ROW 1:** K3, *work Simple Eyelet Lace to marker, yo, sm, K1, yo; repeat from * to last 13 stitches, work Simple Eyelet Lace to last 3 stitches, K3.
- **ROW 2:** K3, purl to last 3 stitches, K3.
- Continue in this manner, increasing before the markers and after the K1, and working Simple Eyelet Lace between increases, until piece measures about 6" (15 cm) and you have 52 sleeve stitches between markers 1 and 2 and 52 sleeve stitches between markers 3 and 4.

Dividing for Fronts and Back

- **NEXT ROW (RS):** Continuing in pattern as established but without further increasing, work 33 stitches, place 52 sleeve stitches on holder, work 60 stitches for back, place 52 sleeve stitches on holder, work 33 stitches. Work one WS row in pattern.

Beginning the Mock Cable Eyelet

- Continuing on these 126 stitches (33+60+33) for fronts and back, keep first and last 3 stitches in garter stitch and work Mock Cable Eyelet (worked flat) for 3 full repeats (12 rows total), binding off on the last WS row. Cut yarn.

Knitting the Sleeves (make two)

- Place 52 sleeve stitches onto double-point needles and join into a round. Decreasing 2 stitches on first round, work Mock Cable Eyelet (in the round) on 50 stitches for 3 full repeats (12 rows total), binding off on the last WS row.

Finishing

- Weave in ends. Sew button opposite buttonhole.

---

stitch pattern

Mock Cable Eyelet (worked flat)

ROW 1: P1, *yo, ssk, K1, P2; repeat from *.

ROWS 2 AND 4: *K2, P3; repeat from * to last stitch, K1.

ROW 3: P1, *K1, yo, ssk, P2; repeat from *.

Repeat Rows 1–4 for pattern.

Mock Cable Eyelet (worked in the round)

ROUND 1: *Yo, ssk, K1, P2; repeat from *.

ROUNDS 2 AND 4: *K3, P2; repeat from *.

ROUND 3: *K1, yo, ssk, P2; repeat from *.

Repeat Rounds 1–4 for pattern.

Fishbowl Baby Hat

Designed by Elizabeth Lenhard, *photo on page 19*

Elizabeth's favorite baby hats are those that plunk something unexpected onto the head, like a bug-eyed frog or a giant strawberry. With that in mind, she made her daughter a hat that looks like a fishbowl, complete with gravel and three funky fish.

stitch pattern

SEED

ROUND 1: *K1, P1; repeat from *.

ROUND 2: Purl the knits and knit the purls.

Repeat Round 2 for pattern.

MEASUREMENTS	To fit infant 6–18 months, 16" (41 cm) circumference
YARN	Cascade Yarns Sierra, 80% pima cotton/20% wool, 3.5 oz (100 g)/192 yds (176 m), 26 Turquoise
NEEDLES	One US 6 (4 mm) circular needle 16" (40 cm) long and set of four US 6 (4 mm) double-point needles or size you need to obtain correct gauge
GAUGE	19 stitches = 4" (10 cm) in stockinette stitch
OTHER SUPPLIES	Stitch markers, tapestry needle
ABBREVIATIONS	**m** marker **M1** make one increase **pm** place marker **ssk** slip 1, slip 1, knit 2 slipped stitches together **ssp** slip 1, slip 1, purl 2 slipped stitches together

Getting Started

- With circular needle, cast on 72 stitches. Join into a round, being careful not to twist stitches. Place marker for beginning of round. Work seed stitch for 6 rounds.
- Change to stockinette stitch (knit every round) and work for 1.5" (4 cm).

Knitting the Fish Motifs

- **SET UP ROUND:** *K9, pm, K15, pm; repeat from * to end of round.
- Slip markers on following rounds.
- **ROUND 1:** *K to m, K3, P4, K8; repeat from * 2 more times.
- **ROUND 2:** *K to m, K2, P6, K5, P2; repeat from * 2 more times.
- **ROUND 3:** *K to m, K1, P8, K3, P3; repeat from * 2 more times.
- **ROUND 4:** *K to m, P10, K1, P3, K1; repeat from * 2 more times.
- **ROUND 5:** *K to m, P13, K2; repeat from * 2 more times.
- **ROUND 6:** Repeat Round 5.

WORSTED WEIGHT

Fishbowl Baby Hat continued

- **ROUND 7:** Repeat Round 4.
- **ROUND 8:** Repeat Round 3.
- **ROUND 9:** Repeat Round 2.
- **ROUND 10:** Repeat Round 1.
- Remove all markers but the beginning of round marker. Work stockinette stitch for 1.5" (4 cm).

Decreasing for the Crown

- Change to double-point needles, placing 24 stitches on each needle.
- **ROUND 1:** *K6, K2tog; repeat from *.
- **ROUND 2:** *K5, K2tog; repeat from *.
- **ROUND 3:** *K4, K2tog; repeat from *.
- Work stockinette stitch for 1" (2.5 cm). Bind off loosely. Roll down last rows of stockinette stitch creating the "rim" of the fishbowl.

Knitting the Top of the Crown

- With straight needles, cast on 8 stitches.
- **ROWS 1, 3, AND 5:** K1, M1, K to last 2 stitches, M1, K1.
- **ROWS 2 AND 4:** P1, M1, P to last stitch, M1, K1. After Row 5, you have 18 stitches.
- **ROWS 6 AND 8:** Purl.
- **ROWS 7 AND 9:** Knit.
- **ROWS 10, 12, AND 14:** Ssp, P to last 2 stitches, P2tog.
- **ROWS 11 AND 13:** Ssk, K to last 2 stitches, K2tog.
- You now have 8 stitches. Bind off. Cut yarn leaving a tail long enough to sew top of crown to hat.

Finishing

- Thread tail from top of crown onto tapestry needle. Place the top of the crown inside the rolled "rim," about .5" (1.25 cm) down. Sew the top of the crown to the hat. Weave in loose ends. To block, place hat over round object such as a balloon or ball, spritz with water, and allow to dry.

WORSTED WEIGHT   183

Fishbowl Baby Hat Chart

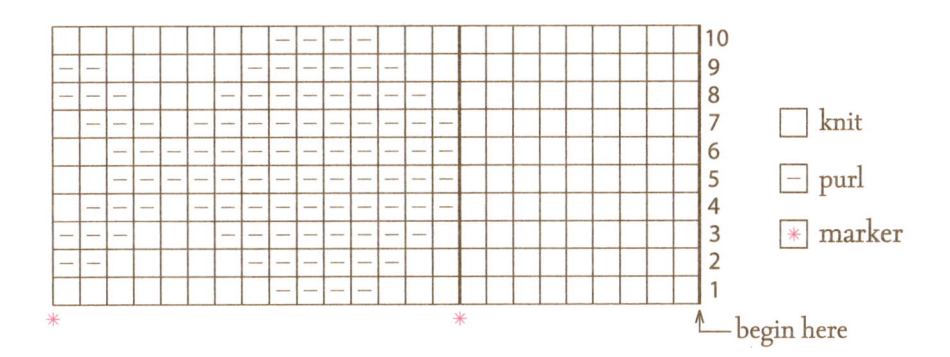

□ knit
— purl
✳ marker

begin here

Heavy Worsted Weight

Cross-Stitch Scarf

Designed by Margaret Halas, *photo on page 27*

This cross-stitch pattern produces a lovely dense fabric that looks like it could have been woven rather than knitted. It makes a great showcase for Manos del Uruguay multicolored yarn.

MEASUREMENTS	Approximately 5" (13 cm) wide and 52" (132 cm) long
YARN	Manos del Uruguay, 100% wool, 3.5 oz (100 g)/138 yds (126 m), color 109
NEEDLES	US 11 (8 mm) straight needles or size you need to obtain correct gauge
GAUGE	14 stitches = 4" (10 cm) in pattern
OTHER SUPPLIES	Stitch markers, tapestry needle
ABBREVIATIONS	**pm** place marker **sm** slip marker

Knitting the Scarf

- Cast on 21 stitches.
- **ROW 1:** K2, pm, work Cross-Stitch pattern on next 17 stitches, pm, K2.
- **ROW 2:** K2, sm, work Cross-Stitch pattern on next 17 stitches, sm, K2.
- Continue as established, working the first and last 2 stitches in garter stitch and working 2-row Cross-Stitch pattern between the markers until scarf measures 52" (132 cm) or desired length. Bind off in purl.

Finishing

- Weave in ends. Block lightly.

stitch pattern

CROSS-STITCH

ROW 1: *Knit the 2nd stitch without removing it from the needle by reaching behind and inserting needle between 1st and 2nd stitch, knit the 1st stitch and take both stitches off left needle; repeat from *, end K1.

ROW 2: *Purl the 2nd stitch without removing it from the needle, purl the 1st stitch and take both stitches off left needle; repeat from *, end P1.

Repeat Rows 1 and 2 for pattern.

April-in-Paris Beret

Designed by Carol Martin, photo on page 28

This beret is worked in reverse stockinette (worn with the purl side as the right side) to best show off the texture in the yarn. But if you prefer the smoother look of stockinette, you can simply turn the finished beret inside out, and wear it with the knit side as the right side.

MEASUREMENTS	Approximately 20" (51 cm) circumference, unstretched
YARN	Farmhouse Yarns Lumpy Bumpy by Charlene, 100% wool, 4 oz (113 g)/150 yds (137 m), Fall Flowers
NEEDLES	One US 10 (6 mm) and one US 9 (5.5 mm) circular needle 16" (40 cm) long and set of four US 10 (6 mm) double-point needles or size you need to obtain correct gauge
GAUGE	14 stitches = 4" (10 cm) on larger needle in stockinette stitch
OTHER SUPPLIES	Tapestry needle

Knitting the Rib

- With smaller circular needle, and using the long tail method (see page 246), cast on 60 stitches very loosely. Place marker and join into a round, being careful not to twist stitches. Work K2/P2 ribbing for 5 rounds.

Increasing the Crown

- **CHANGE TO LARGER SIZE CIRCULAR NEEDLE AND BEGIN PATTERN AS FOLLOWS:**
- **ROUND 1:** *K1, P1 into next stitch (this increases 1 stitch), P5; repeat from *. You now have 70 stitches.
- **ROUND 2 AND EVERY EVEN-NUMBERED ROUND:** Knit the knits and purl the purls.
- **ROUND 3:** *K1, P1 into next stitch, P6; repeat from *. You now have 80 stitches.
- Continue in this manner, purling one more stitch between increases and working one round even knitting the knits and purling the purls between increase rounds until you have 150 stitches.

Decreasing the Crown

- **ROUND 1:** *K1, P6, P2tog, P6; repeat from *. You now have 140 stitches.
- **ROUND 2 AND ALL EVEN-NUMBERED ROUNDS:** Knit the knits and purl the purls.

HEAVY WORSTED WEIGHT

April-in-Paris Beret continued

- ROUND 3: *K1, P6, P2tog, P5; repeat from *. You now have 130 stitches.
- ROUND 5: *K1, P5, P2tog, P5; repeat from *. You now have 120 stitches.
- ROUND 7: *K1, P5, P2tog, P4, repeat from *. You now have 110 stitches.
- Continue in this manner, working one fewer stitch first after and then before the decreases and working one round even between decrease rounds until you have 40 stitches.
- Change to double-point needles when necessary.
- NEXT ROUND: *K1, P1, P2tog; repeat from *. You now have 30 stitches.
- Purl 1 round.
- NEXT ROUND: *K1, P2tog; repeat from *. You now have 20 stitches.
- Purl 1 round.
- LAST ROUND: *P2tog; repeat from *. You now have 10 stitches.

Finishing

- Cut yarn leaving a 10" (25 cm) tail. Thread tail onto tapestry needle and draw through remaining stitches twice. Fasten off on inside. Weave in ends.

Cozy Socks for Kids

DESIGNED BY SUE DIAL, photo on page 28

These quick, cozy socks will fit most kids. Adjust the leg and foot length as needed for "big" kids.

MEASUREMENTS	Approximately 6" (15 cm) foot length
YARN	Harvest Moon Handspun Bulky Singles, 100% hand dyed superwash merino, 1.75 oz (50 g)/110 yds (100 m), Amethyst
NEEDLES	Set of four US 8 (5 mm) double-point needles or size you need to obtain correct gauge
GAUGE	20 stitches = 4" (10 cm) in stockinette stitch
OTHER SUPPLIES	Stitch holder, tapestry needle
ABBREVIATIONS	**ssk** slip 1, slip 1, knit 2 slipped stitches together

Knitting the Cuff

- Using the backward loop method (see page 244), cast on 30 stitches and place 10 stitches on each of three double-point needles.

- **ROUNDS 1–4:** Purl.
- **ROUNDS 5 AND 6:** Knit.
- Repeat Rounds 1–6 three more times.

Knitting the Heel Flap

- Knit 7 and slip next 16 stitches onto holder for instep. Turn, slip the first stitch, and purl 13. You will work the heel flap back and forth over these 14 stitches as follows:
- **ROW 1:** *Slip 1, K1; repeat from *.
- **ROW 2:** Slip 1, P13.
- Repeat Rows 1 and 2 until flap measures 2" (5 cm).

Turning the Heel

- **ROW 1:** *Slip 1, K1; repeat from *.
- **ROW 2:** Slip 1, P8, P2tog, P1.
- **ROW 3:** Slip 1, K5, K2tog, K1.
- **ROW 4:** Slip 1, P6, P2tog, P1.
- **ROW 5:** Slip 1, K7, K2tog, K1.

Knitting the Gussets

- Continuing in the same direction, pick up the slipped stitches along the side of the heel flap. With another needle, knit across 16 held instep stitches. With third needle, pick up same number of stitches along second heel flap and knit 5 heel stitches onto this needle. Knit one round, arranging stitches so you have the same number on needles 1 and 3 and 16 stitches on needle 2.
- **ROUND 1:** Knit to last 3 stitches on needle 1, K2tog, K1; K16 on needle 2; K1, ssk at the beginning of needle 3, knit to end of round.
- **ROUND 2:** Knit.
- Repeat Rounds 1 and 2 until you have 28 stitches total — 16 stitches on needle 2 and 6 stitches each on needles 1 and 3. Move the first and last stitches from needle 2 to needles 1 and 3. You now have 14 stitches on needle 2 and 7 stitches each on needles 1 and 3.

Knitting the Foot

- Continue even in stockinette stitch until sock is 2" (5 cm) less than desired finished length.

Cozy Socks for Kids continued

Shaping the Toe

- **ROUND 1:** Knit to last 3 stitches on needle 1, K2tog, K1; K1, ssk at beginning of needle 2, work to last 3 stitches on needle 2, K2tog, K1; K1, ssk at beginning of needle 3, knit to end of round.
- **ROUND 2:** Knit.
- Repeat Rounds 1 and 2 until there are 6 stitches on needle 2 and 3 stitches each on needles 1 and 3. Knit stitches from needle 1 onto needle 3.

Finishing

- Join toe with Kitchener stitch (see page 245). Weave in ends.

Zigzag Scarf

DESIGNED BY SUSAN GUAGLIUMI, photo on page 28

This delightful scarf is ever changing: ever changing color, and ever changing direction! Finished off with corkscrew fringes, it will make a great addition to your accessories stash.

MEASUREMENTS	Approximately 4" (10 cm) wide and 48" (122 cm) long
YARN	Manos del Uruguay, 100% wool, 3.5 oz (100 g)/135 yds (123 m), 109 Woodland
NEEDLES	US 11 (8 mm) straight needles or size you need to obtain correct gauge
GAUGE	16 stitches = 4" (10 cm) in pattern
OTHER SUPPLIES	US G/6 (4.5 mm) crochet hook, tapestry needle
ABBREVIATIONS	**pwise** purlwise

Knitting the Scarf

- Cast on 12 stitches.

Section A

- **ROW 1:** Knit.
- **ROW 2 AND ALL WRONG-SIDE ROWS:** Purl.
- **ROW 3:** K10, wrap and turn (see Wrap and Turn).

Wrap and Turn

Worked on right-side (knit) rows.

Bring yarn to front, slip next stitch to right needle as to purl, bring yarn to back, place slipped stitch back onto left needle. Turn work.

Worked on wrong-side (purl) rows.

Bring yarn to back, slip next stitch to right needle as to purl, bring yarn to front, place slipped stitch back onto left needle. Turn work.

Knitting the Wrapped Stitches

When knitting stitches that have been wrapped, knit the wrap together with the stitch as follows:

Insert right needle into wrap, then the stitch on the needle, and knit them together.

When purling stitches that have been wrapped, insert the needle into the wrap, then through the stitch and purl them together.

- ROW 5: K8, wrap and turn.
- Continue in this manner, knitting 2 fewer stitches before the wrap and turn on right-side rows and purling wrong-side rows until you have worked all but 2 stitches.

Section B

- ROW 1: K2, knit the wrapped stitch (see Knitting the Wrapped Stitches), turn.
- ROW 2 AND ALL WRONG-SIDE ROWS: Slip 1 pwise, purl to end of row.
- ROW 3: K4, knit the wrapped stitch, turn.
- ROW 5: K6, knit the wrapped stitch, turn.
- Continue in this manner, knitting 2 more stitches on right-side rows and purling wrong-side rows until you have worked all 12 stitches.

Section C

- ROW 1: Purl.
- ROW 2 AND ALL RIGHT-SIDE ROWS: Knit.
- ROW 3: P10, wrap and turn.
- ROW 5: P8, wrap and turn.
- Continue in this manner, purling 2 fewer stitches before the wrap and turn on wrong-side rows and knitting right-side rows until you have worked all but 2 stitches.

Section D

- ROW 1: P2, purl the wrapped stitch, turn.
- ROW 2 AND ALL RIGHT-SIDE ROWS: Slip 1 pwise, knit to end of row.
- ROW 3: P4, purl the wrapped stitch, turn.
- Continue in this manner, purling 2 more stitches on wrong-side rows and knitting right-side rows until you have worked all 12 stitches.
- Repeat Sections A–D until piece measures 48" (122 cm).
- Bind off loosely.

Crocheting the Trim

- With right side facing and starting at lower right corner, insert crochet hook through first edge stitch. *Chain 12, turn work 1 row of single crochet across these 12 stitches, work 1 single crochet in next edge stitch; repeat from * across bottom edge of scarf. Make fringe on the other end.

Finishing

- Weave in all ends. Wash scarf and lay flat to dry, pulling zigzags into shape and curling the fringes.

Loop's Centipede

Designed by Patricia Colloton-Walsh, photo on page 29

Yes, it really does have 100 legs! This amusing little creature will add a unique touch to any child's toy collection. To make a "giant" (36"–38" [95 cm] long) centipede, use Cascade Magnum yarn (123 yds/111 m) and a US 15 (10 mm) circular needle; follow the same directions for Knitting the Body and Finishing.

MEASUREMENTS	Approximately 12" (30 cm) long, stuffed
YARN	Tahki Trio, 55% nylon/20% cotton/25% rayon, 1.75 oz (50 g)/92 yds (84 m), color 005
NEEDLES	US 8 (5 mm) straight needles or size you need to obtain correct gauge
GAUGE	14 stitches = 4" (10 cm) in stockinette stitch
OTHER SUPPLIES	Tapestry needle, polyfil, scrap of black yarn for eyes

Knitting the Body

- Cast on 56 stitches.
- **ROWS 1, 3, AND 5:** Knit.
- **ROWS 2, 4, AND 6:** Purl.
- **ROW 7:** K4, make 50 loops, K2.
- **ROWS 8–15:** Knit.
- **ROW 16:** Repeat Row 7.
- **ROWS 17, 19, AND 21:** Knit.
- **ROWS 18, 20, AND 22:** Purl.
- Bind off.

Finishing

- With right side facing, fold the centipede in half lengthwise and sew the seam starting at the "head" and stuffing with polyfil as you go. Weave in ends. With scrap of black yarn, embroider eyes.

MAKING THE LOOPS

1. Knit the first stitch but do not drop it from the left needle. Pull right needle away from the left. You now have a space between the needles with half the stitch on each needle.

2. Bring the yarn to the front between the needles.

3. Wrap yarn around your thumb of your left hand going under, then over the thumb, creating a loop, then take the working yarn to the back between the needles.

4. Keeping the yarn around your thumb, knit the half of the stitch that is on the left needle, completing the stitch so that it is on the right needle.

5. Bring the first part of the stitch that is still on the right needle over the stitch just made.

Saw-Tooth Companion Bowl
Designed by Miriam G. Briggs, photo on page 29

While you're on the couch or in your favorite chair, keep this little felted bowl at your side to hold your essentials: tape measure, stitch markers, cable needles, scissors, pencil — whatever your knitting calls for!

MEASUREMENTS	Approximately 6" × 7" × 4" (15 × 18 × 10 cm) after felting
YARN	Skacel Unikat, 100% wool, 3.5 oz (100 g)/174 yds (159 m), 07 Autumn
NEEDLES	One US 10.5 (6.5 mm) circular needle 24" (60 cm) long or size you need to obtain correct gauge
GAUGE	12 stitches = 4" (10 cm) in stockinette stitch
OTHER SUPPLIES	Stitch holder, stitch markers, tapestry needle
ABBREVIATIONS	**Kfb** knit into front and back of stitch (one stitch increased)

Knitting the Saw-Tooth Edging

- Cast on 3 stitches.
- **ROW 1:** Knit.
- **ROW 2:** Knit 2, Kfb.
- **ROW 3:** Kfb, K3.
- **ROW 4:** K4, Kfb.
- **ROW 5:** Kfb, K5.
- **ROW 6:** K6, Kfb.
- **ROW 7:** Bind off 5, K2. You now have 3 stitches
- Repeat Rows 2–7 sixteen more times for a total of 17 points. Place remaining 3 stitches on holder.

Knitting the Base

- Cast on 20 stitches.
- **ROW 1:** Knit.
- **ROW 2:** Kfb, P19.
- **ROW 3:** Kfb, K20.
- **ROW 4:** Kfb, P21.

Saw-Tooth Companion Bowl continued

- **ROW 5:** Kfb, K22.
- **ROWS 6–38:** Work even in stockinette stitch for 33 rows.
- **ROW 39:** K2tog, K22.
- **ROW 40:** P2tog, P21.
- **ROW 41:** K2tog, K20.
- **ROW 42:** P2tog, P19.

Picking Up for the Sides

- **ROW 1:** Knit 20 stitches. Pick up and knit 34 stitches along one side of base, pick up and knit the 20 cast-on stitches, pick up and knit 34 stitches along other side of base, pm. You now have 108 stitches.

Knitting the Bowl

- Knit 33 rounds. Bind off.

Attaching the Edging

- Sew edging to top of bowl, easing stitches evenly around.

Felting the Bowl

- Place bowl inside pillowcase or other cloth bag and tie closed. Set the washing machine for the lowest water level, longest washing cycle, and hottest temperature. Place the pillowcase in the machine with a pair of jeans or other heavy garment. Add a tiny amount of liquid soap. Start the washer and check the felting progress frequently. When desired size is reached, remove the bowl and rinse in cold water. Blot excess water with a towel. Shape the bag and allow it to dry.

Nano Nanny

Designed by Gabrielle Bolland, *photo on page 28*

Keep your iPod Nano tucked snuggly inside this little keeper. Frog Tree Alpaca lends itself beautifully to felting, and the chunky size makes this a quick and inexpensive gift to knit for any of your music-loving friends. (Or for yourself!)

MEASUREMENTS	Approximately 6" (15 cm) wide and 2.75" (7 cm) tall before felting
YARN	Frog Tree Chunky Alpaca, 100% alpaca, 1.75 oz (50 g)/54 yds (50 m), 99 Yellow
NEEDLES	US 6 (4 mm) straight needles or size you need to obtain correct gauge
GAUGE	18 stitches = 4" (10 cm) in stockinette stitch
OTHER SUPPLIES	Tapestry needle, iron-on appliqués, Nano-sized piece of waterproof cardboard, butter knife

Getting Started

- Cast on 26 stitches.
- ROW 1: Knit.
- ROW 2: Purl.
- Repeat Rows 1 and 2 until piece measures 6" (15 cm). Bind off loosely.

Finishing

- Fold the Nanny in half with the purl (wrong) side facing out. Sew up side and bottom seams. Work in ends. Turn right-side out.

Hand Felting the Nanny

- Wear rubber gloves to avoid being burned. Immerse the Nanny in very hot water with a little bit of dish soap and agitate. Test the size of the Nanny by slipping it over the cardboard (don't try it on your Nano while it's still wet!). If it's too large, continue to agitate in hot water. When Nanny is felted to correct size, squeeze out excess water and roll in a towel to blot dry. Reshape to correct size and dry upright over a butter knife.

Adding the Patches

- When the Nanny is completely dry, carefully iron on patches following package instructions with iron set no higher than the "wool" setting.

Smock-a-Ruche Scarf

Designed by Bobbe Morris, photo on page 27

Knitted in a smocking pattern that creates ruches between the smocks, this pattern is fun to knit. The wavy silhouette gives the scarf lots of places to interlock, creating a nice snug fit for a cold winter day — or night!

Measurements	Approximately 6" (15 cm) wide and 52" (132 cm) long
Yarn	Wool Around the World Wool Pak, 100% wool, 8.8 oz (250 g)/310 yds (283 m), Apple Blossom
Needles	US 8 (5 mm) and US 10 (6 mm) straight needles or size you need to obtain correct gauge
Gauge	14 stitches = 4" (10 cm) in stockinette stitch on larger needle
Other Supplies	Tapestry needle
Abbreviations	**K1b** knit 1 through the back loop **WS** wrong side **wyib** with yarn in back

Knitting the Beginning Ruffle

- With smaller needles, cast on 96 stitches.
- **Row 1:** Knit.
- **Row 2:** *K2tog; repeat from *. You now have 48 stitches.
- Change to larger needles.

Knitting the Smocking Pattern

- **Row 1 and all odd-numbered rows through 11:** Knit.
- **Row 2 and all even-numbered rows through 12:** Purl.
- **Row 13:** *K2tog; repeat from *. You now have 24 stitches.
- **Row 14 (WS):** K1, *P1, K2; repeat from * to last 2 stitches, P1, K1.
- **Row 15:** P1, *K1, P2; repeat from * to last 2 stitches, K1, P1.
- **Row 16:** Repeat Row 14.
- **Row 17:** P1, *wyib, insert right needle between 4th and 5th stitches on left needle, yo and draw yarn through, slip loop just made onto left needle, knit this loop together with next stitch tightly, P2, K1, P2; repeat from *, ending last repeat with P1 instead of P2.
- **Rows 18 and 20:** Repeat Row 14.
- **Row 19:** Repeat Row 15.

- **ROW 21:** P1, K1, P2, *wyib, insert right needle between 4th and 5th stitches on left needle, yo and draw yarn through, slip loop just made onto left needle, knit this loop together with next stitch tightly, P2, K1, P2; repeat from * to last 2 stitches, K1, P1.
- **ROWS 22 AND 24:** Repeat Row 14.
- **ROW 23:** Repeat Row 15.
- **ROW 25:** Repeat Row 17.
- **ROW 26 (WS):** *(P1, K1) in next stitch; repeat from *. You now have 48 stitches.
- Repeat these 26 rows 8 more times.

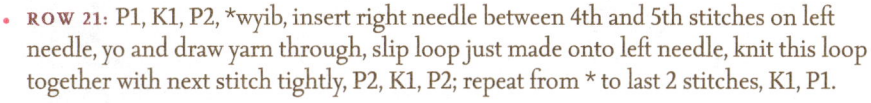

Knitting the Ending Ruffle

- Work 12 rows stockinette stitch. Change to smaller needle.
- **ROW 1:** *K1, yo; repeat from *. You now have 96 stitches.
- **ROW 2:** *K1, K1b; repeat from *.
- Bind off in knit.

Finishing

- Weave in ends.

Vermont Felted Bag

DESIGNED BY KATHY ELKINS, photo on page 26

But for the handles, this bag is knitted in one piece. What begins as a large and somewhat floppy bag magically becomes a compact and very useful handbag with just some hot water and agitation. (Don't worry. The agitation happens after you've finished with the knitting!)

MEASUREMENTS	Approximately 12" (30 cm) tall and 4" (10 cm) deep before felting; approximately 9" (23 cm) wide, 7" (18 cm) tall, and 3" (8 cm) deep after felting
YARN	Valley Yarns Berkshire Hand Dyed, 85% wool/15% alpaca, 3.5 oz (100 g)/141 yds (129 m), Antique
NEEDLES	US 15 (10 mm) straight needles or size you need to obtain correct gauge
GAUGE	12 stitches = 4" (10 cm) in stockinette stitch
OTHER SUPPLIES	Tapestry needle, four 1" (2.5 cm) buttons

Vermont Felted Bag continued

Knitting the Bag

- Cast on 34 stitches. Knit 4 rows. Work in stockinette stitch (knit a row, purl a row) until piece measures 13" (33 cm). Bind off 3 stitches at the beginning of the next 2 rows. You now have 28 stitches for the bottom of the bag. Continue in stockinette stitch until bottom of bag measures 6.75" (17 cm).
- Cast on 3 stitches at the beginning of the next 2 rows. Knit the other side of the bag to match the first. Bind off.

Knitting the Straps (make two)

- Cast on 4 stitches. Work in garter stitch for 3" (8 cm). Change to stockinette stitch and continue until strap measures 18" (46 cm). Change to garter stitch and continue until strap measures 21" (53 cm). Bind off.

Assembling the Bag

- Pin the bag together, bringing the outer bottom edge points to the center of the bottom of the bag. Sew the bottom and side seams. Weave in ends.

Felting the Bag

- Place bag and the straps inside pillowcase or other cloth bag and tie closed. Set the washing machine for the lowest water level, longest washing cycle, and hottest temperature. Place bag in machine with a pair of jeans or other heavy garment. Add a tiny amount of liquid soap. Start the washer and check the felting progress frequently. If necessary, reset the machine and run again. When desired size is reached, remove the bag and rinse in cold water. Blot excess water with a towel. Shape the bag and allow it to dry.

Finishing

- Measure 4" (10 cm) in from side seams and sew straps to bag with buttons.

Zane's Coming Home Sweater

Designed by Tara Jon Manning, photo on page 29

Made in a brushed merino blend, this sweater is almost felt-like, and the color is quintessentially little boy blue. Soft, quick knitting, easy and economical, this is a perfect cuddly gift for baby's arrival.

MEASUREMENTS	To fit infant 0–3 months, approximately 20" (51 cm) chest
YARN	Crystal Palace Merino Frappe, 80% merino/20% nylon, 1.75 oz (50 g)/140 yds (128 m), 011 Forget-me-not
NEEDLES	US 8 (5 mm) straight needles or size you need to obtain correct gauge
GAUGE	14 stitches = 4" (10 cm) in stockinette stitch
OTHER SUPPLIES	Stitch holders, safety pins (optional, for marking placement of buttonholes), sewing needle and thread, US J/10 (6 mm) crochet hook, four ½" (1.3 cm) buttons, tapestry needle
ABBREVIATIONS	**yo** yarn over

YO Buttonhole

Make yarn over buttonholes where desired by yo, K2tog. That's it!

Knitting the Back

- Cast on 36 stitches. Work stockinette stitch for 4" (10 cm). Bind off 2 stitches at the beginning of the next 2 rows for armhole shaping. Continue even until piece measures 8.5" (22 cm) from cast-on edge. K9, bind off center 14 stitches, knit to end of row. Place 9 stitches for each shoulder on two separate holders.

Knitting the Fronts

- Make two, reversing shaping and placing the buttonholes on the left for a boy/unisex or on the right for a girl, if you subscribe to that sort of thing. Knit the side without buttonholes first, then place the four buttons along center front. Mark these spots with safety pins. When you are knitting the side with buttonholes, work to the marker and make a YO Buttonhole two stitches in from center front.

- Cast on 20 stitches. Work stockinette stitch for 4" (10 cm). Bind off 2 stitches at armhole edge. When piece measures 5.5" (14 cm), shape V neck by decreasing 1 stitch at neck edge every other row 9 times.

- Continue in stockinette stitch until piece measures 8.5" (22 cm) from cast-on edge. Place 9 shoulder stitches on holder.

- Repeat for other side, reversing armhole and neck shaping.

Zane's Coming Home Sweater continued

Joining the Shoulders

- With right sides facing, join fronts to back at shoulders using the 3-needle bind-off (see page 251).

Knitting the Sleeves *(make 2)*

- With right sides facing, pick up 30 stitches evenly spaced between armhole notches. Working in stockinette stitch, decrease 1 stitch at each end of every 6th row 4 times. Continue even until sleeve measures 6.5" (17 cm). Bind off loosely.

Finishing

- Sew sleeves and side seams. With right side facing and beginning at lower right front, work single crochet along right front, around neck and along left front; continue along bottom edge if desired. Sew buttons opposite buttonholes. Weave in ends. Block.

Mitered Square Belt with Beads

Designed by Judy Warde, photo on page 26

A technique featured in Domino Knitting by Vivian Hoxbro and Modular Knitting by Iris Schreier, the centered double decrease shapes a square. Wear the belt just below the waist.

MEASUREMENTS	Approximately 34" (86 cm) long, excluding ties
YARN	Noro Kureyon, 100% wool, 1.75 oz (50 g)/109 yds (100 m), color 157
NEEDLES	US 6 (4 mm) straight needles or size you need to obtain correct gauge
GAUGE	20 stitches = 4" (10 cm) in stockinette stitch
OTHER SUPPLIES	Nine 20 mm beads (more or fewer depending on length of finished belt), tapestry needle, 6 yds beading thread or heavy carpet thread, six 10 mm beads
ABBREVIATIONS	**RS** right side **S2KP** slip 2 together kwise, knit 1, pass the 2 slipped stitches over the knitted stitch **WS** wrong side

Knitting the Squares

- Cast on 21 stitches.
- ROW 1 (WS): K10, P1, K10.
- ROW 2 (RS): K9, S2KP, K9.
- ROW 3: K9, P1, K9.
- ROW 4: K8, S2KP, K8.
- ROW 5: K8, P1, K8.
- Continue in this manner, working double decrease on right-side rows and purling the center stitch on wrong-side rows, until you have 1 stitch remaining. Cut yarn leaving a 6" (15 cm) tail, and pull it through remaining stitch.
- Make as many squares as necessary for desired length, accounting for size of beads between the squares.

Finishing

- Weave in cast-on tails. Block squares. Using the 6" (15 cm) tails, join the squares, placing a 20 mm bead between each square. *Thread tapestry needle with a double strand of heavy thread and carefully weave through the squares and the bead joins. Repeat from * with a second strand of thread.
- Cut six strands of yarn about 20" (51 cm) long. *Pull one strand through end point of diamond to half its length. Work two overhand knots next to end of belt; repeat from * two more times. Work an overhand knot with all six strands next to end of belt. **At 8" (20.5 cm) from knot, work an overhand knot over two strands held together. Slide one 10 mm bead over the two strands and tie in a knot to secure. Repeat from ** for the other groups of two strands. Repeat for other side of belt. Weave in ends.

Waterfall Scarf

DESIGNED BY LINDA O'LEARY, photo on page 27

This scarf is knit in twisted garter stitch from beginning to end. The fun comes when you bind off and encourage dropped stitches to drop from one end to the other.

MEASUREMENTS	Approximately 8" (20 cm) wide and 50" (127 cm) long
YARN	Kaolin Designs Aspen, 55% wool/45% mohair, 4 oz (113 g)/180 yds (165 m), 742 Shimmer
NEEDLES	US 10 (6 mm) straight needles or size you need to obtain correct gauge
GAUGE	16 stitches = 4" (10 cm) in stockinette stitch
OTHER SUPPLIES	Tapestry needle

Knitting the Scarf

- Cast on 19 stitches using the simple loop method (see page 250).
- ROW 1: Knit.
- ROW 2 AND ALL REMAINING ROWS: Knit through the back loop.
- Repeat Row 2 for desired length of scarf. Be careful not to drop or add stitches while knitting: Any variation from the 19 stitches will not allow the required number of stitches to drop.

Binding Off

- *Bind off 2 stitches. Enlarge the loop on the right needle and pull remaining ball of yarn through the loop and pull up to close. This makes 3 bound off stitches. Knit the next stitch. Repeat from *, ending by binding off 3 stitches. Pull the yarn through the last loop.

Finishing

- Remove needle from live stitches. Encourage the live stitches to drop the entire length of the scarf. Weave in ends.

Square Hole Hat and Wristlets

Designed by Valentina Devine, photo on page 27

These are actually two one-skein projects: one skein for the hat, one skein for the wristlets. Choose one or both.

MEASUREMENTS	Hat: approximately 21" (53 cm) circumference; wristlets: approximately 9" (23 cm) circumference and 7" (18 cm) length
YARN	Noro Kureyon, 100% wool, 1.75 oz (50 g)/109 yds (100 m), color 170
NEEDLES	US H/8 (5 mm) crochet hook or size you need to obtain correct gauge
GAUGE	8 chain stitches = 2" (5 cm)
OTHER SUPPLIES	Tapestry needle

Crocheting the Hat

- Ch 4 and join with slip stitch to form ring.
- **ROUND 1:** Ch 3 (counts as 1 dc) work 15 dc into ring, slip stitch in top of beginning ch 3 to join. You now have 16 dc.
- **ROUND 2:** Ch 5 (counts as 1 dc, ch 2) skip first dc, *dc in next dc, ch 2; repeat from *, slip stitch in third ch of beginning ch 5 to join.
- **ROUND 3:** Repeat Round 2.
- **ROUND 4:** Ch 5 (counts as 1 dc, ch 3) skip first dc, *dc in center of ch-3 space of previous row, dc in next dc, ch 3; repeat from * 15 times, dc in next ch-3 space, slip stitch in third ch of beginning ch 5 to join. You now have 32 dc.
- **ROUND 5:** Ch 5 (counts as 1 dc, ch 4) skip first dc, *dc in next dc, ch 4; repeat from *, slip stitch in third ch of beginning ch 5 to join.
- Continue with Round 5 until there are 15 rounds of square holes.

Adding the Picot

- Ch 3, *2 sc in ch-3 space of previous row, sc in top of next dc, ch 3, slip stitch in same dc; repeat from *. Cut thread and draw through last loop. Weave in end.

Crocheting the Flower

- Ch 4 and join with slip stitch to form ring.
- **ROUND 1:** Ch 3 (counts as 1 dc) work 15 dc into ring, slip stitch in top of beginning ch 3 to join. You now have 16 dc.

Square Hole Hat and Wristlets continued

- **ROUND 2:** Ch 5 *skip 1 dc in row below, 1 dc into second dc in row below; repeat from * around, slip stitch in beginning of ch 5 to join. You now have 8 ch-5 loops.
- **ROUND 3:** To work petals, into each ch-5 loop, crochet (1 sc, 1 hdc, 3 dc, 1 hdc, 1 sc).
- **ROUND 4:** Ch 5 into each dc below, wrapping the yarn in front of the dc.
- **ROUND 5:** Repeat Row 3 except work 5 dc instead of 3.

Finishing

- Weave in ends. Attach flower with a few stitches through the petals onto hat.

Crocheting the Wristlets

- Ch 30 and join with slip stitch to form ring.
- **ROUND 1:** Ch 5 (counts as 1 dc, 2 ch), *skip 1 ch below, dc into next ch; repeat from * until you have 15 square holes. Slip stitch in third ch of beginning ch 5 to join.
- Repeat Round 1 thirteen more times.
- Finish with one row of picots on top and bottom of wristlets as for hat.

Crocheting the Flowers

- Ch 4 and join with slip stitch to form ring.
- **ROUND 1:** Ch 3 (counts as 1 dc) work 15 dc into ring, slip stitch in top of beginning ch-3 to join. You have 16 dc.
- **ROUND 2:** *Ch 8, sc in next dc of previous row; repeat from *. You now have 16 loops.

Finishing

- Weave in ends. Attach flowers with a few stitches through the petals onto wristlets. Work one French knot (see below) into center of flower.
- **DESIGNER NOTE:** Since the pattern stitch is very open, the thumb can fit easily into a square hole.

FRENCH KNOT

With yarn threaded on a tapestry needle, bring yarn from wrong side to right side where you want your knot to be. With the tip of the needle close to where the yarn exits the fabric, wrap the yarn around the needle twice. (A)

Hold the thread so the wrap stays on the needle and insert the needle close to where it originally exited but not in the same spot. Pull the yarn to the back to form the knot. (B)

Felt Ruffle Bag

Designed by Barbara Breiter, photo on page 30

This cute little bag can hold a small gift or just what you need to run to the store — keys, cell phone, and money. It may also make a nice tote for a bottle of your favorite wine.

MEASUREMENTS	Approximately 6.5" (17 cm) wide and 8" (20 cm) tall, excluding ruffle before felting; approximately 4" (10 cm) wide and 7" (18 cm) tall, excluding ruffle after felting
YARN	Noro Kureyon, 100% wool, 1.75 oz (50 g)/109 yds (100 m)
NEEDLES	US 11 (8 mm) straight needles or size you need to obtain correct gauge
GAUGE	12 stitches = 4" (10 cm) in stockinette stitch
OTHER SUPPLIES	Tapestry needle
ABBREVIATIONS	**Kfb** knit into front and back of stitch (one stitch increased)

Knitting the Bag

- Cast on 26 stitches. Work stockinette stitch until piece measures 14" (36 cm). Bind off.

Knitting the Ruffle

- With right side facing, pick up 44 stitches along one long edge.
- **INCREASE ROW:** *Kfb; repeat from *. You now have 88 stitches.
- Knit 7 rows. Bind off.

Felt Ruffle Bag continued

Knitting the Handles (make two)

- Cast on 80 stitches. Bind off.

Assembling the Bag

- Fold the bag in half and seam the bottom, side, and ruffle. Sew handles to the inside of the bag, at the base of ruffle on the side seam and directly opposite. Weave in ends.

Felting the Bag

- Place bag inside pillowcase or other cloth bag and tie closed. Set the washing machine for the lowest water level, longest washing cycle, and hottest temperature. Place the pillowcase in the machine with a pair of jeans or other heavy garment. Add a tiny amount of liquid soap. Start the washer and check the felting progress frequently. If necessary, reset the machine and run again. When desired size is reached, remove the bag and rinse in cold water. Blot excess water with a towel. Shape the bag and allow it to dry.

Blanket Buddy

Designed by Mary Anne Thompson, *photo on page 26*

This little critter is as easy to knit as it is to cuddle and it is small enough for baby to carry anywhere. You can get creative and make up your own favorite animal by reshaping the ears.

MEASUREMENTS	Approximately 12" (30 cm) square (not counting ears!)
YARN	Sirdar Denim Chunky, 60% acrylic/25% cotton/15% wool, 3.5 oz (100 g)/171 yds (156 m), 560 Wavecrest
NEEDLES	US 10.5 (6.5 mm) and US 7 (4.5 mm) straight needles or size you need to obtain correct gauge
GAUGE	14 stitches = 4" (10 cm) on larger needles in stockinette stitch
OTHER SUPPLIES	Tapestry needle, fiberfill, scrap of contrasting yarn for eyes
ABBREVIATIONS	**Kfb** knit into front and back of stitch (one stitch increased) **pwise** purlwise **yo** yarn over

Knitting the Body

- With larger needles, cast on 1 stitch.
- ROWS 1–6: Kfb, knit to end of row. You now have 7 stitches.
- ROW 7: K3, yo, knit to end of row.
- Repeat Row 7 until you have 40 stitches.

Knitting the Paws

- Cast on 12 stitches at the beginning of the next 2 rows. Knit 6 rows on these 64 stitches. Bind off 12 stitches at the beginning of the next 2 rows. You now have 40 stitches.

Continuing the Body

- NEXT ROW: K2, K2tog, yo, K2tog, knit to end of row.
- Repeat this row until you have 28 stitches.
- Change to smaller needles.
- NEXT ROW: *K2tog; repeat from *.
- NEXT ROW: *Kfb; repeat from *.

Blanket Buddy continued

Shaping the Head

- You will be working both the front and back of the head at the same time by slipping the stitches for one and purling the stitches for the other. This forms a pocket for stuffing.
- ROW 1: *P1, slip 1 pwise; repeat from *.
- Repeat Row 1 until head measures 3.5" (9 cm).

Knitting the Ears

- *P3tog, return stitch to left needle, cast on 17 stitches. You now have 43 stitches.
- P3tog, P15, turn. P14, P2tog, turn.
- P16, turn. P12, turn, P14, turn. P16, P2tog, turn.
- P18, turn. P16, P2tog, turn.
- Bind off 18.
- Work P1, slip 1 to end of row.
- Turn work and repeat from * for second ear. You now have 12 stitches.

Finishing

- Cut yarn leaving a 10" (25 cm) tail. Thread tail onto tapestry needle and draw through stitches 1, 3, 5, 7, 9, and 11. Turn work and draw through stitches 12, 10, 8, 6, 4, and 2. Slide stitches off needle. Stuff head with fiberfill. Draw needle through stitches again. Pull up snug and fasten off. Weave in ends. Tie knots in "paws." Embroider eyes with scrap of yarn.

Power Flowers

Designed by Tamara Del Sonno, photo on page 26

Power to the flowers! Or is that power from the flowers? Whatever your idea, these fabulous felted blossoms will brighten up your wardrobe or your home. Attach a pin back and pin them anywhere you need a little color. You can make all four from one skein of yarn.

MEASUREMENTS	From 3" (8 cm) to 7" (18 cm) diameter
YARN	Zitron Loft, 100% new wool, 1.75 oz (50 g)/110 yds (101 m), color 910
NEEDLES	One US 10.5 (6.5 mm) circular needle 16" (40 cm) long or size you need to obtain correct gauge
GAUGE	12–16 stitches = 4" (10 cm) in stockinette stitch
OTHER SUPPLIES	Tapestry needle, decorative buttons, pin backs

Knitting the Small Sea Anemone

- *Cast on 5 stitches using the knitted cast-on method (see page 246). Bind off to last stitch, but do not break yarn; repeat from * 7 more times. Do not break yarn.
- *Cast on 6 stitches using the knitted cast-on method. Bind off to last stitch, but do not break yarn; repeat from * 7 more times. Do not break yarn.
- *Cast on 7 stitches using the knitted cast-on method. Bind off to last stitch, but do not break yarn; repeat from * 7 more times. Do not break yarn.
- *Cast on 8 stitches using the knitted cast-on method. Bind off to last stitch, but do not break yarn; repeat from * 7 more times. Do not break yarn.

Assembling the Flower

- Pick up and knit 1 stitch in each attached stitch along the bottom. Bind off. Break yarn leaving a 12" (30 cm) tail. Thread tail onto tapestry needle. Roll up petals starting with the smallest in the center and sew them together through the bottom edge with the tail. Fasten off. Weave in ends.

Knitting the Large Sea Anemone

- *Cast on 5 stitches using the knitted cast-on method. Bind off to last stitch, but do not break yarn; repeat from * 5 more times. Do not break yarn.
- *Cast on 7 stitches using the knitted cast-on method. Bind off to last stitch, but do not break yarn; repeat from * 5 more times. Do not break yarn.

Power Flowers continued

- *Cast on 9 stitches using the knitted cast-on method. Bind off to last stitch, but do not break yarn; repeat from * 5 more times. Do not break yarn.
- *Cast on 13 stitches using the knitted cast-on method. Bind off to last stitch, but do not break yarn; repeat from * 5 more times. Do not break yarn.
- *Cast on 15 stitches using the knitted cast-on method. Bind off to last stitch, but do not break yarn; repeat from * 7 more times. Do not break yarn.

Assembling the Flower

- Pick up and knit 1 stitch in each attached stitch along the bottom. Bind off. Break yarn leaving a 12" (30 cm) tail. Thread tail onto tapestry needle. Roll up petals starting with the smallest in the center and sew them together through the bottom edge with the tail. Fasten off. Weave in ends.

Knitting the Small Poppy

- Cast on 72 stitches. Join into a round being careful not to twist stitches.
- ROUND 1: *K4, P4; repeat from *.
- Repeat Round 1 until piece measures 2.75" (7 cm).
- DECREASE ROUND: *K2tog twice, P2tog twice; repeat from *.
- NEXT ROUND: *K2, P2; repeat from *.

Finishing

- Cut yarn leaving a 12" (30 cm) tail. Thread tail onto tapestry needle and draw through remaining stitches twice. Fasten off. Weave in ends.

Knitting the Large Poppy

- Cast on 64 stitches. Join into a round being careful not to twist stitches.
- ROUND 1: *K4, P4; repeat from *.
- Repeat Round 1 until piece measures 1.5" (4 cm).
- DECREASE ROUND: *K2tog twice, P2tog twice; repeat from *.
- NEXT ROUND: *K2, P2; repeat from *.

Finishing

- Cut yarn leaving a 12" (30 cm) tail. Thread tail onto tapestry needle and draw through remaining stitches twice. Fasten off. Weave in ends.

Felting the Flowers

- Place flowers inside pillowcase or other cloth bag and tie closed. Set the washing machine for the lowest water level, longest washing cycle, and hottest temperature. Place the pillowcase in the machine with a pair of jeans or other heavy garment. Add a tiny amount of liquid soap. Start the washer and check the felting progress frequently, resetting the machine if necessary. When desired flower size is reached, remove and rinse in cold water. Blot excess water with a towel. Shape the flowers and allow them to dry.

Embellishing the Flowers

- Add buttons to centers and pin backs as desired.

Infant's Rolled Neck Pullover

Designed by Wendy Banks, *photo on page 28*

This brightly colored baby sweater is warm, wooly, and wonderful. And because the front and back are identical, it's easy to slip on and off your little one.

MEASUREMENTS	To fit infant 0–12 months, approximately 20" (51 cm) chest
YARN	Schaefer Yarns Elaine, 100% merino wool, 8 oz (227 g)/ 300 yds (274 m), Snoopy's Crayons
NEEDLES	US 11 (8 mm) straight and one US 11 (8 mm) circular needle 12" (30 cm) long or set of four US 11 (8 mm) double-point needles or size you need to obtain correct gauge
GAUGE	14 stitches = 4" (10 cm) in garter stitch
OTHER SUPPLIES	Stitch holder, tapestry needle

Knitting the Front and Back *(make one each)*

- Cast on 34 stitches. Work in garter stitch until piece measures 11" (28 cm) from cast-on edge.

Shaping the Shoulders

- **ROW 1:** Bind off 8, knit to end.
- **ROW 2:** Bind off 8, knit to end.
- Place remaining 18 stitches on a holder for neck edge(s).

Knitting the Sleeves *(make two)*

- Cast on 18 stitches. Knit 2 rows.
- **NOTE:** Sleeve increases are worked 2 stitches in from each edge: in other words, on increase rows you knit 2, increase 1, knit to last two stitches, increase 1, knit 2.
- Continue in garter stitch and increase 1 stitch at each end of every 4th row seven times. You now have 32 stitches. Continue even until sleeve measures 7" (18 cm). Bind off all stitches.

Working the Neck

- Sew shoulder seams together. Place 18 held back neck and 18 held front neck stitches on circular or double-point needles. Join into a round and knit 8 rounds. Bind off loosely.

Finishing

- Sew top of sleeves to body, matching center of sleeve to shoulder seam. Sew side and underarm seams. Weave in ends.

Bulky Weight

Two-Hour Handbag
Designed by Cindy Yoshimura, photo on page 30

This quick and easy handbag uses less than 150 yards of bulky wool. Worked in the round, all you do is knit. (Well, okay, you have to cast on, bind off, and decrease a few times, but that's it.) Estimated time to complete: two hours!

MEASUREMENTS	Approximately 13" (33 cm) wide and 10" (25 cm) tall before felting, 10" (25 cm) wide and 7.5" (19 cm) tall after felting
YARN	Imperial Stock Ranch Wool Lopi, 100% wool, 4 oz (113 g)/150 yds (137 m), Black Cherry
NEEDLES	One US 13 (9 mm) circular needle 24" (60 cm) long or size you need to obtain correct gauge
GAUGE	12 stitches = 4" (10 cm) in stockinette stitch
OTHER SUPPLIES	Tapestry needle, 1.25" (3 cm) button for decoration

Getting Started

- Cast on 68 stitches. Join into a round, being careful not to twist stitches.
- Knit 6 rounds.
- **NEXT ROUND:** *K9, K2tog; repeat from * to last 13 stitches, K11, K2tog.
- Knit 5 rounds.
- **NEXT ROUND:** *K8, K2tog; repeat from * to last 12 stitches, K10, K2tog. You now have 56 stitches.
- Knit even until piece measures 9.5" (24 cm).

Knitting the Handle

- Use the backward loop method to cast on where necessary (see page 244). Be careful not to twist stitches and keep tension tight.
- **ROUND 1:** K9, bind off 10, K18, bind off 10, K9.
- **ROUND 2:** K8, cast on 10, K18, cast on 10, K10.
- Knit 6 rounds. Bind off.

Assembling the Bag

- With right sides together, sew bottom edge of seam with overcast stitch. Stitch over seam again. Weave in ends. If a gap appears at handle edge, weave an 8"–10" (20–25 cm) length of yarn in and out from inside of bag close to gap. This will disappear during felting.

Felting the Bag

- Place bag inside pillowcase or other cloth bag and tie closed. Set the washing machine for the lowest water level, longest washing cycle, and hottest temperature. Place the pillowcase in the machine with a pair of jeans or other heavy garment. Add a tiny amount of liquid soap. Start the washer and check the felting progress frequently. When desired size is reached, remove the bag and rinse in cold water. Blot excess water with a towel. Shape the bag and allow it to dry.

Fuchsia Felted Bowl

Designed by Lucie Sinkler, photo on page 30

Made with a super-bulky yarn and then felted, this little catch-all bowl will hold its shape with or without contents. It is knitted in the round from top to bottom in only thirty-four rounds.

MEASUREMENTS	Approximately 17" (43 cm) circumference and 4" (10 cm) tall
YARN	Cascade Yarns Lana Grande, 100% wool, 3.5 oz (100 g)/87.5 yds (80 m), Color 6033
NEEDLES	One US 13 (9 mm) circular needle 24" (60 cm) long and set of five US 13 (9 mm) double-point needles or size you need to obtain correct gauge
GAUGE	11 stitches = 4" (10 cm) in stockinette stitch
OTHER SUPPLIES	Tapestry needle
ABBREVIATIONS	**M1** make 1 increase (see page 247)

Knitting the Rim

- Using circular needle, cast on 108 stitches.
- K1, *bind off 4, K1; repeat from * to last 4 stitches, bind off 4. You now have 36 stitches.

Knitting the Body

- Place 9 stitches on each of 4 double-point needles. Join into a round, being careful not to twist stitches.
- ROUNDS 1–6: Knit.
- ROUND 7: *K6, M1; repeat from *. You now have 42 stitches.
- ROUNDS 8 AND 9: Knit.
- ROUND 10: *K7, M1; repeat from *. You now have 48 stitches.
- ROUNDS 11 AND 12: Knit.
- ROUND 13: *K8, M1; repeat from *. You now have 54 stitches.
- ROUNDS 14–25: Knit.

Decreasing for the Bottom

- ROUND 26: *K7, K2tog; repeat from *. You now have 48 stitches.
- ROUND 27: *K6, K2tog; repeat from *. You now have 42 stitches.
- ROUND 28: *K5, K2tog; repeat from *. You now have 36 stitches.
- ROUNDS 29-32: Continue in this manner, knitting 1 fewer stitch between decreases, until you have 12 stitches remaining.
- ROUND 33: *K2tog; repeat from *. You now have 6 stitches.

Finishing

- Cut the yarn leaving a 10" (25 cm) tail. Thread tail onto tapestry needle and draw through remaining stitches twice. Pull up snug and fasten off on the inside. Weave in ends.

Felting the Bowl

- Place bowl inside pillowcase or other cloth bag and tie closed. Set the washing machine for the lowest water level, longest washing cycle, and hottest temperature. Place the pillowcase in the machine with a pair of jeans or other heavy garment. Add a tiny amount of liquid soap. Start the washer and check the felting progress frequently. If necessary, reset the machine and run again. When desired size is reached, remove the bowl and rinse in cold water. Blot excess water with a towel. Shape the bowl and allow it to dry.

Novelty Yarn

Flirty Ribbon Purse

Designed by Laura Militzer Bryant, photo on page 32

This flirty little purse really shows off the ribbon it's knitted with by using unknitted ribbon for fringe. The ribbon is knitted at a nice firm gauge, so you don't have to worry about anything falling through the cracks.

MEASUREMENTS	Approximately 5.5" (14 cm) square
YARN	Prism ½" Sparkle Ribbon, 95% rayon/5% lurex, 3.5 oz (100 g)/95 yds (87 m), Woodlands
NEEDLES	One US 9 (5.5 mm) circular needle 16" (40 cm) long or size you need to obtain correct gauge
GAUGE	14 stitches = 4" (10 cm) in stockinette stitch
OTHER SUPPLIES	US H/8 (5 mm) and J/10 (6 mm) crochet hooks, one 24 mm bead, tapestry needle
ABBREVIATIONS	**RS** right side **WS** wrong side

stitch pattern

Loop

Knit the first stitch but leave on left needle. Bring yarn to front between the needles, wrap yarn around thumb forming a 2" (5 cm) loop, and return yarn to back. Knit the stitch on the left needle again and remove it to right needle, dropping the loop. Pass first stitch on right needle over the second to lock the loop in place.

Knitting the Bag

- Cast on 20 stitches. Work stockinette stitch back and forth for 5.5" (14 cm), ending with a RS row.
- **NEXT WS ROW:** Knit. This makes a turning ridge.
- Resume stockinette stitch and continue until piece measures 11" (28 cm) ending with a wrong-side row.

Knitting the Looped Fringe

- Work a row of the Loop pattern. Fold bag along turning ridge and work Loop pattern on other side, picking up stitches from the cast-on edge. Join and work another row of Loop pattern, making the loops slightly smaller than for the first row and binding off stitches as you go. Fasten off, but do not cut yarn.

Crocheting the Strap

- With J hook, work strap of chain stitch about 36" (91 cm) long. With H hook, work 1 row of reverse single crochet along one side of chain, then work 1 row of reverse single crochet along one side of bag, attaching the strap and joining the seam. Cut the yarn and fasten off.

- Join ribbon to bottom of bag on opposite side and, with H hook, join the seams with reverse single crochet and continue along other side of chain strap. Without cutting yarn, slip stitch to top of bag and work reverse single crochet around top edge of bag.

Finishing

- Cut a 16" (41 cm) length of yarn. Fold in half and feed fold through bead. Pull loop through and tie a knot about 4" (10 cm) from end, snug to bead. Tie knot on other side of bead. Tie loose ends to inside of bag near the center top of one side. Fasten off and weave in all ends.

Catnip Kick Pillow

Designed by Karen Mortensen, photo on page 32

Yes, you read that right, a kick pillow for a cat. Fill the core of this pillow with catnip and watch your furry little friend romp and roll. Held with the front paws, the back paws will kick up a storm.

stitch pattern

Double Cable

Rows 1, 3, and 5 (wrong side): K2, P4, K1, P4, K2.

Rows 2 and 4 (right side): P2, K9, P2.

Row 6: P2, C4B, K1, C4F, P2.

Repeat Rows 1–6 for pattern.

Measurements	Approximately 4" (10 cm) wide and 12" (30 cm) long
Yarn	LanaKnits Hemp for Knitting-All Hemp 6, 100% hemp, 3.5 oz (100 g)/165 yds (150 m), Red
Needles	US 5 (3.75 mm) straight needles or size you need to obtain correct gauge
Gauge	20 stitches = 4" (10 cm) in stockinette stitch
Other Supplies	Cable needle, fiberfill, catnip, crochet hook, tapestry needle
Abbreviations	**wyif** with yarn in front **C4F** place 2 stitches on cable needle and hold in front, knit 2, knit 2 from cable needle **C4B** place 2 stitches on cable needle and hold in back, knit 2, knit 2 from cable needle

Knitting the Pillow Front

- **Cast on 21 stitches. Note:** Slip the first stitch of every row wyif.
- **Row 1:** Slip 1 wyif, K3, work Double Cable pattern over next 13 stitches, K4.

Catnip Kick Pillow continued

- **ROW 2:** Slip 1 wyif, K3, work Double Cable pattern over next 13 stitches, K4.
- Continue in this manner, working the first and last 4 stitches in garter stitch and working the Double Cable pattern over the center 13 stitches, until piece measures 12" (30 cm), ending with Row 3 of Double Cable pattern.
- **NEXT ROW:** Purl. This creates a turning ridge.

Knitting the Pillow Back

- Work as for front, but reverse the direction of the cable crosses by working the 13 center stitches of Row 6 of Double Cable pattern as follows:
- P2, C4F, K1, C4B, P2.
- Continue until piece measures same as front, ending with Row 3 of Double Cable pattern.

Finishing

- Fold piece in half at turning ridge. Seam both sides with whipstitch or single crochet. Stuff pillow halfway with fiberfill, add catnip, stuff remaining pillow with fiberfill. Seam the top with whipstitch or single crochet. Weave in ends.

Neck Warmer

DESIGNED BY ANNI KRISTENSEN, *photo on page 31*

This little warmer is the perfect weight to wear at the office or around the home to keep the chill off your neck. Made of recycled silk, it is as comfortable as it is colorful.

MEASUREMENTS	Approximately 16" (41 cm) long and 5" (13 cm) wide
YARN	Himalaya Yarn Tibet, 100% recycled silk, 3.5 oz (100 g)/80 yds (73 m), Random Multi-Color
NEEDLES	US 8 (5 mm) straight needles and one US 8 (5 mm) circular needle 24" (60 cm) long or size you need to obtain correct gauge
GAUGE	13 stitches = 4" (10 cm) in pattern
OTHER SUPPLIES	Tapestry needle, 2 buttons
ABBREVIATIONS	**Kfb** knit into front and back of stitch (one stitch increased)

stitch pattern

TWISTED RIB

ROWS 1–3: *K2, P2; repeat from *.

ROW 4: *K second stitch on left needle and leave on needle, K first stitch and drop both stitches from needle, P2; repeat from *.

Repeat Rows 1–4 for pattern.

Knitting the First Ruffle

- With straight needles, cast on 104 stitches.
- **ROW 1 (WS):** Knit.
- **ROW 2:** Knit.
- **ROW 3:** *K2tog; repeat from *. You now have 52 stitches.

Knitting the Center of the Warmer

- Work in Twisted Rib pattern over 52 stitches for 4" (10 cm), ending with a wrong-side row. Cut yarn leaving a 10" (25 cm) tail, but leave stitches on needle.

Knitting the Buttonholes and Second Ruffle

- With circular needle and right side facing, begin just above first ruffle and pick up 3 stitches along short side, yo twice, skip 1 stitch and pick up 4 stitches, yo twice, skip 1 stitch and pick up 3 stitches, knit across stitches on straight needle then 14 stitches on opposite short edge. (The circular needle aids in going around the corner.)
- Working on 14 end stitches and 52 stitches on straight needle, *Kfb; repeat from *. You now have 132 stitches. K3, K2 into double yo, K4, K2 into double yo, K3.
- Bind off.

Finishing

- Weave in ends. Sew on buttons opposite buttonholes.

Square-Hole Shrug

Designed by Valentina Devine, photo on page 32

Dress up your summer wardrobe with this cool and airy shrug. No added warmth here, this light and lacy ribbon design is as easy to crochet as it is to wear. Gauge is not crucial — start with your desired width measurement and crochet to the end of the skein.

MEASUREMENTS	Approximately 12" (30 cm) wide and 32" (81 cm) long
YARN	Tess' Designer Yarns Micro Fiber Ribbon, 100% nylon, 5 oz (150 g)/ 333 yds (304 m), Rainbow Pastels
NEEDLES	US E/4 (3.5 mm) crochet hook or size you need to obtain correct gauge
GAUGE	As desired
OTHER SUPPLIES	Tapestry needle, one large button

Getting Started

- Chain stitches to reach desired width. The model shown has 47 chains.
- Chain 47.
- **ROW 1**: Tc into 4th chain from hook (this counts for 2 tc), *ch 2, skip 2 chains, tc into next 2 chs; continue to end of chain. You now have 11 square holes. Ch 4, turn.
- **ROW 2**: Tc in top of second tc of previous row, *ch 2, skip ch 2 of previous row, tc in top of next 2 tc of previous row; repeat from * ending 2 tc in last tc of previous row. Ch 4, turn.
- Repeat Row 2 for 68 rows or desired length. Do not cut yarn.

Finishing

- Cut a piece of yarn off the other end of the ball approximately 24" (61 cm) long. Thread yarn onto tapestry needle. Fold crocheted piece in half and mark Center Back. Count 6 holes on either side of Center Back (this is point A). Bring one short edge (B) to point A at the neck edge and stitch together for the width of one hole (from A to C). Repeat for second short end. This will form shoulders and an approximate 9" (23 cm) armhole.

```
B          C A    Center Back    A C          B
```

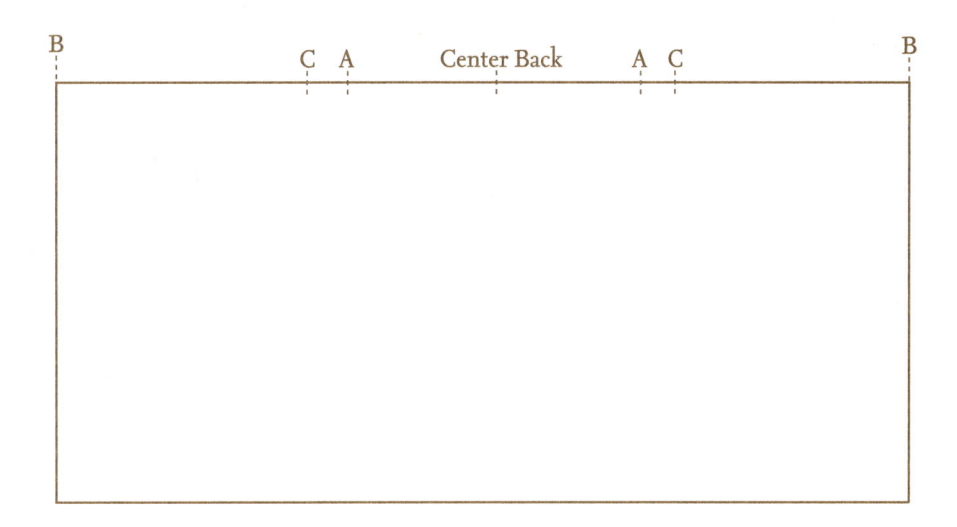

- Pick up the loop of yarn still attached to the ball and crochet a picot edge along front and neck edge as follows:

- Ch 3, turn, work dc in next tc, *2 dc in ch 2 space, 1 dc in top of each of next 2 tc; repeat from * across short end, back neck (between shoulder stitching), and second short end.

- Ch 3, turn, slip stitch in first dc, *2 sc in next 2 ch, ch 3, slip stitch in first ch of ch 3; repeat from * to end. Cut yarn, and draw end through last chain.

- Weave in ends. Sew button to center front.

Soft Clutch Purse

Designed by Nancy Brown for Dark Horse Yarn, photo on page 31

This furry little purse has a spring-loaded frame inside so it will stay firmly closed. It is knitted in reverse stockinette stitch.

MEASUREMENTS	Approximately 7" (18 cm) wide and 5" (13 cm) deep
YARN	Dark Horse Yarn Soft, 100% nylon, 3.5 oz (100 g)/54 yds (49 m), Color 103
NEEDLES	One US 10 (6 mm) circular needle 16" (40 cm) long or size you need to obtain correct gauge
GAUGE	14 stitches = 4" (10 cm) in stockinette stitch
OTHER SUPPLIES	Stitch holder, tapestry needle, one 6" (15 cm) straight hex open frame

Knitting the Purse

- Cast on 50 stitches. Work reverse stockinette stitch (purl every round) until piece measures approximately 4" (10 cm).

Decreasing for Top of Purse

- **ROUND 1:** Purl, decreasing 4 stitches evenly spaced.
- **ROUND 2:** Purl.
- Repeat Rounds 1 and 2 two more times. You now have 38 stitches.

Working the Top Front and Back

- Purl 19 stitches and place remaining 19 stitches on hold for back. Work back and forth for 6 rows even in reverse stockinette stitch. Bind off.
- Place 19 held stitches on needle and work as for front. Bind off.

Attaching the Frame

- Thread a tapestry needle with a 24" (61 cm) length of yarn and anchor at one side of purse. Holding frame inside the purse, fold the front flap over the frame and stitch flap to inside of purse. Repeat for back of purse.

Finishing

- Sew cast-on edge together for bottom of purse. Weave in ends.

Tokyo Scarf

Designed by Emre Koc, photo on page 31

This scarf proves that you really can't get too much of a good thing. Beautiful yarns that "do the work for you" are many, and this one is great. Knitted on large needles in stockinette stitch, the resulting pattern looks almost like lace. It comes in great colors, too.

MEASUREMENTS	Approximately 12" (30 cm) wide and 50" (127 cm) long
YARN	Feza Tokyo, 100% polyamide, 1.75 oz (50 g)/170 yds (155 m), Color 106
NEEDLES	US 15 (10 mm) straight needles or size you need to obtain correct gauge
GAUGE	12 stitches = 4" (10 cm) in garter stitch
OTHER SUPPLIES	Tapestry needle

Knitting the Scarf

- Cast on 35 stitches.
- Knit until you have just enough yarn left to bind off.

Finishing

- Bind off loosely. Weave in ends.

Buttons on Belts

Designed by Jane M. Brown, photo on page 32

Now that you've knitted a scarf for every outfit, it's time to move on to belts! The knitting is quick, and there's no end to the type of embellishment you can add.

MEASUREMENTS	Approximately 2" (5 cm) wide and 56" (142 cm) long without tassels
YARN	Berroco Suede or Suede Deluxe, 100% nylon or 85% nylon/10% rayon/5% polyester, 1.75 oz (50 g)/120 yds (110 m), 3704 Wrangler or 3901 Dale Evans Gold
NEEDLES	US 8 (5 mm) straight needles or size you need to obtain correct gauge
GAUGE	20 stitches = 4" (10 cm) in stockinette stitch
OTHER SUPPLIES	Crochet hook, tapestry needle, forty ⅝" (1.5 cm) buttons

Knitting the Belt

- Cut 20 pieces of 9"–14" (23–36 cm) yarn for tassels. Set aside. Cast on 12 stitches.
- **ROW 1:** K2, P2, K4, P2, K2.
- **ROW 2:** K1, P1, K2, P4, K2, P1, K1.
- Repeat Rows 1 and 2 until belt is desired length, 50"–60" (127–152 cm).

Adding the Tassels

- Fold 10 precut pieces in half and pull the centers through one end of the belt with a crochet hook, working one or two pieces at a time. Even up the ends and wrap one strand around the others near the belt and tie into a knot to form the tassel and secure. Repeat on other end of belt.

Adding the Buttons

- Thread a tapestry needle with a long strand of yarn. Pull the yarn through the center of the belt at one end. Working yarn through buttons and belt stitches twice, sew the buttons to the belt evenly spaced along entire length of belt (at approximately 1.5" [3.8 cm] intervals).

Finishing

- Weave in all ends.

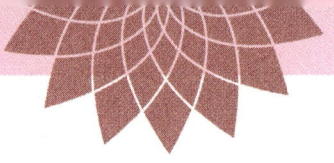

About the Designers

Nancy Abel

A licensed clinical social worker who works in a private practice in Portland, Maine, Nancy has a small hobby business called "Nancy Knits!" She sells knitted hats, scarves, and shawls at craft shows.

Betty Balcomb

Knitty City
208 W. 79th St.
New York, NY 10024

Betty is a teacher, designer, knitting consultant, and all-purpose promoter of knitting at Knitty City in New York City. Her specialties are socks and lace, but she will knit most anything.

Wendy Banks

The Village Sheep
369 Litchfield Rd.
New Milford, CT 06783
www.thevillagesheep.com

Wendy is owner of The Village Sheep with "the most beautiful yarns in the most wonderful store." Nestled in the Litchfield Hills in Northwestern Connecticut, The Village Sheep is a new breed of yarn shop with luxurious yarns, necessary notions, and fabulous accessories. Having spent many years of her career in the fashion industry, Wendy Banks has filled the shop with a glorious selection of well-edited fibers and colors. "Our approach to knitting and crocheting is from a fashion, not a craft point of view." The store samples rotate on a seasonal basis, and they are inspiring!

Leslie Barbazette

A knitter from age eight, Leslie currently works in product development for a large apparel company. She knits and lives in Berkeley, California with her husband and daughter. Her first knitting book, *Viva Poncho* (Stuart, Tabori and Chang), was published in the spring of 2005.

Libby Beiler

Mad About Ewes
429 Market St.
Lewisburg, PA 17837

Libby has been knitting since the age of ten, handspinning for twelve years, and weaving for eight years; creating original patterns is a recent pursuit. Her passion is for taking a raw fleece and producing wearable art through knitting or weaving. She is the weaver for her local sheep to shawl team, "Carl and the Not-So-Lazy Kates," which has won the state sheep to shawl competition twice in the past three years. The event takes place at the PA State Farm Show, held annually in January.

Anastasia Blaes

Anastasiaknits
www.anastasiaknits.com

Anastasia Blaes owns Anastasiaknits, a pattern company that publishes the Yarn Cocktails and Yarn Candy pattern lines. Created to educate as well as entertain, these patterns teach technique in easy increments. In addition to designing for yarn companies and magazines such as *Cast On*, Anastasia co-authored the companion books *The Knitter's Guide to Yarn Cocktails* and *The Crocheter's Guide to Yarn Cocktails* with Kelly Wilson. Anastasia is thankful to her test knitter, Katie Kemp.

Marci Blank

Th'Red Head
7817 Woodstone Ln.
Lenexa, KS 66217
www.thredhead.com

Knitting since she was in the third grade, Marci has turned her love of the craft into a full-time career. As owner of Th'Red Head, she designs, knits, and markets garments for art fairs, galleries, and shops. She also dyes and spins yarns that she sells or makes into fabulous one-of-a-kind garments.

Memberships: Association of Knitwear Designers, The Knitting Guild Association, Kansas City Weaver's Guild, and Fiber Guild of Greater Kansas City.

About the Designers

Gabrielle Bolland
Posh Knits
http://poshknits.com

Frog Tree Yarns designer Gabrielle is a seventeen-year-old homeschooler who has been designing crochet and knitting patterns since the age of six. When she's not knitting, crocheting, beading, sewing, reading, or working at the local library, she runs her own design company, Posh Knits, which has knitting patterns in shops across America.

Nancy Bowron
Haus of Yarn
Paddock Pl.
73 Nashville, TN 37205
www.hausofyarn.com

Opened in 2003, Haus of Yarn is a full-service knit and crochet center with the most comprehensive yarn selection in Middle Tennessee. Knitted models are displayed throughout the store to spark creativity and help with yarn and pattern selection. The staff have more than 250 combined years of knitting experience, so they can accurately answer your knitting questions. Classes are offered for knitters of all skills and ages. Customers enjoy a cozy atmosphere, a helpful and courteous staff, competitive prices, and an incomparable selection of patterns, books, needles, accessories, and of course, yarn. Nancy manages the store and enjoys both textured and color knitting.

Barbara Breiter
Knit a Bit
www.knitabit.net

Barbara Breiter has been knitting and designing for more than twenty years. Her work has been written about in *People* and many other publications. She was commissioned to design a special sweater for *US News & World Report* for a story on the "Unraveling of Enron." Her book, *The Complete Idiot's Guide to Knitting and Crocheting* (second edition), was published in August, 2003 and a third revised edition was published in September, 2006. Information on the book and a preview of the patterns included is available at Knit a Bit. You can also visit Barbara online at www.knittingonthenet.com.

Kelly Bridges
The Elegant Ewe
71 South Main St.
Concord, NH 03301

Kelly is the manager of The Elegant Ewe yarn and fiber shop in Concord, New Hampshire, where she also designs patterns and teaches classes of all fiber sorts. Her love of handwork started in high school, when her beautiful grandmother taught her to knit.

Miriam G. Briggs
Wool Away!
443 Railroad St.
St. Johnsbury, VT 05815

A devoted fiber enthusiast since childhood, Miriam took to knitting with gusto in the late 1970s. Moving to northern Vermont in the early 1990s, and finding no yarn shop, Miriam invented and opened Wool Away! Fiber Arts, the most complete yarn shop in the Northeast Kingdom.

Having always been a recipe tweaker and re-thinker, it was only natural, with a yarn shop and discerning customers to satisfy, for her to begin writing down her thoughts and tweaks. Thus *Northeast Kingdom Knits* was born and currently only available from Wool Away!

Jane M. Brown
After retiring from teaching (academic testing and art classes), Jane opened a quilt and knit shop. The craft skills she learned as a young girl blend well with her master's degree in art. Developing designs for crochet and knitting has given Jane much satisfaction.

Nancy Brown
Dark Horse Yarn, LLC

Nancy learned to knit as a young adult, so you can say she has been knitting for decades. Having been a manufacturer's representative since 1989, Nancy has had the good fortune of being able to make a living in the yarn industry. Nancy is currently heading up the design department of a new and innovative yarn company, Dark Horse Yarn, LLC, and she says that life in the yarn world is very exciting.

Laura Militzer Bryant

Laura Militzer Bryant began knitting as a child, and received a Bachelor of Fine Arts from the University of Michigan, where she concentrated in textile arts. She then worked in retail knitting and as a knitting yarn sales representative, and in 1984 founded her company, Prism Arts, Inc.

Laura has received individual artist grants from both the National Endowment for the Arts and the State of Florida. She has published more than forty pattern books for Prism, writes frequently for a variety of knitting publications, teaches nationally, and is on the Advisory Board for The Knitting Guild Association. Laura has written four books for Martingale Publishers: Knitting with Novelty Yarns, A Knitter's Template, and The Ultimate Knitted Tee with Barry Klein; and most recently, The Yarn Stash Workbook.

Linda Burt

WEBS
75 Service Center Rd.
Northampton, MA 01061
www.yarn.com

Linda Burt is the customer service manager at WEBS Yarn Store and in her spare time dabbles in design for Valley Yarns.

Cathy Campbell

Vermont Organic Fiber Co.
52 Seymour St., Suite 8
Middlebury, VT 05753

As program manager for O-Wool hand knitting yarns, Cathy has been fortunate in supporting her two biggest passions: knitting and preserving the environment. She has designed for O-Wool and Crystal Palace Yarns and has appeared on an episode of the DIY Network Series, Knitty Gritty. Cathy currently lives in Highlands, New Jersey.

Cathy Carron

Knitwear designer and author Cathy Carron left behind a corporate career in marketing once her daughters Emma and Lydia were born. Ever since, her focus has been on handknitting, first as a small business owner and importer of children's sweaters, then as a writer and researcher on hand knitting for the military during wartime. She recently wrote two books on handknitting technique: Hip Knit Hats (2005) now in its fifth printing and Knitting Sweaters From the Top-Down (2007). Her design work can be seen in Vogue Knitting, Interweave Knits, Knit Simple, Knit 1, Knitscene, Vogue Knitting On the Go: Bags Two, Rowan International Vol. #42, and the forthcoming Vogue Knitting: The Ultimate Sock Book and Vogue Gift Book II.

Lily M. Chin

www.lily-chin.com

Lily M. Chin is an internationally famous knitter and crocheter who has worked in the yarn industry for nearly twenty-five years as a designer, instructor, and author of four books on knitting and crochet. She was the first American knitwear designer to create a line of fashion yarns under her own name, The Lily Chin Signature Collection, launched in 2005 with CNS Yarns. She has lived in New York City nearly all her life and has been involved in some aspect of the fashion industry since age thirteen. She is a graduate of the Fashion Institute of Technology, Queens College, City University of New York, and The Bronx High School of Science.

Therese Chynoweth

Dale of Norway
4750 Shelburne Rd, Suite 20
Shelburne, VT 05482
www.daleofnorway.com

As Product Manager for Dale of Norway, Therese divides her time between editing Dale's Norwegian patterns for the North American market, designing for the U.S. Market, and handling questions from shops and knitters. Her hand knitting designs combine her graphics training, design experience, and love of texture and color. Using her interest in traditional knitting techniques, Therese's creations often work finishing details into a garment as part of its construction. Therese recently relocated to Vermont from Wisconsin when Dale of Norway relocated its U.S. Sales office.

About the Designers

Patricia Colloton-Walsh
Loop Yarn Shop
2999 North Humboldt Ave.
Milwaukee, WI 53212

Visit Loop, Milwaukee! Enjoy and explore a store committed to the creativity and resourcefulness of the fiber lover. Caitlin Colloton-Walsh, owner and designer, teams with Patricia, teacher and designer, to create an environment that inspires and instructs. Whether novice or expert, there are classes, yarns, and products for all knitters, crocheters, and fiber enthusiasts.

Kimberly Conterio
Bella Yarns
508 Main St.
Warren, RI 02885

Kim Conterio is the owner of Bella Yarns, established in 2003. She lives to play with yarn and to share the joy of knitting with anyone and everyone. A math major in college, Kim loves the technical side of knitting. Whether it's converting a pattern to a different gauge or creating new designs, she's always up for a challenge!

Tamara Del Sonno
Clickity Sticks & Yarns
2722 East 50th St.
Minneapolis, MN 55417

Tamara has been knitting since she was eight, making pin money knitting and crocheting hats and "hippie" vests for high-school classmates. As an adult she continued to design and sell custom sweaters, dresses, hats, and scarves, along with working, studying, and teaching in yarn shops in both San Diego and Minnesota. In 2000, she became a founding partner, with Camille Meyer, of Clickity Sticks, in south Minneapolis, MN, a block from Lake Nokomis. In a cottage-like atmosphere, you can test-drive a swatch before buying your needles and yarn. Help for a quick question is always at hand; classes are available for all levels of expertise. Clickity Sticks & Yarns has been named the Best of the Best by both MPLS/STP magazine and City Pages newspaper. Known as "Knit 'n Purl Girl," Tamara has also been called a Trendsetter by Minnesota Monthly magazine.

Marlaine DesChamps
Marlaine lives in upstate New York, where she enjoys playing with all different types of fiber arts, her family, and her two dogs.

Catherine Devine
Schaefer Yarn Co.
3514 Kelly's Corners Rd.
Interlaken, NY 14847

Catherine's grandmother taught her to knit when she was six, but more importantly, she showed her that "you don't need no stinkin' pattern" by knitting doll clothes and small garments on the fly from odds and ends of yarn. Those lessons resurfaced years later when Catherine began to spin her own yarn and wanted to knit to the yarn rather than to a pattern. These days her right brain dreams up designs and the math geek left brain works out the details.

Valentina Devine
Valentina has always enjoyed knitting. It started at an early age and is continuing into old age. Her first interest in yarn is the color, and design ideas come from the use of it. Valentina teaches creative knitting throughout the U.S. and Germany, and she designs and knits garments for publications and for sale through local boutiques in New Mexico.

Sue Dial
Harvest Moon Handspun
24 7th St.
York, SC 29745

Sue Dial got her first spinning wheel in 1988 and has been knitting exclusively with her own handspun yarn ever since. She raises angora rabbits and, whenever possible, she uses their fiber along with fiber from her dogs and other locally produced animal fibers in her work. She's happy to receive custom spinning, knitting, and/or dyeing orders.

About the Designers

Anne Dill
Pine Tree Yarns
75 Main St.
Damariscotta, ME 04543

Known to her friends and colleagues as a computer wizard and gourmet cook, Anne Dill has been designing textiles for many years. "I particularly enjoy taking a line and turning it into an intricate plane," says Anne.

Susan Dirk
The Big Wooly
www.thebigwooly.com

Susan was taught to knit by her mother at the age of six. While she was a photographer for the Seattle Art Museum and the Frye Art Museum, knitting and felting began to take over her life. Instruction Manager at Hilltop Yarn in Seattle, Susan teaches knitting to adults and children and has taught classes to help benefit Woodland Park Zoo, Plymouth Housing Group, and the Linus Project. She has organized after-school knitting programs and summer fiber arts camps in the Seattle area. Currently Susan is combining weaving, dyeing, knitting, and felting to create three-dimensional art.

Jenny Dowde
J'Designs
www.jennydowde.com

Australian Jenny Dowde began her creative life in 1984, spending six years at art school before venturing into textiles. She has been teaching freeform knitting and crochet since 1998, working with fibers and, more recently, with wire and beads. She is a regular columnist for *Textile Fibre Forum* and the author of three books: *Freeform Knitting and Crochet* (2004), *Freeformations* (2006), and *Surface Works* (2007).

Judith Durant
judithdurant@earthlink.net

Judith Durant is author of *Never Knit Your Man a Sweater* (*unless you've got the ring!)* and editor of *101 Designer One-Skein Wonders* and *One-Skein Wonders: 101 Yarn Shop Favorites*. She also authored *Ready, Set, Bead* and coauthored *The Beader's Companion*. Judith is a freelance technical and copy editor who currently lives in Lowell, Massachusetts.

Kathy Elkins
WEBS
75 Service Center Rd.
Northampton, MA 01061
www.yarn.com

Kathy Elkins, along with her husband, Steve, is the owner of WEBS – America's Yarn Store in Northampton, MA. She holds an MBA in marketing and has extensive experience in corporate marketing and branding. Her love of modern design elements, coupled with her belief that items should be "knittable, wearable, and usable," provide a solid foundation for her designs. You can catch up with Kathy at WEBS on her blog websyarnstore.blogspot.com, or on the podcast, "Ready, Set, Knit!" she and her husband host weekly.

Katherine Eng

Katherine learned to crochet when she was eight years old from her grandma and a neighbor who loved to make doilies. She has worked as a crochet designer for the past twenty years, and also assists her daughter with the Argentine Tango classes she teaches at CCSF.

Diana Foster
Lowell Mountain Wools
194 Mitchell Rd.
Lowell, VT 05847

Lowell Mountain Wools is a farm shop with sheep, knitting and spinning fibers, Storey books, patterns, wooden needles, and organic herbs. It is affiliated with the Old Stone House Museum in Brownington, Vermont, for classes and with the TKGH Knitters. The shop is located off Route 58E, at the top of Lowell Mountain.

About the Designers

Chrissy Gardiner
Gardiner Yarn Works
3415 NE 40th Ave.
Portland, OR 97212
www.gardineryarnworks.com

Chrissy Gardiner is a knit designer and mom living in Oregon.

Patti Ghezzi
pattighezzi@hotmail.com

Patti Ghezzi started knitting in 1999 after reading a column in the *New York Times Magazine*. Her first published pattern appears here in *101 Designer One-Skein Wonders*.

Mary C. Gildersleeve
By Hand, With Heart
282 Oneida Ct.
Denver, CO 80220

Mary's been a knitter since she was eight years old (when she taught herself) and a designer since the age of twelve. Currently working on a book of designers tied to great family read-alouds, she teaches and talks about knitting every chance she gets and is an active member of the Association of Knitwear Designers.

Anne Carroll Gilmour
Anne lives in the beautiful Wasatch Mountains of Utah where she works full-time in her fiber studio. She has been teaching classes in spinning, weaving, and knitting since 1990. Every Monday, Anne comes down from the mountains to work at the Black Sheep Wool Company in Salt Lake City. She sells her work at galleries and art shows all over the U.S., and her patterns are available at Black Sheep and in the Woolly West Catalog.

Wendy Gross
All Knit Up
www.allknitup.com

Wendy Gross is the creative talent behind All Knit Up, a web-based retail store focusing on hand knit toys. Wendy began knitting in her Pennsylvania home in order to make herself a simple scarf. She instantly found a love of the craft and quickly progressed to more adventurous designs, eventually leading her to create the lovable toys dubbed "Little Monsters."

Susan Guagliumi
Susan Guagliumi is a hand- and machine-knit author and designer. She has written *Hand Manipulated Stitches for Machine Knitters* (Taunton Press) and *12 Sweaters One Way: Knitting Cuff to Cuff* and *12 Sweaters One Way: Knitting Saddle Style* (both for Creative Publishing International). She lives in Connecticut with her artist husband, Arthur. When she isn't knitting or sewing, you'll find her in the garden.

Margaret Halas
Sew Krazy
142 E. Liberty St.
Wooster, OH 44691
www.sew-krazy.com

Margaret's Italian grandmother taught her to knit at age six. After an extended period as an adult spinning and knitting with handspun, she discovered Sew Krazy. The shop's fabulous selection of yarns has inspired her to design scarves, shawls, and other accessories to do them justice.

Kirsten Hipsky
Kirsten learned to knit almost as soon as her fingers could hold needles and hasn't wanted to put them down since. Fed up with the patterns that needed tweaking, she started designing her own sweaters as a teenager in her parents' yarn store. She now designs for WEBS while struggling to knit down her own stash at home. As a designer, she loves giving new life to classic shapes and incorporating elements from her classical education and from the inspiring landscapes of western Massachusetts.

Sarah Keller
Knot Another Hat
16 Oak St. Suite 202
Hood River, OR 97031
www.knotanotherhat.com

Located in the Columbia River Gorge National Scenic Area, Sarah's shop is where you can find everything hip and knit-worthy. The shop specializes in fine yarns and friendly, down-to-earth service. With a complete web presence, Knot Another Hat is like your favorite LYS online! If you're in the area, bring your latest project to sit and knit in the comfy sitting area.

About the Designers

Barry Klein
Trendsetter Yarns
16745 Saticoy St. #101
Van Nuys, CA 91406

Owner and designer for Trendsetter Yarns since 1987, Barry teaches for retail stores and at the trade show Stitches. Past President for TNNA and winner of the Excellence in Needlearts award, he is author of *Knitting with Novelty Yarns*, *The Ultimate Knitted Tee*, *A Knitter's Template*, and *Knitovations*. Barry has been seen on television's Knitty Gritty, Uncommon Threads, and Needle Arts Studio.

Emre Koc
Feza Yarns
161 Jamaica Ave.
Brooklyn, NY 11207
www.fezayarns.com

"Feza Yarns is the only correct address for fashion and classical yarns. Its world famous ALP yarns make knitting more enjoyable for everyone around the world."

Anni Kristensen
Himalaya Yarn
149 Mallard Dr.
Colchester, VT 05446
www.himalayayarn.com

Anni feels fortunate to be doing exactly what she loves to do: She works with wonderful people, she works with wonderful colors, and she gets to play with yarn whenever she wants to!

Lori Law
Oceanwind Knits
http://oceanwindknits.ca

Lori Law is a knitting designer and yarn dyer located in Teeswater, Ontario, Canada. Her patterns and hand-dyed yarn are available online at oceanwindknits.ca and through other select retailers in Canada and the U.S.

Dawn Leeseman
Crystal Palace Yarns
1709 Lawler St.
Chico, CA 95928

Dawn is a freelance designer, as well as knitting instructor at HeartStrings Yarn Studio. She has been an avid knitter for over twenty-five years, and has been designing professionally for the past six years. Dawn currently writes and designs for Crystal Palace Yarns. She has several designs that will appear in upcoming books. She is currently coauthoring a book with Faina Goberstein, *Casual Elegant Knits*, to be published by Martingale the fall of 2008. Dawn lives in Chico, California.

Elizabeth Lenhard
www.elizabethlenhard.com

Elizabeth Lenhard is the author of the Chicks with Sticks trilogy for young adults: *Chicks with Sticks (It's a Purl Thing)*, *Chicks with Sticks (Knit Two Together)*, and *Chicks with Sticks (Knitwise)* (Dutton Books). The knitty novels are about four very different Chicago teenagers who develop unlikely fiber fetishes and become best friends in the process. Elizabeth learned to knit alongside her characters and soon became addicted to baby hats. The Fishbowl Baby Hat is her first published pattern. Elizabeth lives in Atlanta with her husband and daughter.

About the Designers

Tara Jon Manning
Tara Handknitting Designs
429 Dewey Ave.
Boulder, CO 80304
www.tarahandknitting.com

A knitting author of five books including Men in Knits (Interweave Press, 2003), The Gift Knitter (Berkley Books, 2004), Mindful Knitting (Tuttle Publications, 2004), Compassionate Knitting (Tuttle Publications, 2006) and Nature Babies: Organic Knits and Natural Crafts for Babies, Moms, and a Better World (Potter Craft, 2006), Tara Jon pioneered the "Mindful Knitting" movement, which continues to gain popularity through her lectures, workshops, and knitting retreats. Her design work can be seen in magazines, books, and the collections of major yarn companies. She holds a Master of Arts Degree in Apparel & Textile Design and Fiber Arts, an undergraduate degree in Fine Arts, and is a Crafts Yarn Council of America Certified Knitting instructor. Tara lives with her husband and two young sons in Boulder, Colorado.

Carol Martin
Farmhouse Yarns
383 Mt. Parnassus Rd.
East Haddam, CT 06423
www.farmhouseyarns.com

A hand dyer recently featured on NBC's Today Show and also in More magazine, Carol left her corporate job in industrial sales to pursue her dream of raising sheep and producing beautiful hand-knitting yarns.

Carol Metzger
CFM Designs

An artist her whole life, Carol will try to make art out of just about anything. She especially loves combining colors, textures, and materials in unexpected ways, and textiles offer a rich variety of media and method for such exploration. Carol learned to knit from a neighbor when she was nine, and it was only a matter of time before she tried to turn knitting into art. Her obsession for knitting with beads came after she saw a beaded scarf in a local yarn shop.

Nancy Miller
Nancy Miller has been knitting for over fifteen years. She is a fiber addict who also loves to felt and spin. She teaches workshops in a variety of fiber topics. Nancy has had several of her designs and patterns appear in recent publications. Along with her husband and two girls who have already gotten hooked on felting, she lives in Maine, in a big old house by the sea that is bursting with fiber.

Karen J. Minott
WEBS
75 Service Center Rd.
Northampton, MA 01061
www.yarn.com

While working at WEBS, Karen found herself eyeing a wonderful yarn by Great Adirondack called Sierra. When the challenge of another one-skein project came along, she knew that she had to use this particular yarn — the only question was "What will I make?" The answer was a vest, her favorite garment to knit and wear.

Lorna Miser
Lorna Miser is the founder of Lorna's Laces Yarns, which she sold in 2003. Since then, Lorna has designed for many yarn companies, has written two booklets, and is working on her first knitting book, to be published in winter 2008. Lorna's favorite things to knit and design are baby sweaters and purses.

Bobbe Morris

Haus of Yarn
Paddock Pl.
73 Nashville, TN 37205
615-354-1007
www.hausofyarn.com

Opened in 2003, Haus of Yarn is a full-service knit and crochet center with the most comprehensive yarn selection in Middle Tennessee. Knitted models are displayed throughout the store to spark creativity and help with yarn and pattern selection. The staff have more than 250 combined years of knitting experience, so they can accurately answer your knitting questions. Classes are offered for knitters of all skills and ages. Customers enjoy a cozy atmosphere, a helpful and courteous staff, competitive prices, and an incomparable selection of patterns, books, needles, accessories, and of course, yarn. Bobbe is known for adding embellishments and ruffles to most items she designs.

Karen Mortensen

Hilltop Yarn
2224 Queen Anne Ave., North
Seattle, WA 98109

Karen works at Hilltop Yarn in Seattle, located in a beautiful old Craftsman-style house. Her first shop pattern was released to the world in 2006, and, since then, she has enjoyed designing small knit and crochet patterns, perfect for showing off her single-skein yarn "collection."

Ranée Mueller

Arabian Knits

Ranée Mueller lives in the beautiful Puget Sound area with her husband, five children, thirty chickens, and 60,000 honeybees. She knits and designs in her spare time (usually between 1:00 a.m. and 3:00 a.m.). You can occasionally find her behind the counter at The Yarn Garden of Gig Harbor and almost always at http://arabianknits.blogspot.com.

Laura Nelkin

Laura has been knitting for only a few years and has become utterly obsessed with it. She is the head designer at Schaefer Yarn. When she is not knitting, she can be found playing with her daughter, gardening, or cooking up a yummy storm.

Leah Oakley

Haus of Yarn
Paddock Pl.
73 Nashville, TN 37205
www.hausofyarn.com

Read more about the Haus of Yarn in the bio for Nancy Bowron (page 233) or Bobbe Morris (at left). Leah is known as the sock queen at the Haus.

Cheryl Oberle

Cheryl Oberle Designs
www.cheryloberle.com

Cheryl Oberle is owner of Cheryl Oberle Designs, which specializes in hand-dyed yarns and knitting kits. She is the author of *Folk Shawls* and *Folk Vests*, and her work has been seen in many knitting magazines as well as in *One-Skein Wonders: 101 Yarn Shop Favorites*.

About the Designers

Linda O'Leary
Kaolin Designs
727 Archie Whitesides Rd.
Gastonia, NC 28052
kaolindesigns@earthlink.net

Linda is owner and designer at Kaolin Designs, which offers a unique selection of hand-painted yarns for the handknitter and crocheter. The shop offers wools, mohairs, and silk blends, as well as hand-painted wool rovings and kits. Custom color orders are welcome.

Kristin Omdahl
Styled By Kristin
www.styledbykristin.com

Kristin Omdahl is a freelancer who writes, knits, crochets, and designs for publishers and for her own pattern collection, which can be found on her Web site.

Gail Owens
Fiberworks
4013 Dayton-Xenia Rd.
Beavercreek, OH 45432

Gail's scarf idea came while she was with the Tuesday-After-Lunch Knit & Nibble regulars at Fiberworks (www.fiberworks-dayton.blogspot.com). The discussion began, "Why must spiral scarves have 500 plus stitches?" With encouragement from Arlene and pestering from the nibblers, Gail's first knitting pattern became a reality. She says we are all designers: We choose our yarns, make pattern adjustments, do things an easier way, and pass on advice or suggestions to other knitters.

Elizabeth Prusiewicz
Knit Knot Studio
1238 NW Glison St.
Portland, OR 97209
www.knitknotstudio.com

Elizabeth Prusiewicz learned to knit from her mother when she was five years old in her native Poland. Since 2003, she has been passing on the skill and creating custom designs at Knit Knot Studio, her cozy yarn shop in the Pearl District of northwest Portland, Oregon.

Margaret Radcliffe
Maggie's Rags
www.maggiesrags.com

Margaret Radcliffe teaches everything from beginning knitting to design, promoting creativity and independence in all knitters. Her own designs are published in Maggie's Rags line of knitting patterns and she is the author of The Knitting Answer Book (Storey, 2005).

Dorothy T. Ratigan
Dorothy T. Ratigan is author of Knitting the Perfect Pair: Secrets to Great Socks, to be published in 2008. Her career in fiber arts spans thirty years, as a shop owner, designer, and editor. Dorothy is technical editor for 101 Designer One-Skein Wonders and One-Skein Wonders: 101 Yarn Shop Favorites. One of her designs is featured in The Vogue Knitting Book.

Marci Richardson
Elegant Ewe
71 South Main St.
Concord, NH 03301

Marci is owner of a very successful yarn shop, the Elegant Ewe, in Concord, New Hampshire, which is now in its tenth year of operation. Featured in 2000 in Knitter's Stash and as an editor's choice "must visit shop" in the Yankee Magazine Travel Guide to New England, the shop has become a destination for knitters around the world.

Hélène Rush
Hélène began knitting at age eight and she sold her first design to a magazine in 1979. After writing five books in the 1980s, including the best-selling Maine Woods Woolies, she became editor of McCall's Needlework & Crafts in the early 1990s, and editor of Cast On in 2001. In 2003 Hélène purchased the yarn company Knit One, Crochet Too, and she has been living in yarn paradise ever since!

About the Designers

Carol Scott
TrueThreads
474 Sunset Ct.
Glen Ellyn, IL 60137

A professor of fashion design and merchandising for twenty-six years, Carol recently retired to pursue her passion for knitting and sewing, which began at an early age, when she decided that creating unique garments and looking different were good things. Carol continues to teach knitting and sewing, and she designs knit garments for adults and children under the labels TrueThreads and TrueThreads2. As with all of us with the fiber addiction, Carol says there aren't enough hours in the day to do all the knitting, sewing, and teaching that she would like to do!

Lucie Sinkler
CloseKnit
622 Grove St.
Evanston, IL 60201

Lucie Sinkler is the owner of CloseKnit Yarn Store in Evanston, Illinois.

Shelagh Smith
Vermont Designs by Shelagh
342 Hooker Rd.
Leicester, VT 05733

Shelagh is a Vermont-based member of the Association of Knitwear Designers. Her knitting and crochet patterns offer wearable garments and fun accessories for all skill levels.

Myrna A. I. Stahman
Myrna, author and publisher of *Stahman's Shawls and Scarves: Lace Faroese-Shaped Shawls from the Neck Down and Seamen's Scarves*, is currently working on a book that features Feather and Fan lace pattern stitches. She designed the Alix Lace Prayer Shawl featured in Debbie Macomber's latest knitting-related novel, *Back on Blossom Street*.

Kathleen Taylor
Kathleen Taylor is a writer, spinner, crafter, wife, mother, grandma, and life-long knitter. She has written six Tory Bauer Mysteries, three knitting books: *Knit One, Felt Too* (Storey Publishing, 2003), *Yarns to Dye For* (Interweave Press, 2005), and *I Heart Felt* (Taunton Press, 2008), many magazine articles (most recently: "Spindle-Spun Christmas Stocking," *Spin-Off*, Winter 2006), and has designed exclusive sock and sweater patterns for the Knit Picks yarn company. She lives in northeastern South Dakota.

Mary Anne Thompson
Mary Anne has been knitting for about sixty years and is still excited to learn new techniques. With eleven grandchildren, she is always looking for small, fun projects to knit for the little ones; sometimes she has to make up her own patterns. "I'm looking forward to the publication of the new one-skein book not only for the fun of the new ideas, but as a way to reduce my considerable 'stash' of extra yarns."

Jolene Treace
Kristmen's Design Studio

Jolene Treace is a designer from the Midwest. She has had designs published in *Interweave Knits*, the British magazine *Knitting*, *Handknit Holidays* by Melanie Falick, Jamison's Shetland Knitting books two and three, and for various yarn companies. In addition she self publishes a line of pattern leaflets. She is a professional member of the Association of Knitwear Designers; the name of her business is Kristmen's Design Studio.

Judy Warde
A committed fiber "geek" who has recently taken up spinning as well as knitting, Judy was also a contributor to *One-Skein Wonders: 101 Yarn-Shop Favorites*. She teaches classes at her local yarn shop, KnitWit in Portland, Maine.

Megan B. Wright
Megan knits, spins, and designs in Seattle while she awaits the arrival of her first son.

Cindy Yoshimura

Cindy Yoshimura lives and knits in Hood River, Oregon. She is addicted to felting and loves bringing new knitters under the spell of its creative magic. Cindy designs felted bags and teaches felting in her home and at Hood River's premier local yarn shop, Knot Another Hat.

Shirley Young

Universal Yarn

Shirley began working for Universal Yarn approximately two years ago. She now edits and writes patterns with Universal's in-house and freelance designers. In her "spare" time, she spins, knits, weaves, and dyes.

Abbreviations

bo	bind off
CF	center front
ch	chain
cn	cable needle
co	cast on
dc	double crochet
dec	decrease
hdc	half double crochet
inc	increase
K	knit
K2tog	knit 2 stitches together
Kfb	knit into the front, then the back of 1 stitch
kwise	knitwise, as if to knit
m	marker
M1	make 1 increase (see page 247)
M1L	make 1 increase, left leaning (see page 247)
M1R	make 1 increase, right leaning (see page 247)
P	purl
pm	place marker
psso	pass slipped stitch over
P2tog	purl 2 stitches together
pu	pick up and knit
pwise	purlwise, as if to purl
RS	right side
rsc	reverse single crochet
sc	single crochet
sl	slip
sl st	slip stitch
sm	slip marker
ssk	slip 1, slip 1, knit 2 slipped stitches together
st(s)	stitch(es)
tbl	through the back loop
tr	triple crochet
WS	wrong side
wpi	wraps per inch
wyib	with yarn in back
wyif	with yarn in front
yo	yarn over

Glossary

Backward loop cast-on. Hold the end of the yarn and a needle in your right hand. Hold the working yarn in your left hand. Bring your left thumb over the top, down behind, and up in front of the yarn creating a loop. Insert needle into loop on thumb as if to knit and slide loop onto needle. You may also use the loop cast-on to add stitches to the end of a row of knitting.

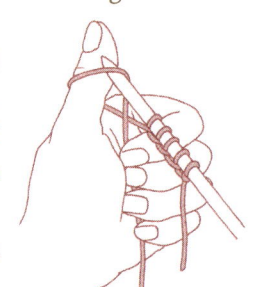

Bind off loosely. This method is sometimes called a suspended bind-off. Knit 2 stitches. *Lift the first stitch over the second stitch as for a regular bind-off but leave the lifted stitch on the left needle. Pass your right needle in front of the suspended stitch, knit the next stitch, and drop both from the left needle. Repeat from * until all stitches are bound off.

Cable cast-on. Make a slipknot and place it on your left needle. Follow Steps 1 and 2 for knitted cast on below.

1. Place the second needle between the two stitches on the first needle.

2. Knit a new stitch between the two stitches, pull it long, and place in on the first needle.

Continue in this manner, knitting between the last two stitches on the first needle, until you have the required number of stitches.

GLOSSARY 245

Chain (crochet). Begin with a slipknot on the hook. Wrap yarn over hook and pull the loop through the slipknot. Yarn over hook, pull loop through loop on hook to make second chain. Repeat for the required number of chain stitches.

Double crochet. Yarn over hook. Insert hook through both loops of next stitch. Draw loop through stitch. Yarn over hook. Draw loop through first 2 loops on hook. Yarn over hook. Draw loop through 2 loops on hook.

Garter stitch. When knitting back and forth in rows, knit all rows. When knitting circularly, knit one row, purl one row.

Half double crochet. Yarn over hook. Insert hook through both loops of next stitch. Yarn over and draw loop through stitch. Yarn over hook and draw through all 3 loops on hook.

I-cord. Use 2 double-point needles to make I-cord. Cast on required number of stitches. *Knit all stitches. Without turning work, slide the stitches to the other end of the needle. Pull the working yarn across the back. Repeat from * until cord is desired length. Bind off.

Kitchener stitch. This grafting technique is used to join two sets of live stitches invisibly. It is most often used for sock toes, but can be used to join shoulder seams or two halves of a scarf.

1. Place the two sets of live stitches to be bound off on separate needles. Hold the needles parallel in your left hand with right sides of the knitted fabric touching.

2. Insert the tapestry needle into the first stitch on the front needle as if to knit, and slip the stitch off the needle. Then insert the tapestry needle into the next stitch on the front needle as if to purl, and leave the stitch on the needle.

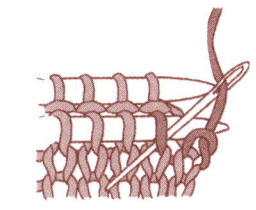

3. Insert the tapestry needle into the first stitch on the back needle as if to purl, and slip the stitch off the needle.

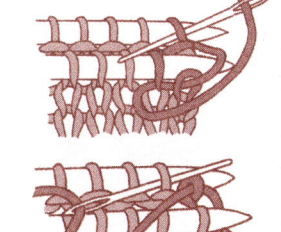

4. Insert the tapestry needle into the next stitch on the back needle as if to knit, and leave the stitch on the needle.

Repeat steps 2, 3, and 4 until all stitches have been joined.

K2tog bind off. Knit 1 stitch and slip the next stitch knitwise. Insert the left needle into the 2 stitches on the right needle from left to right.

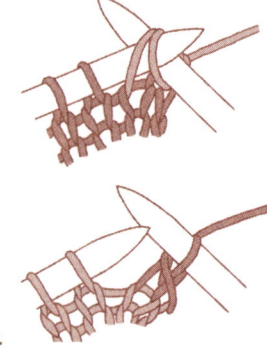

Knit the two stitches together.

Continue until all stitches are bound off. Cut the yarn and pull through last stitch.

Knit the knits and purl the purls. This simply means that you work the stitches as they appear on your needles. For example, if a stitch was knitted on the right-side row, it appears as a purl on the wrong side and should be purled on the wrong-side row.

Knitted cast-on. Make a slipknot and place it on your left needle.

1. Knit a stitch into the slipknot, leaving the slipknot on the needle.

2. Place the new stitch onto left needle by inserting the left needle into the front of the new stitch.

3. Tighten stitch and continue until you have the required number of stitches.

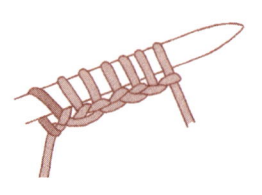

Knitwise. When a pattern says "slip the next stitch knitwise" or "slip the next stitch kwise," insert your needle into the next stitch from front to back as if you were going to knit it, then slip it to the right needle without knitting it.

Long tail cast-on. Leaving a tail long enough to cast on the desired number of stitches (a generous guess would be one inch per stitch), make a slip knot and place it on the needle. Wrap one of the threads around your thumb and the other around your index finger. Hold the tails with your other three fingers.

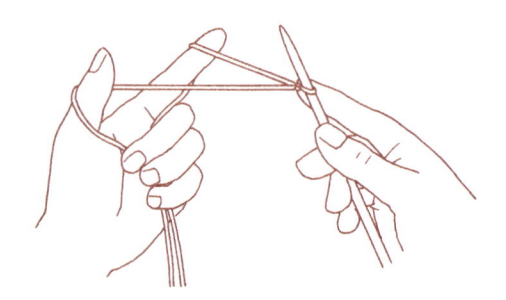

Insert the needle into the loop around your thumb from front to back (a) and over the yarn around your index finger (b).

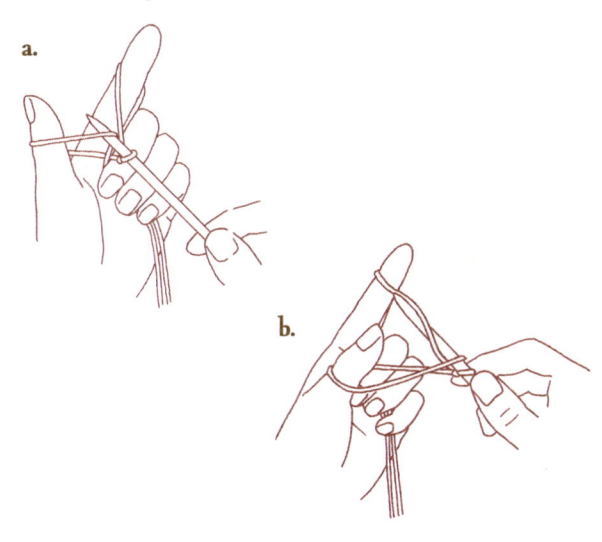

a.

b.

With the needle, bring the yarn from in front of your index finger down through the loop around your thumb.

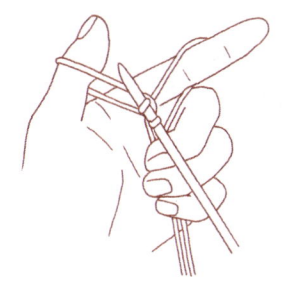

Drop the loop off your thumb, tighten the stitch, and form a new loop around your thumb.

M1 increase.

1. Work in pattern to where you'll need to begin increasing. Insert the tip of the left needle underneath the strand of yarn between the two needles, and place the lifted strand on the left needle.

2. Knit the lifted strand, twisting it to avoid leaving a hole.

The illustrations that follow show two versions of this technique. Choose right or left slant according to need.

MAKE 1, RIGHT SLANT

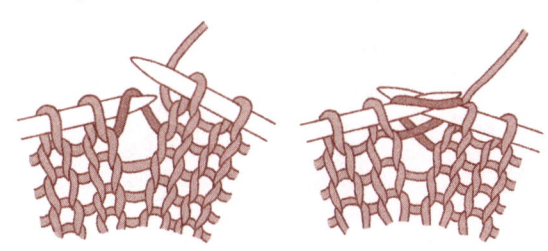

MAKE 1, LEFT SLANT

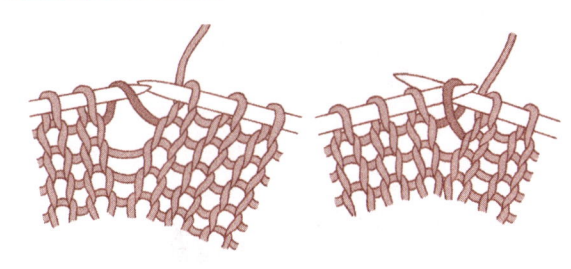

Mattress stitch. With a threaded tapestry needle, right sides facing, and working from bottom of garment to top, go under two bars between the first and second stitches on one edge, then under the two corresponding bars between the first and second stitches on the other edge.

Continue in this manner, pulling the yarn upward in the direction of the seaming to draw the two pieces together with an invisible seam. Try to match the tension of the knitting and don't pull the seaming yarn so tight that the seam puckers.

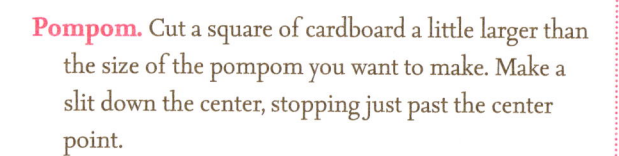

Pompom. Cut a square of cardboard a little larger than the size of the pompom you want to make. Make a slit down the center, stopping just past the center point.

1. Center a 12" piece of yarn in the slit, leaving both ends hanging.

2. Wrap yarn around the cardboard to desired thickness of pompom. Cut the yarn.

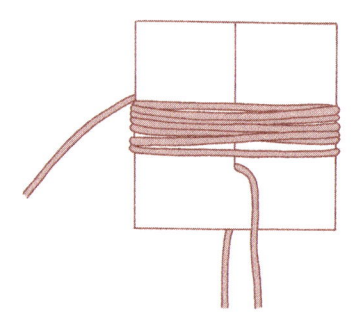

3. Tie the wrapped yarn tightly together with the piece of yarn that's hanging in the slit.

4. Cut the wrapped yarn along both edges of the cardboard.

5. Remove the cardboard, fluff up the pompom, and trim any uneven ends.

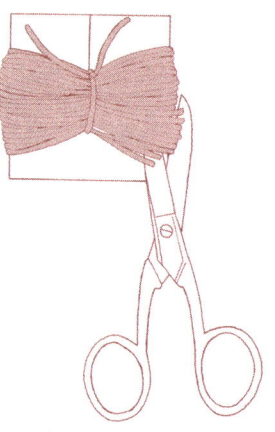

Provisional cast-on (crochet over needle).

1. Make a slip knot and place it on a crochet hook. Hold your knitting needle on top of a long strand of yarn.

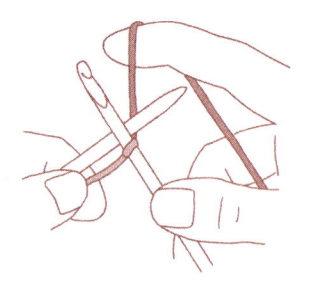

2. * With the crochet hook, draw the yarn over the needle and through the loop on the hook. To cast on another stitch, bring yarn behind knitting needle into position as for step 1, and repeat from *. Note: If you find it awkward to cast on the first couple of stitches, work a few crochet chain stitches before casting onto the needle so you have something to hold on to.

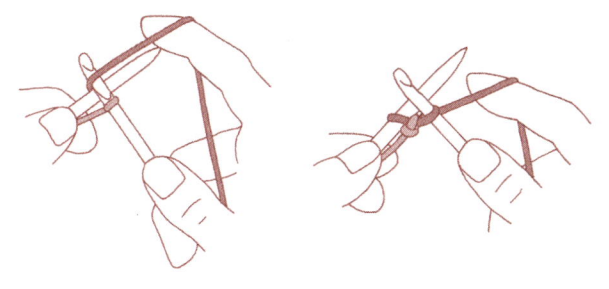

3. When the last stitch has been cast on, work two or three extra crochet chain stitches without taking the yarn around the knitting needle, then cut the yarn, leaving a 10" tail, draw the tail through the last loop on the hook, and pull the tail to close the loop loosely — just enough so the tail can't escape. To remove the scrap yarn when you've finished the knitting, pull the tail out of the last loop and gently tug on it to "unzip" the chain and carefully place the live stitches on a needle, holder, or separate length of scrap yarn as they are released.

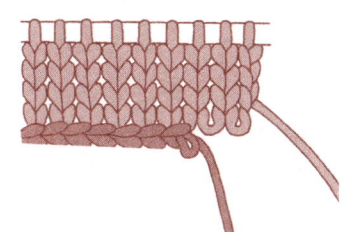

Purlwise. When a pattern says, "slip the next stitch purlwise" or "slip the next stitch pwise," keep the working yarn to the back and insert your needle into the next stitch from back to front as if you were going to purl it, then slip it to the right needle without purling it.

Reverse single crochet. This is worked the same as single crochet, only you work from left to right. Reverse single crochet creates a "braided" edge.

Seed stitch. This is an alternating K1, P1 stitch. When knitting back and forth, on wrong-side rows knit the stitches that were knit on the right side (they will look like purls on the wrong side) and purl the stitches that were purled on the right side (they will look like knits on the wrong side). When working circularly, purl the stitches that were knit on the previous round and knit the stitches that were purled on the previous round.

Short rows (WT). Work the number of stitches specified; this will leave some stitches unworked at the end of the row.

On a knit row, bring the yarn to the front of the work and slip the next stitch from the left needle to the right needle as if to purl. Bring the yarn to the back again and return the slipped stitch to the left needle. The first stitch on the left needle now has the working yarn wrapped around its base.

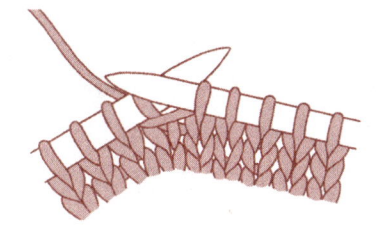

On a purl row, bring the yarn to the back of the work and slip the next stitch from the left needle to the right needle as if to purl. Bring the yarn to the front again and return the slipped stitch to the left needle.

If you're working short rows in stockinette stitch, you'll have to close the gaps and hide the wraps. **To hide the wraps on a right-side row,** insert the right needle tip under the wrap from front to back and from bottom to top and then into the wrapped stitch as if to knit. Knit the stitch together with its wrap. **To hide the wraps on a wrong-side row,** use the right needle tip to lift the back loop of the wrap from back to front and from bottom to top, and place it on the left needle. Purl the stitch together with its wrap.

Simple loop cast-on. Hold the cut end of the yarn and the needle in your left hand and hold the working yarn in your right hand. Move your right thumb down behind then up in front of the working yarn.

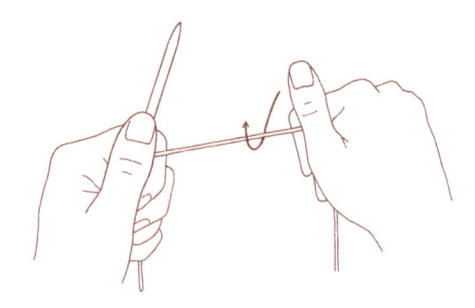

Insert the needle into the loop on your thumb from front to back.

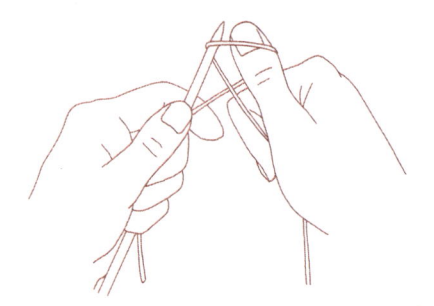

Remove your thumb. Repeat until you have the desired number of stitches on the needle.

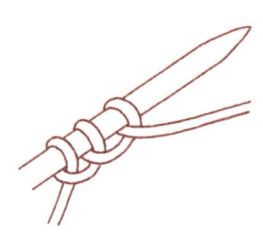

Single crochet. Insert hook into next stitch, wrap yarn over hook and draw the loop through the stitch. You now have 2 loops on the hook. Yarn over hook and draw loop through both loops on hook.

Single crochet decrease. Insert hook into next stitch, wrap yarn over hook and draw the loop through the stitch. Insert hook into next stitch, wrap yarn over hook and draw the loop through the stitch. Yarn over needle and draw through all three loops on hook.

Slip stitch crochet. Insert hook into next stitch, wrap yarn over hook and draw the loop through the stitch and the loop on the hook.

Stockinette stitch. When knitting back and forth in rows, knit the right-side rows, purl the wrong-side rows. When knitting circularly, knit all rounds.

Three-needle bind off. This technique is used to join two sets of live stitches.

1. Place the two sets of stitches to be bound off on separate needles. Hold the needles parallel in your left hand with right sides of the knitted fabric touching.

2. Insert the tip of a third needle into the first stitch on both needles and knit these two stitches together.

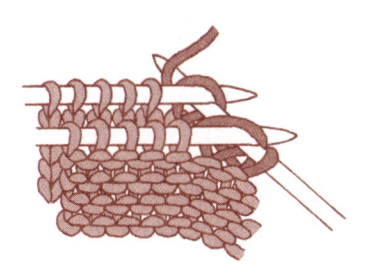

3. Repeat step 2. You now have two stitches on the right needle. With one of the needles in your left hand, lift the first stitch on the right needle over the second and off the needle as for a regular bind-off. Repeat until all stitches are bound off.

Triple Crochet. Yarn over hook twice. Insert hook through both loops of next stitch. Draw loop through stitch. Yarn over hook. Draw loop through first 2 loops on hook. Yarn over hook. Draw loop through 2 loops on hook. Yarn over hook. Draw loop through remaining 2 loops on hook.

Wraps per inch. This is the number of wraps it takes to cover one inch of a ruler with the yarn. The heavier the yarn, the fewer number of times it will wrap around one inch; the finer the yarn, the more times it will wrap.

Index

Page numbers in *italics* indicate photographs.

a

abbreviations, 244
Abel, Nancy, 111–12, 232
All Knit Up, 237
Alpaca Warmers, *5*, 44–46
April-in-Paris Beret, *28*, 187–88, 232
Arabian Knits, 240
Aran, miniature, 145

b

baby
    Basket Hat, *18*, 154–55
    Blue-Wave Sweater, *8*, 74–75
    Christening Shawl, *4*, 47–50
    Feather-and-Fan Sweater, *12*, 92–94
    Ostrich Plume Bonnet, *6*, 65–66
    Pink Tweed for, *13*, 105–6
    Pullover, Rolled Neck, *28*, 212–13
    Squash Hat, *13*, 112–13
    Wave Jumper, *7*, 73–74
    See also toy
backward loop cast-on, 244
bags
    Cabled Baglet, *23*, 169–71
    Felt Ruffle, *30*, 205–6
    Knitted Humbug, *9*, 70–71
    Mini Messenger, *17*, 151–53
    Sachets and Keepsake Pouches, *14*, 107–8
    Vermont Felted, *26*, 197–98
    See also Purse
Balcomb, Betty, 81–83, 232
Banks, Wendy, 212–13, 232
Barbazette, Leslie, 73–74, 232
Basket Lattice Cap, *16*, 167–68
beads
    Mitered Square Belt with, *26*, 200–201
    Scallop-Edge Beaded Necklace, *14*, 102
    Tiers-of-Waves Beaded Scarf, *15*, 118–19

beanie. *See under* cap
Bear, Little Monster, *25*, 155–57
Beiler, Libby, 60–64, 232
Bella Yarns, 235
belts
    Blossom, *18*, 178
    Buttons on, *32*, 230–31
    Mitered Square, with Beads, *26*, 200–201
    Plaited Cable Men's, *11*, 99
berets
    April-in-Paris, *28*, 187–88
    miniature, *20*, 143–44
Between-Seasons Cap, *13*, 109–10
Big Woolly, The, 236
bind off loosely, 244
Blaes, Anastasia, 99, 232
Blank, Marci, 164–65, 232
Blanket Buddy, *26*, 207–8
Blossom Belt, *18*, 178–79
BlueBells Socks, *9*, 79–81
Blue-Wave Baby Sweater, *8*, 74–75
Bolland, Gabrielle, 88–89, 195, 233
Bonnet, Ostrich Plume Baby, *6*, 65–66
bowls
    Fuchsia Felted, *30*, 218–19
    Saw-Tooth Companion, *29*, 193–94
Bowron, Nancy, 147–49, 150, 233
Boy-O-Boy, *16*, 135–37
Breiter, Barbara, 205–6, 233
Bridges, Kelly, 66–67, 233
Briggs, Miriam G., 142–45, 193–94, 233
Broken Rib Socks, *16*, 138–40
Brooch, Flower, *19*, 173–74
Brown, Jane M., 230–31, 233
Brown, Nancy, 228–29, 233
Bryant, Laura Militzer, 222–23, 234
Burt, Linda, 38–40, 234
Buttons on Belts, *32*, 230–31
By Hand, With Heart, 237

c

cable cast-on, 244
Cabled Baglet, *23*, 169–71

Campbell, Cathy, 109–10, 167–68, 234
caps
    Basket Lattice, *16*, 167–68
    Between-Seasons, *13*, 109–10
    Lacy Beanie, *11*, 94–95
    Lavender Lace Beanie, *21*, 160
    See also beret; hat
Carron, Cathy, 128, 234
Catch-Me-If-You-Can Socks, *6*, 83–85
Catnip Kick Pillow, *32*, 223–24
Centipede, Loop's, *29*, 192
CFM Designs, 239
chain (crochet), 245
Checkbook Cover, Missy's, *9*, 64–65
Cheryl Oberle Designs, 240
Chicly Chevroned "Broadway" Hat, *15*, 117
Child's Hat with Pompom, *14*, 111–12
Chin, Lily M., 117, 234
Christening Shawl, *4*, 47–50
Chullo, miniature, *20*, 144–45
Chynoweth, Therese, 162–63, 234
Clickity Sticks & Yarns, 235
CloseKnit Yarn Store, 242
Colloton-Walsh, Patricia, 192, 235
Conterio, Kimberly, 92–94, 235
covers
    Knitted Notebook, *22*, 130
    Missy's Checkbook, *9*, 64–65
Cowl, Lace Kid Merino, *15*, 116
Cozy Socks for Kids, *28*, 188–90
Crochet Ruffle Scarf, *16*, 161
Cross-Stitch Scarf, *27*, 186
Crystal Palace Yarns, 238

d

Dale of Norway, 234
Dark Horse Yarn, LLC, 228–29, 233
Del Sonno, Tamara, 79–81, 112–13, 209–11, 235
DesChamps, Marlaine, 129, 130, 235
Devine, Catherine, 36–37, 235
Devine, Valentina, 74–75, 203–5, 226–27, 235

INDEX

Dial, Sue, 188–90, 235
Dill, Anne, 47–50, 236
Dirk, Susan, 96–98, 236
Dogwood Blossom Wrap, *5*, 36–37
double crochet, 245
Dowde, Jenny, 173–75, 178–79, 236
Durant, Judith, 44–46, 77–78, 236

e

Edge-of-Lace Hat and Cuffs, The, *20*, 165–66
Egg-Cozy Hats, Four, *20*, 142–45
Elegant-and-Easy Cable Mittens for the Family, *19*, 140–42
Elegant-and-Easy Garter Stitch Tie, *14*, 104
Elegant Ewe, The, 233, 241
Elizabeth Lenhard (Web site), 238
Elizabeth's Perfect Hat, *20*, 175–76
Elkins, Kathy, 197–98, 236
Eng, Katherine, 137–38, 236
Essentials Mini-Purse, *23*, 158–59
Eyelet Shruglet, *25*, 179–80

f

Farmhouse Yarns, 239
Feather-and-Fan Baby Sweater, *12*, 92–94
Felt Ruffle Bag, *30*, 205–6
Feza Yarns, 238
Fiberworks, 241
Fishbowl Baby Hat, *19*, 181–83
Flirty Ribbon Purse, *32*, 222–23
flowers
    Brooch, *19*, 173–74
    Power (adornments), *26*, 209–11
Forest Park Dresser Scarf, *4*, 51–53
Foster, Diana, 64–65, 124–25, 236
Fuchsia Felted Bowl, *30*, 218–19

g

Gardiner, Chrissy, 169–71, 237
Gardiner Yarn Works, 237
Garterlac Bath Rug, *19*, 131–33
garter stitch, 245

Garter Stitch Loop-Through Scarf, *11*, 90–91
Ghezzi, Patti, 154–55, 237
Gildersleeve, Mary C., 179–80, 237
Gilmour, Anne Carroll, 42–43, 237
glossary, 244–51
Grampie's Tie, *10*, 66–67
Gross, Wendy, 155–57, 237
Guagliumi, Susan, 190–91, 237
Guilty Pleasures Socks, *12*, 88–89

h

Halas, Margaret, 186, 237
half double crochet, 245
Handbag, Two-Hour, *30*, 216–17
hand warmers
    Alpaca Warmers, *5*, 44–46
    Hugs-and-Kisses-with-Love, *22*, 147–49
    Scrunchie, *10*, 68–69
    See also wristlets
Harvest Moon Handspun, 235
hats
    April-in-Paris Beret, *28*, 187–88
    Baby Basket, *18*, 154–55
    Baby Squash, *13*, 112–13
    Chicly Chevroned "Broadway", *15*, 117
    Child's, with Pompom, *14*, 111–12
    Edge-of-Lace, Cuffs and, *20*, 165–66
    Egg-Cozy, Four, *20*, 142–45
    Elizabeth's Perfect, *20*, 175–76
    Fishbowl Baby, *19*, 181–83
    Kat's, *23*, 124–25
    miniature, *6*, 60–61
    New Directions, *17*, 133–34
    Spiral, *22*, 164–65
    Square Hole, Wristlets and, *27*, 203–5
    See also beret; cap
Haus of Yarn, 233, 240
headbands
    Hand Warmers, *22*
    Hugs-and-Kisses-with-Love, *22*, 150
    Poems Easy, *25*, 177
    Ribbed, *18*, 129
Hilltop Yarn, 240

Himalaya Yarn, 238
Hipsky, Kirsten, 41, 237
His 'n' Hers Shower Soap Holders, *18*, 128
Horseshoe Cable Socks, *10*, 77–78
Hugs-and-Kisses-with-Love
    Hand Warmers, *22*, 147–49
    Headband, *22*, 150

i

I-cord, 245
Indian Cross Scarf, *19*, 146
Infant's Rolled Neck Pullover, *28*, 212–13
iPod Nano Nanny, *28*, 195

j

J'Designs, 236
Jumper, Wave, *7*, 73–74

k

K2tog bind off, 246
Kaolin Designs, 241
Kat's Hat, *23*, 124–25
Keepsake Pouches and Sachets, *14*, 107–8
Keller, Sarah, 131–33, 237
kitchener stitch, 245
Klein, Barry, 161, 238
Knit a Bit, 233
Knit Knot Studio, 241
Knit One, Crochet Too, 241
knitted cast-on, 246
Knitted Humbug Bag, *9*, 70–71
Knitted Notebook Cover, *22*, 130
knit the knits and purl the purls, 246
Knitty City, 232
knitwise, 246
Knot Another Hat, 237
Koc, Emre, 229, 238
Kristensen, Anni, 224–25, 238
Kristmen's Design Studio, 242

l

La Cancion Amulet Purse and Flower Brooch, *19*, 173–75

l

Lace Kid Merino Cowl, *15*, 116
Lace Spiral Scarf, *15*, 120–21
Lacy Beanie, *11*, 94–95
Lavender Lace Beanie, *21*, 160
Law, Lori, 151–53, 238
Leeseman, Dawn, 116, 126–27, 238
Lenhard, Elizabeth, 181–83, 238
Lily Chin Signature Collection, The, 234
Little Green Wristlets, *24*, 162–63
Little Monster Bear, *25*, 155–57
Lola Flip-Flop Mittens, *10*, 56–58
long tail cast-on, 246–47
Loop's Centipede, *29*, 192
Loop Yarn Shop, 235
Lorna's Laces Yarns, 239
Lowell Mountain Wools, 236

m

M1 increase, 247
Mad About Ewes, 232
Maggie's Rags, 241
Magic Loop Minis, *6*, 60–64
Manning, Tara Jon, 199–200, 239
Marialis End-to-End Scarf, *7*, 75–76
Martin, Carol, 187–88, 239
mattress stitch, 248
Megan's Ruffled Neck Warmer, *7*, 71–72
Metzger, Carol, 102, 239
Miller, Nancy, 43, 239
Mini Messenger Bag, *17*, 151–53
Minis, Magic Loop, *6*, 60–64
Minott, Karen J., 103, 239
Miser, Lorna, 105–6, 158–59, 160, 239
Missy's Checkbook Cover, *9*, 64–65
Mitered Square Belt with Beads, *26*, 200–201
mittens
    Elegant-and-Easy Cable, for the Family, *19*, 140–42
    Lola Flip-Flop, *10*, 56–58
    miniature, *6*, 61–62
Morris, Bobbe, 196–97, 240
Mortensen, Karen, 223–24, 240
Mueller, Raneé, 65–66, 240

n

Nancy Knits!, 232
Nano Nanny, *28*, 195
Necklace, Scallop-Edge Beaded, 14
neck warmer, *31*, 224–25
    Megan's Ruffled, *7*, 71–72
    See also scarf
Nelkin, Laura, 56–58, 240
New Directions Hat, *17*, 133–34
Notebook Cover, Knitted, *22*, 130
Not-Your-Average Washcloths, *17*, 172

o

Oakley, Leah, 68–69, 240
Oberle, Cheryl, 165–66, 240
Oceanwind Knits, 238
O'Leary, Linda, 202, 241
Omdahl, Kristin, 118–19, 241
Oriel Lace Scarf, *5*, 42–43
ornaments and adornments
    Flower Power, *26*, 209–11
    Magic Loop Minis, *6*, 60–64
Ostrich Plume Baby Bonnet, *6*, 65–66
Owens, Gail, 120–21, 241

p

Picot Edge Socks, *6*, 81–83
pillows
    Catnip Kick, *32*, 223–24
    Ring Bearer, *12*, 96–98
Pine Tree Yarns, 236
Pink Tweed for Baby, *13*, 105–6
Plaited Cable Men's Belt, *11*, 99
Pocketbook. *See* Bag; Purse
Poems Easy Headband, *25*, 177
pompom, 248
Posh Knits, 233
Power Flowers, *26*, 209–11
Prism Arts, Inc., 234
provisional cast-on (crochet over needle), 248–49
Prusiewicz, Elizabeth, 172, 175–76, 241
Pullover, Infant's Rolled Neck, *28*, 212–13
purlwise, 249

purses
    Essentials Mini-, *23*, 158–59
    Flirty Ribbon, *32*, 222–23
    La Cancion Amulet, *19*, 173–75
    Missy's Checkbook Cover, *9*, 64–65
    Soft Clutch, *31*, 228–29
    Two-Hour Handbag, *30*, 216–17
    See also bag

r

Radcliffe, Margaret, 133–34, 241
Ratigan, Dorothy T., 107–8, 241
reverse single crochet, 249
Rhea Lace Stole, *5*, 41
Ribbed Headband, *18*, 129
Richardson, Marci, 90–91, 104, 140–42, 146, 241
Ring Bearer Pillow, *12*, 96–98
Roll Brim Hat, miniature, *20*, 143
Rug, Garterlac Bath, *19*, 131–33
Rush, Hélène, 94–95, 241

s

Sachets and Keepsake Pouches, *14*, 104
Saw-Tooth Companion Bowl, *29*, 193–94
Scallop-Edge Beaded Necklace, *14*, 102
scarves
    Crochet Ruffle, *16*, 161
    Cross-Stitch, *27*, 186
    Forest Park Dresser, *4*, 51–53
    Garter Stitch Loop-Through, *11*, 90–91
    Indian Cross, *19*, 146
    Lace Spiral, *15*, 120–21
    Marialis End-to-End, *7*, 75–76
    Oriel Lace, *5*, 42–43
    Smock-a-Ruche, *27*, 196–97
    Sock-It-To-Me, *9*, 59
    Tiers-of-Waves Beaded, *15*, 118–19
    Tokyo, *31*, 229
    Tweed Silk, *20*, 137–38
    Waterfall, *27*, 202
    Zigzag, *28*, 190–91
    See also neck warmer
Schaefer Yarn Co., 235, 240

INDEX

Scott, Carol, 59, 135–37, 242
Scrunchie Hand Warmers, *10*, 68–69
seed stitch, 249
Sew Krazy, 237
shawls
    Christening, *4*, 47–50
    Tucson Lattice, *4*, 43
short rows (WT), 249–50
Shrug, Square-Hole, *32*, 226–27
Shruglet, Eyelet, *25*, 178–80
simple loop cast-on, 250
Simple Mistake Rib Vest, *13*, 103
single crochet, 250
single crochet decrease, 250
Sinkler, Lucie, 218–19, 242
Slippers, Taos, *25*, 126–27
slip stitch crochet, 250
Smith, Shelagh, 70–71, 242
Smock-a-Ruche Scarf, *27*, 196–97
Soap Holders, His 'n' Hers, *18*, 128
Sock-It-To-Me Scarf, *9*, 59
socks
    BlueBells, *9*, 79–81
    Broken Rib, *16*, 138–40
    Catch-Me-If-You-Can, *6*, 83–85
    Cozy, for Kids, *28*, 188–90
    Guilty Pleasures, *12*, 88–89
    Horseshoe Cable, *10*, 77–78
    miniature, *6*, 63–64
    Picot Edge, *6*, 81–83
Soft Clutch Purse, *31*, 228–29
Spiral Hat, *22*, 164–65
Square Hole Hat and Wristlets, *27*, 203–5
Square-Hole Shrug, *32*, 226–27
Stahman, Myrna A.I., 75–76, 242
stockinette stitch, 250
Stole, Rhea Lace, *5*, 41
Styled By Kristin, 241
sweaters
    Blue-Wave Baby, *8*, 74–75
    Boy-O-Boy, *16*, 135–37
    Feather-and-Fan Baby, *12*, 92–94
    Infant's Rolled Neck Pullover, *28*, 212–13
    miniature, *6*, 62–63
    Pink Tweed for Baby, *13*, 105–6
    Zane's Coming Home, *29*, 199–200

t

Taos Slippers, *25*, 126–27
Tara Handknitting Designs, 239
Taylor, Kathleen, 138–40, 242
Thompson, Mary Anne, 207–8, 242
Th'Red Head, 232
three-needle bind off, 251
Three-Season Lace Vest, *4*, 38–40
ties
    Elegant-and-Easy Garter Stitch, *14*, 104
    Grampie's, *10*, 66–67
Tiers-of-Waves Beaded Scarf, *15*, 118–19
Tokyo Scarf, *31*, 229
toys
    Blanket Buddy, *26*, 207–8
    Little Monster Bear, *25*, 155–57
    Loop's Centipede, *29*, 192
Treace, Jolene, 51–53, 242
Trendsetter Yarns, 238
triple crochet, 251
TrueThreads, 242
Tucson Lattice Shawl, *4*, 43
Tweed Silk Scarf, *20*, 137–38
Two-Hour Handbag, *30*, 216–17

u

Universal Yarn, 243

v

Vermont Designs by Shelagh, 242
Vermont Felted Bag, *26*, 197–98
Vermont Organic Fiber Co., 234
vests
    Simple Mistake Rib, *13*, 103
    Three-Season Lace, *4*, 38–40
Village Sheep, The, 232

w

Warde, Judy, 200–201, 242
Washcloths, Not-Your-Average, *17*, 172
Waterfall Scarf, *27*, 202
Wave Jumper, *7*, 73–74
WEBS – America's Yarn Store, 234, 236, 237, 239
Wool Away!, 233
Wrap, Dogwood Blossom, *5*, 36–37
wraps per inch, 251
Wright, Megan B., 71–72, 242
wristlets
    Little Green, *24*, 162–63
    Square Hole Hat and, *27*, 203–5
    See also hand warmers

y

Yoshimura, Cindy, 216–17, 243
Young, Shirley, 83–85, 177, 243

z

Zane's Coming Home Sweater, *29*, 199–200
Zigzag Scarf, *28*, 190–91

The following items were supplied by:

Greenjeans — Handmade for Conscientious Living
www.greenjeansbrooklyn.com
718-907-5835

Hand-built Canterbury shaker rocker, page 4, Tuscan Lattice Shawl

Handcrafted round basket with mahogany bottom, page 5, Oriel Lace Scarf

Other Storey Titles You Will Enjoy

2-at-a-Time Socks, by Melissa Morgan-Oakes.
An easy-to-learn new technique to banish Second Sock Syndrome forever!
144 pages. Hardcover with concealed wire-o. ISBN 978-1-58017-691-0.

Felt It!, by Maggie Pace.
Hats, shawls, belts, bags, home accessories — the perfect introduction to the magic of felting, for all levels of knitters.
152 pages. Paper. ISBN 978-1-58017-635-4.

The Knitting Answer Book, by Margaret Radcliffe.
Answers for every yarn crisis — an indispensable addition to every knitter's project bag.
400 pages. Flexibind with cloth spine. ISBN 978-1-58017-599-9.

Knitting Rules!, by Stephanie Pearl-McPhee.
A sourcebook of invaluable advice, woven with witty insights and wry reflections in celebration of the knitting life.
224 pages. Paper. ISBN 978-1-58017-834-1.

Kristin Knits, by Kristin Nicholas.
Hats, mittens, scarves, socks, and sweaters — inspired designs for bringing your knitting alive with color.
208 pages. Hardcover with jacket. ISBN 978-1-58017-678-1.

One-Skein Wonders: 101 Yarn Shop Favorites, edited by Judith Durant.
One hundred and one projects for all those single skeins in your stash, collected from yarn shops across America.
240 pages. Paper. ISBN 978-1-58017-645-3.

Stephanie Pearl-McPhee Casts Off.
A journey deep into the heart of the Land of Knitting, with the witty, zany Yarn Harlot as a guide to its customs, features, and inhabitants.
224 pages. Paper. ISBN 978-1-58017-658-5.

These and other books from Storey Publishing are available wherever quality books are sold or by calling 1-800-441-5700.
Visit us at *www.storey.com*.